The Bedside, Bathtub and Armchair Companion
to Virginia Woolf and Bloomsbury

# The Bedside, Bathtub and Armchair Companion to Virginia Woolf and Bloomsbury

Sarah M. Hall

continuum

**Continuum**

The Tower Building
11 York Road
London SE1 7NX

80 Maiden Lane, Suite 704
New York
NY 10038

www.continuumbooks.com

British Library Cataloguing-in-Publication Data
A catalogue record for this book is available from the British Library.

ISBN-10:  HB: 0-8264-8674-6
          PB: 0-8264-8675-4
ISBN-13:  HB: 978-0-8264-8674-5
          PB: 978-0-8264-8675-2

Typeset by Fakenham Photosetting Ltd, Fakenham, Norfolk
Printed and bound in the USA.

# Contents

· · · · · · · · · · · ·

# Acknowledgements

· · · · · · · · · · · ·

Any Woolf researcher finds Virginia Woolf's *Letters*, ed. Nigel Nicolson and Joanne Trautmann, and the *Diary*, ed. Anne Olivier Bell, invaluable, and I am no exception. I frequently consulted *The Bibliography of Virginia Woolf*, by B.J. Kirkpatrick and Stuart N. Clarke (fourth edition, 1997).

All due efforts have been made to trace and acknowledge copyright holders, but please contact the publisher in the case of errors or omissions, which can be corrected in subsequent editions.

Thanks to . . .

Vanessa Curtis, partly responsible for the shape of this book. She very kindly donated the engraving of Fitzroy Square (p. 148) and allowed me to reprint a few bars from her composition, 'The Waves' (p. 113).

Geoff Licence, for drawings that appear on pp. 6, 14, 43, 65, 118, 127, 131, 139, 156, 159, 168 and 177.

Sheila Wilkinson for the photographs on pp. 9 and 10.

Bryan Greene for the photographs on pp. 15, 19, 49, 76, 92, 144, 154 and 194.

Stephen Barkway for the photograph on p. 61.

A.J. Matravers for the photograph on p. 100.

Milo Keynes for the photograph on p. 101.

Mark Scott for the photographs on pp. 159 and 195.

Thomas Pakenham, Moira Eddy, Mary Gray, Erika and Joachim Lukas, and the Bagenal family for permission to use photographs. The Virginia Woolf Society of Great Britain for permission to reproduce the cover images on pp. 2 and 199, and Random House for permission to use those on pp. 46, 59, 117, 174 and 181.

Peter Lofts for the Ramsey and Muspratt photographs on pp. 73, 77 and 158.

The Tate for the photograph on p. 78 © Tate, London 2006.

The National Portrait Gallery for the photograph by A.C. Cooper on p. 81, and the photograph on p. 93 © National Portrait Gallery, London.

King's College Modern Archive for the photograph by Edward Leigh on p. 108 © King's College Modern Archive, Cambridge.

Catherine Trippett at Random House; Patricia McGuire, archivist at the King's College Modern Archive at the University of Cambridge; Chris Jakes, curator of the Cambridgeshire Collection, Cambridge Central Library; Matthew Bailey at the National Portrait Gallery; Sarah Fahmy at the Tate, for help with pictures.

S.P. Rosenbaum for pointing out a detail I had missed, and members of the Reading Group of the VWSGB, who provide new insights into Woolf each time we meet.

My competent and friendly editor at Continuum, Anna Sandeman, who gave helpful advice very tactfully, and her assistants, Rebecca Simmonds and Colleen Coalter. Also to copy-editor Kate Reeves, for her care and courtesy.

And most of all, Bryan Greene again, for continual help and support in ways unfortunately too numerous to relate here.

London Underground logo (featuring on pp. 147–52) reproduced with kind permission from Transport for London.

Drawings that appear on pp. 18, 27 (adapted from a painting by Henry Lamb), 28, 41, 44, 48, 51, 67, 70, 75 (adapted from an Omega design by Duncan Grant), 83 (adapted from the poster advertising the Second Post-Impressionist Exhibition), 97, 102, 106, 110, 115, 131, 161, 176 and 190, plus the puzzle on p. 31, were by the author. Photographs on pp. 38, 45, 63, 69, 80, 83, 94, 137, 150, 151, 188, 189, 196, 198, 199, 201 and 203 were taken by the author.

# Major Works of Virginia Woolf

· · · · · · · · · · · ·

**Novels**

| | |
|---|---|
| 1915 | *The Voyage Out* |
| 1919 | *Night and Day* |
| 1922 | *Jacob's Room* |
| 1925 | *Mrs Dalloway* |
| 1927 | *To the Lighthouse* |
| 1928 | *Orlando* |
| 1931 | *The Waves* |
| 1937 | *The Years* |
| 1941 | *Between the Acts* (posthumous) |

**Other**

| | |
|---|---|
| 1917 | *Two Stories* (includes 'The Mark on the Wall') |
| 1919 | *Kew Gardens* |
| 1921 | *Monday or Tuesday* |
| 1924 | *Mr Bennett and Mrs Brown* |
| 1925 | *Common Reader*, Series 1 |
| 1929 | *A Room of One's Own* |
| 1932 | *Common Reader*, Series 2 |
| 1933 | *Flush* |
| 1938 | *Three Guineas* |
| 1940 | *Roger Fry* |

# Bloomsbury Lives

**(Arthur) Clive (Heward) Bell**
Born 16 September 1881
Died 18 September 1964

**Vanessa Bell**
Born 30 May 1879
Died 7 April 1961

**(Dora) Carrington**
Born 29 March 1893
Died 11 March 1932

**Roger (Eliot) Fry**
Born 14 December 1866
Died 9 September 1934

**David Garnett ('Bunny')**
Born 9 March 1892
Died 17 February 1981

**Duncan (James Corrowr) Grant**
Born 21 January 1885
Died 9 May 1978

**(John) Maynard Keynes**
Born 5 June 1883
Died 21 April 1946

**(Charles Otto) Desmond MacCarthy**
Born 20 May 1877
Died 7 June 1952

**Mary MacCarthy ('Molly')**
Born August 1882
Died 29 December 1953

**Frances Marshall, later Partridge**
Born 15 March 1900
Died 5 February 2004

**Adrian (Leslie) Stephen**
Born 27 October 1883
Died 3 May 1948

**(Julian) Thoby Stephen**
Born 8 September 1880
Died 20 November 1906

**(Giles) Lytton Strachey**
Born 1 March 1880
Died 21 January 1932

**Saxon (Arnoll) Sydney-Turner**
Born 28 October 1880
Died 4 November 1962

**(Adeline) Virginia Woolf**
Born 25 January 1882
Died 28 March 1941

**Leonard (Sidney) Woolf**
Born 25 November 1880
Died 14 August 1969

# Bloomsbury – What, Why and Who?

· · · · · · · · · · ·

## What Does 'Bloomsbury' Mean Today?

On the surface, 'Bloomsbury' means simply a geographical area of London, postcoded WC1. But, although this would seem odd to the group of people who were named after the area, it has connotations of smart fashionability. With its regency buildings, built in squares with gardens at their centres, the district, even the name, conjures up early nineteenth-century images of ladies with parasols, linen and muslin, and delicate floral patterns.

But what does it mean to the person in the street, the 'man on the Clapham omnibus', as the Victorians would have said? Most people, because of the meteoric rise of Harry Potter, know of Bloomsbury Publishing, so named because of its geographical roots in that district. To locals, Bloomsbury is the home of the University of London. Others are familiar with the Bloomsbury area of London because of the 'Bloomsbury Group', who lived in WC1 in the first half of the twentieth century. They know the Bloomsbury Group were a scandalous lot, who broke society's rules and got away with it because they were artists and writers, and therefore 'bohemians' who could not be expected to follow laws laid down by others.

A search on the internet brings a variety of results bearing the Bloomsbury name: book and magazine publishers, literary sites, a theatre, a church, an auction house, an English-language school, financial consultants, a London chamber orchestra, an au pair agency, a dental practice, even a fleet of expensive cars. Further afield there are a restaurant in North Carolina, a Canadian interior design company, a garden furniture outlet in Minneapolis (based on the domestic designs at Charleston Farmhouse), a florist in Sydney, a Hong Kong bookshop.

So there we have it. 'Bloomsbury' is synonymous, apparently, with literature and the arts, high culture, good taste and comfortable living. Not a bad legacy.

## Why Are We Fascinated by Virginia Woolf and Bloomsbury?

When Frances Partridge died a few weeks before her 104th birthday on 5 February 2004 it was generally agreed that she had been the last survivor of Bloomsbury, the avant-garde group of friends who flourished in the first half of the twentieth century. Most had died many years earlier. Yet the appeal of Virginia Woolf and the Bloomsbury Group remains. An annual conference is held to report on Virginia Woolf studies; there are Virginia Woolf societies in the UK, the US, France, Japan and Korea (see pp. 199–200); new editions and translations of her books appear regularly; and new critical and biographical studies of Woolf and Bloomsbury find eager readers throughout the world. An internet search comes up with over half a million results for 'Virginia Woolf' and 40,000 for 'Bloomsbury Group' and 'Bloomsbury Set' added together. Why, eighty years after its heyday, does Bloomsbury still attract so much attention?

As you might expect, there is no single reason, but there are a number of factors in the continued appeal. Chief among these is that Bloomsbury was composed of talented people: Virginia Woolf is generally considered one of the best writers of the twentieth century; Maynard Keynes's economic theories

*An issue of the* Virginia Woolf Bulletin, *the journal of the Virginia Woolf Society of Great Britain*

# Six Degrees of Separation

It is interesting to play 'six degrees of separation' with Bloomsbury – think of someone famous who would have been in London in the first half of the twentieth century, and a connection can almost certainly be made with one or more of the Bloomsbury Group, usually in less than six moves.

---

### H.H. Asquith – Violet Asquith – Rupert Brooke – James Strachey – Lytton Strachey

Prime Minister Herbert Asquith's daughter Violet developed a close friendship with the poet Rupert Brooke, on whom James Strachey, brother of Lytton, had a violent crush for many years.

---

### Captain R.F. Scott – Kathleen Scott – Hilton Young – Virginia Woolf

Scott's widow, Kathleen, later became the wife of politician Hilton Young, one of Virginia Woolf's former suitors.

---

A couple of Duncan Grant's links stretched further afield:

---

### Adolf Hitler – Unity Mitford – Duchess of Devonshire – Violet Hammersley – Duncan Grant

Duncan's friend Violet introduced him to the Duke and Duchess of Devonshire. The Duchess's sister was Unity Mitford, a great friend and admirer of Hitler.

---

Sometimes the links form a circular chain, or lead to another Bloomsbury figure:

---

### Lytton Strachey – James Strachey – Rupert Brooke – Elisabeth van Rysselberghe – André Gide – Dorothy Bussy – Lytton Strachey

Lytton Strachey's brother James was friends with Rupert Brooke, whose ex-lover Elisabeth van Rysselberghe was later impregnated by André Gide, for whom Lytton's sister Dorothy nursed an unrequited passion for many years.

---

### Clive Bell – Mary Hutchinson – Jeremy Hutchinson – Peggy Ashcroft – E.M. Forster – Leonard Woolf

Clive Bell's mistress, Mary Hutchinson, had a son who married Peggy Ashcroft, who played Mrs Moore in the film of E.M. Forster's book, *A Passage to India*. Forster was a friend of Leonard Woolf, as indeed was Ms Ashcroft in Leonard's later years.

are still studied; Roger Fry and Clive Bell introduced the Impressionists and Post-Impressionists to Britain; Lytton Strachey's irreverent writing style revolutionized the art of biography. Bloomsbury included some very modern thinkers, whose ideas were ahead of their time. They believed in many things that find an echo in our beliefs today, such as liberalism, democracy and the value of friendship; they scorned insincerity and false logic, and subjected commonly held convictions to the acid test of discussion and argument. Their advanced views on sexual relations and child-rearing were worlds away from the opinions of their Victorian parents. Young adults of the 1960s would have seen them as advocates of 'free love', and approved their experiments in communal living and in the schooling of their children. The 'radical' concepts they supported – socialism, women's suffrage, stream-of-consciousness writing – are now embedded in our society and culture.

But there is another, lesser, reason for the fascination with which the Bloomsbury group are regarded – they apparently knew *everyone*. They were a close-knit group of friends, but this did not prevent them from making new friends, and their circle of acquaintances was extremely wide. Between them, they were in contact with many of the well-known figures of their time and especially with anyone connected with or interested in the arts. Most of them lived at least part of the year in London, and London had a much smaller population then than it does

now. Society hostesses such as Sibyl Colefax and Ottoline Morrell threw parties with the intention of introducing talented people to other talented people. Virginia Woolf's reputation as a writer and the Hogarth Press's reputation as a publisher brought her and her husband Leonard into close contact with other writers; the art critic Roger Fry acted as a conduit to the world of fine art; there were even a few aristocrats in the mix – Virginia could never resist a title!

## Some Common Misconceptions

Occasionally people who know little about the Bloomsbury Group jump to the wrong conclusions. There are several Bloomsbury myths that need to be dispelled before going any further.

### Myth 1: The Bloomsbury 'Club'

Many assume that Bloomsbury was an organized club, each member of which shared the others' beliefs. Nothing could be further from the truth. The guru of early Bloomsbury was Cambridge philosopher G.E. Moore, but while Lytton Strachey and his friends were great admirers, Roger Fry positively was not. Virginia Woolf came late to Moore's famous book, *Principia Ethica*, and Vanessa Bell probably never read it. Likewise, their views on art differed widely. Roger Fry influenced the thinking of Clive and Vanessa Bell and Virginia Woolf on art, but Lytton Strachey and Maynard Keynes remained unmoved by Roger's passion for the French Post-

≈ Bloomsbury Club ≈
Members Only

≈ Rules ≈

All members should:

≈ Believe unquestioningly in the philosophy of G.E. Moore.
≈ Promote the aims of Post-Impressionist art.
≈ Support pacifism in every conflict.
≈ Have several sexual partners simultaneously, of the same sex wherever possible.

≈ ≈ ≈ ≈ ≈ ≈

Impressionists. Keynes, in the opinion of his Bloomsbury friends, had no aesthetic sense at all. (Unfortunate, if true, since he later married a ballerina and chaired the Arts Council of Great Britain.) While Bloomsbury shared a few fundamental beliefs, such as a rejection of established religion, they had very different attitudes to war, for instance. They were fairly united in their opposition to the First World War, but their views of the Second World War were less straightforward and more diverse (see pp. 165–6).

## Myth 2: Promiscuous Bloomsbury

Because of their enlightened views on sex and marriage, the Bloomsbury Group have developed a reputation for sexual licence and bed-hopping. Virginia was chastised by relatives for sharing 38 Brunswick Square with several young men, to some of whom she was not related; she and Vanessa shocked a don's wife by dressing

as women from Gauguin paintings at the Post-Impressionist Ball in early 1911 (see p. 128); a rumour began (quite unsubstantiated) that Vanessa had had sexual relations with Maynard Keynes.

But despite a few youthful rebellions, on the whole this reputation was unjustified. Virginia and Leonard Woolf, for instance, were almost certainly completely faithful during their marriage (though Vita Sackville-West told her husband Harold Nicolson that she had bedded Virginia). Virginia's sister Vanessa Bell had only two intimate relationships with other men after the breakdown of her marriage to Clive Bell. Her husband, on the other hand, was extremely susceptible to female charms, and had a series of lady-friends until his death. The homosexual men in the group were the most sexually active, though generally not promiscuous – with the exception of the charming but vague Duncan Grant, who attracted the attentions of Adrian Stephen, Lytton Strachey, Maynard Keynes, David ('Bunny') Garnett and many more outside Bloomsbury. Lytton Strachey, even when he lived with Carrington, often had a young man in tow, but only one at a time. Interestingly, even though homosexually-inclined Bloomsbury men had affairs and lived with other men in their youth, most settled down with a female companion in later life: Lytton Strachey set up house with Carrington; Maynard Keynes married the Russian ballerina Lydia Lopokova; Duncan Grant lived with Vanessa Bell for forty-five years; Adrian Stephen married Karin Costelloe; James

Strachey married Newnham graduate Alix Sargant-Florence; David Garnett married Angelica Bell, the daughter of his ex-lover Duncan.

### Myth 3: The Invalid or Mad Virginia

Because she was periodically ill, Virginia Woolf is often envisaged as a fragile invalid of delicate sensibilities, permanently wrapped up in old lace and surrounded by an aroma of lavender. But one only has to read Virginia Woolf's books to see that, though she is subtle and acute, her thinking is as sharp and vigorous as you could wish. *Orlando* testifies to her gift for full-bodied fantasy; *The Waves* to her avant-gardism; and six volumes of letters to her robust and mischievous sense of humour.

If people know two 'facts' about Virginia Woolf, they are that she was mad, and that she eventually committed suicide. Actually, she suffered from what we now call manic depression or bipolar disease, and killed herself at the age of fifty-nine, fearing that she was about to enter into one of the worst bouts of mental illness of her life. In the film *The Hours*, Nicole Kidman played Woolf as an unhappy, self-obsessed woman. While this may have been a more-or-less accurate portrayal of Woolf's state of mind during her periods of illness, for much of her life she was healthy and happy and was a stimulating and fascinating companion, as her friends confirm in letters and memoirs.

### Who Was 'Bloomsbury'?

There are as many opinions as to the composition of Bloomsbury as there

are Bloomsbury biographers. Most would agree that the core comprised the Woolfs, the Bells, Duncan Grant, Lytton Strachey, Maynard Keynes; most classifications would also include Roger Fry and Desmond MacCarthy. Opinions about its composition were given by a few Bloomsbury members: Virginia Woolf, Clive Bell, Leonard Woolf and Quentin Bell.

### Virginia Woolf's Bloomsbury

In the early 1920s Virginia Woolf defined 'Old Bloomsbury' as that group of friends that began to meet in late 1904; that is the four Stephen siblings, Clive Bell, Lytton Strachey and Saxon Sydney-Turner (see 'Old Bloomsbury', in *Moments of Being*). She does not make a list, but it seems reasonable to assume that, although her half-brother Gerald Duckworth was present at the first meetings, she would not have counted him as 'Old Bloomsbury'. His attendance in any case appears to have dropped off, and he is not mentioned as contributing to the philosophical discussions that characterized early Bloomsbury. On the other hand, the presence of Adrian Stephen may be inferred even though his name does not occur in what Virginia refers to as 'Chapter One' Bloomsbury. 'Chapter Two' Bloomsbury emerged after Vanessa's marriage to Clive Bell in 1907, continuing until the advent of the First World War in 1914. In Virginia's view the circle widened from the gathering of Cambridge graduates it had been, and included additional 'members' Roger Fry,

Desmond MacCarthy, Duncan Grant and Maynard Keynes. Oddly, Leonard Woolf is not referred to, although he had returned to England from Ceylon in 1911 and married Virginia in 1912, but his presence must also be assumed.

### Clive Bell's Bloomsbury

In Clive Bell's essay, 'Bloomsbury' (*Old Friends*, 1956), he pretends scepticism of any group that could have been called 'Bloomsbury'. The term, he says, originates from a letter written by Molly MacCarthy in 1910 or 1911, though the original group of friends – Clive, Lytton, Leonard, Saxon and Thoby Stephen – had become acquainted at Cambridge a decade earlier. The second incarnation emerged in 1907 when Bell married Vanessa Stephen, and she and her siblings Virginia and Adrian can be said to have become members. By this time Thoby Stephen was dead, Leonard Woolf was a colonial administrator in Ceylon (now Sri Lanka), and a number of other friends were frequent visitors to 46 Gordon Square (Clive and Vanessa's home) or to 29 Fitzroy Square (where Virginia and Adrian Stephen shared a house). 'Old Bloomsbury', as Bell refers to the group, came to an end with the First World War. Although he includes Duncan Grant and Maynard Keynes in the 1907–14 group, two major omissions in Bell's list are Roger Fry and Desmond MacCarthy. For post-1918 Bloomsbury he adds several young men who became acquainted with the circle, as well as Ralph Partridge (though not Carrington, who was married to him and had known the group for longer), Frances Marshall (Ralph's second wife) and Duncan Grant's lover David Garnett.

### Leonard Woolf's Bloomsbury

Leonard Woolf, in his autobiography, does not acknowledge a pre-1912 Bloomsbury, for purely geographical reasons: very few of the group actually lived in Bloomsbury, he says, although the Stephens had lived in Gordon Square since 1904. In his opinion, the group came into being after he returned to England from Ceylon. His 'Old Bloomsbury', as distinct from Clive Bell's, dates from 1912 to the beginning of the First World War in 1914, and includes the Bells, the Woolfs, Adrian Stephen, Lytton Strachey, Duncan Grant, Maynard Keynes, Roger Fry, Desmond *and* Molly MacCarthy, and E.M. Forster. For the interwar period, from 1918 to 1939, he includes Vanessa's children and David Garnett in the mix.

### Quentin Bell's Bloomsbury

Clive and Vanessa's younger son, Quentin Bell, took on the task of defining two phases of Bloomsbury in his 1968 book, *Bloomsbury*. His 1913 version includes all the main players: the Bells, Woolfs and MacCarthys, Adrian Stephen, Lytton Strachey, Duncan Grant, Roger Fry and Maynard Keynes, plus Morgan Forster and a number of others on the fringes. After the First World War his version has narrowed to the core named above, minus Adrian Stephen, and with Forster a more frequent visitor.

### On the Fringes

As we can see, even within Bloomsbury there is no consensus as to its composition. It is particularly odd, however, that Clive Bell does not mention Desmond and Molly MacCarthy. Desmond was a disciple of G.E. Moore at Cambridge and was later intimate with the Bells and Woolfs. But the omission of Roger Fry on any of Bell's three lists is, frankly, bizarre. Fry was arguably the artistic heart of Bloomsbury and an essential part of its composition after 1910.

Also strangely unacknowledged but on the fringes after 1916 were Carrington and her friends, the young, crop-haired 'Bloomsbury bunnies', as Virginia Woolf referred to them: (Dora) Carrington, Barbara Bagenal, Dorothy Brett, Faith Henderson and Alix Sargant-Florence. Several had strong Bloomsbury connections: Carrington was Lytton Strachey's companion for many years; Barbara Bagenal was a great friend of both Saxon Sydney-Turner and Clive Bell; Alix Sargant-Florence pursued Lytton Strachey's brother James and eventually married him. There were also several young men: Francis Birrell, a critic and journalist; Raymond Mortimer, a literary critic; Ralph Partridge, a friend of Lytton Strachey's who married Carrington and then Frances Marshall; Stephen Tomlin, a sculptor who married Lytton's niece Julia and in 1931 produced the only three-dimensional image of Virginia Woolf during her lifetime; psychologist W.J.H. ('Sebastian') Sprott, and critic and poet F.L. Lucas. (See pp. 108–12 for more about Bloomsbury's fringes.)

# Virginia Stephen At Home

· · · · · · · · · · · ·

## Background

For a writer at the forefront of the modernist movement, Virginia Woolf's background and early life were surprisingly Victorian. Her father was a historian, writer and critic, the first editor of the *Dictionary of National Biography* (still going strong today). Her mother, Julia Duckworth, née Jackson, came from a family of renowned beauties. Both had been married before: Julia's first husband, barrister Herbert Duckworth, left her a widowed mother of three at twenty-four; Leslie's first wife was the daughter of novelist William Makepeace Thackeray, Harriet Marian ('Minny'), by whom he had one daughter, Laura, who had mental difficulties.

At the time of Minny's death, Julia Duckworth was the Stephens' neighbour. Sympathetic, practical, austerely beautiful and an admirer of Leslie's writing, Julia became Leslie's prop. His gratitude for her kindness turned to love, and in 1878 Julia eventually accepted

*22 Hyde Park Gate in Kensington, the Stephen family home until 1904*

his marriage proposal. She was thirty-two and Leslie forty-five. Between them they already had four children: George,

9

Stella and Gerald Duckworth, and Laura Stephen. Four more were added in quick succession: Vanessa in 1879, Julian Thoby in 1880, Adeline Virginia in 1882 and Adrian Leslie in 1883.

This large family lived at 22 Hyde Park Gate in Kensington, a tall town house with five floors plus basement. Together with the servants, there were seventeen or eighteen people living in the house. Virginia remembered chiefly the lack of privacy and the claustrophobic atmosphere. Her parents, while not didactic, had a strong moral sense and ruled the household by expressing or withholding their approval. Thoby and Adrian were sent away to school to get a traditional education and were expected to enter a profession such as the law or politics. Most of the schooling the girls received took place in the home. Julia expected her daughters only to marry and be of service – she was a born matchmaker, and Virginia remembered being taught to regard an engagement as a joyous and almost mystical event.

Once a year the Stephens escaped their tall, dark London house to spend the summer in St Ives, Cornwall. It is a long journey from London to Cornwall even now, and at the end of the nineteenth century was almost as arduous as moving house. The family stayed in Talland House, situated on high ground overlooking the bay. For Virginia, the Cornish summers were idyllic; her happiest childhood memories were of St Ives, and it inspired one of her best-loved novels, *To the Lighthouse*.

## Virginia's Family

### *Julia Stephen (1846–95)*

The daughter of a Calcutta doctor, Julia Stephen was known for her beauty. In her youth she was a model for several Pre-Raphaelites, one of whom proposed to her, and was photographed extensively by her aunt, Julia Margaret Cameron. By the time she was in her early twenties she was married to a handsome barrister and had two children, with another on the way. Then a disaster struck which was to change her rose-tinted life completely. Her husband died suddenly from a burst abscess, and she was left a widow.

*The nursery window at Talland House*

By the time Virginia was born in 1882, all this was more than a decade in the past. The Julia Stephen she knew was very different to Julia Duckworth, the young woman with a happy future ahead of her. Beautiful but grave, Mrs Stephen devoted her life to others. She ran a large household, took the troubles of friends and neighbours on her own shoulders, and paid frequent visits to the poor and the sick, accompanied by her dutiful daughter Stella Duckworth.

### Leslie Stephen (1832–1904)

Though after his wife's death Leslie Stephen was tyrannical and egotistical, he was also a man of great intelligence and integrity. As an undergraduate he had been awarded a fellowship that obliged him to be ordained as a clergyman. Several years later Leslie underwent a loss of faith and decided he must resign, sacrificing the chance of a comfortable academic career. With the same strength of mind he trained his slight frame to physical pursuits and became an accomplished rowing coach, walker and well-known alpinist. He was the first to climb the Schreckhorn in Switzerland (Thomas Hardy wrote a sonnet about it), and he became President of the Alpine Club in 1865. His mental endeavours were equally arduous. He worked constantly, writing articles and books on literature, philosophy and history, and driving himself to the point of exhaustion editing the *Dictionary of National Biography*.

Virginia Woolf wrote about the less severe side of her father in her essay 'Leslie Stephen' (*The Captain's Death Bed*), describing how he entertained his children, his sympathy with the working man, his support of his daughters' ambitions. Virginia inherited from her father his taste for literature, his work ethic and his partiality for walking long

distances. She was his favourite child. Intelligent and enquiring, she borrowed extensively from her father's library, and talked to him about what she had read. Her precociousness was such that Leslie began to think of her as a future historian. Despite her talent for imaginative and surprisingly mature storytelling, it never seemed to occur to him that she had the makings of a novelist.

### Vanessa Stephen (1879–1961)

Vanessa, the first-born of the four children of Leslie and Julia, adopted Julia's solicitous attitude towards her younger siblings, attending to them with a sense of responsibility far beyond her years. There were the usual childhood spats, and a rivalry between the girls for the attention of their elder brother Thoby (Adrian was too young to compete for). Vanessa and Thoby would occasionally tease Virginia until she turned purple. Unfortunately, Virginia's quick wit was more than a match for her sister's, and she nicknamed Vanessa 'Saint' for her inability to tell a lie. But when the boys had gone away to school, she and Virginia grew very close. Though both had skills in writing and drawing, they resolved between themselves that Vanessa was to be an artist, Virginia a writer.

Vanessa, though quietly determined to go her own way, had many of her mother's qualities – she was beautiful, reserved, maternal and dependable. For Virginia she was a surrogate mother, but Vanessa, like Julia, was always slightly distant and enigmatic. Virginia's adult

letters to Vanessa express a yearning for affection as well as mock-worship of her as a goddess. Vanessa would not, as her mother did, have signed a petition against women's right to vote – she simply took no interest in politics or current affairs. Her world centred increasingly on her family – especially her children – and her painting. (See pp. 73–6 for more on the adult Vanessa Bell.)

### Thoby Stephen (1880–1906)

Virginia's elder brother was widely adored by family and friends. As a small boy he was characterized by wilfulness and was prone to tantrums. He was bright, though not intellectual, with untidy handwriting but a facility for drawing birds and animals inherited from Leslie. He seemed to be a normal schoolboy, but caused his parents some anxiety. When he was eleven, a classmate stabbed him in the thigh with a knife – Leslie suggested it had been done out of a sense of playfulness, and that Thoby had 'allowed' him to do it. On another occasion, he walked through a window while sleepwalking during a bout of influenza. These mysterious incidents hint at a darker side to Thoby's character. But his schooldays appear to have been happy on the whole. During the holidays he would summarize for his eager younger sister what he had been taught that past term. They discussed Shakespeare and the Greeks, and Virginia was inspired to take Greek lessons of her own.

But it was Thoby's undergraduate career that had the greatest impact on his siblings. At Trinity College, Cambridge, he befriended those young men who would become the core of Bloomsbury. He was popular among the hothouse intellectuals, such as Lytton Strachey, as well as those who favoured open-air pursuits, such as Clive Bell, with whom he shared an interest in hunting. Leonard Woolf remembered Thoby as good-natured but unsentimental, and one of the most charming men he had ever met. Virginia adored him and envied his university education. She missed the cut and thrust of lively debate that finally came to her through Thoby's friends.

### Adrian Stephen (1883–1948)

Adrian had the misfortune of being the 'baby' brother – he was only a year younger than Virginia, but a late developer. He and Virginia, the two youngest, could have been expected to pair up, but his precocious sister always tagged onto the older children, and Adrian was often left out. As he would in later life, he tried to make a virtue of his exclusion. Despite being his mother's favourite, Adrian was eclipsed by his charismatic and handsome elder brother. Small for his age in boyhood, Adrian more than made up for it when he shot up to 6'5" in his teens. He was slightly built compared to Thoby and developed a self-conscious stoop, unable to come to terms with his height.

He showed a similar reluctance to face his future career and his sexuality. After a less-than-successful time at Cambridge, he began – as Thoby had – to train as a lawyer. But he gave it up, hoping to become an actor. This, together with his fondness for hoaxes and fancy-dress parties, suggests that he liked trying out different roles, in preparation for a self that had not yet solidified. In 1909 he began a liaison with Duncan Grant, Lytton Strachey's cousin, later transferring his affections to the young and beautiful Noel Olivier. Then he was snapped up by an energetic American, Karin Costelloe, a niece (by marriage) of Bertrand Russell. Though the marriage was not entirely happy, Karin's energy and sense of purpose played a large part in finally finding Adrian a career – she decided that they should both become psychoanalysts.

### Stella Duckworth (1869–97)

Julia and Herbert Duckworth's only daughter is generally seen as a tragic figure. Although she had inherited her mother's beauty, Stella did not have her strength of mind. She was a demure girl with a conventional outlook, a paler version of Julia – a fine example, in fact, of the 'Angel in the House' (see pp. 139–40). She took on many of Julia's domestic duties: accompanying the children to medical appointments, nursing them through illness, running errands, calming irritable relatives and comforting troubled ones.

Unlike her younger half-sisters, Stella had no outstanding talent that might have provided her with a profession (though she was an accomplished pianist). Julia's

greatest ambition for her eldest daughter was for her to serve others and to marry. There were several suitors for Stella, but eventually, after a lengthy courtship and much soul-searching prompted by the thought of leaving her family, Stella married a man of whom her mother had approved. But tragedy was to follow hard upon the heels of her happiness.

### George (1868–1934) and Gerald (1870–1937) Duckworth

George was a toddler and Gerald in the womb at the time of their father's death. They spent much of their childhood fatherless until Julia remarried in 1878. Until the birth of Adrian, George was his mother's favourite: a handsome, conventional boy with impeccable manners and a pronounced sense of etiquette.

The George who emerges from Virginia's autobiographical essay '22 Hyde Park Gate' is sentimental, self-indulgent, easily shocked and hypocritical. Worse, he exploits his position as the girls' sponsor to caress Virginia in private, claiming that he is trying to comfort her during her father's final illness (for more about '22 Hyde Park Gate', see pp. 64–5). Gerald, in Virginia's letters, seems harmless enough, but in 'A Sketch of the Past' he fares little better than his brother. Virginia writes of a childhood incident in which he explored her body until she squirmed with discomfort.

Virginia's reminiscences, and the speculations based on them, account for the almost demonic reputation of the Duckworth brothers in Woolf circles. But we shall never know to what extent actual abuse took place. Virginia wrote her memories of George to amuse her friends, and was prone to exaggeration. Did she wilfully misunderstand George's motives; or did he misunderstand his own? Virginia's report of Gerald's misdemeanour, more straightforwardly written, bears the stamp of truth. His seems a lesser crime, a sexually innocent young lad inquisitive about the difference between boys and girls, deciding to use his little sister as an anatomical model – but he was fifteen or more at the time, a little old for such experiments. However, it is important to note that, whatever the effect of these incidents on Virginia, she never became completely estranged from her half-brothers: George lent her his house when she was going through a bout of mental illness, and she expressed in later life an amused affection for him; Gerald was present at the first Bloomsbury meetings, and was the publisher of Virginia's first two novels.

### Laura Stephen (1870–1945)

Laura was the unacknowledged sister – as the mentally deficient (or possibly autistic) and badly behaved daughter of a learned man, she was no doubt something of an embarrassment to the family. She was born prematurely, which may have been a contributory factor to her condition, but there were also hereditary mental problems. Her grandmother, William Makepeace Thackeray's wife Isabella, was unstable – Thackeray's biographer D.J. Taylor has suggested a form of autism aggravated by post-natal depression. Nor was the Stephen family entirely free from instability: Leslie's favourite nephew Jem Stephen died in an insane asylum, and it has been suggested that Virginia's parents and siblings all suffered from different types of clinical depression.

Virginia, in 'Old Bloomsbury' (*Moments of Being*) remembers Laura's illiteracy, her stammering and her inexplicable behaviour. Leslie had tried to teach her at home, but became frustrated by her disobedience. To his credit, he kept Laura in the family home until 1891, when she was sent to a mental institution. Only when Virginia read her father's letters, full of his worries and hopes for Laura, did she realize how significant a role she had played in Leslie's life. Sadly, it seems as though Laura was neglected by her half-siblings – visits to her are seldom mentioned in diaries and letters. But she lived in mental hospitals for over fifty years, outliving her famous sister and dying at psychiatric hospital, The Priory, Roehampton, in 1945.

### Deaths of Julia, Stella, Leslie and Thoby

Between 1895 and 1906, Virginia lost four members of her immediate family. Julia's death at forty-nine from rheumatic fever was devastating for the whole family, and her sensitive thirteen-year-old daughter suffered her first breakdown in its aftermath. Leslie was unable to hide his grief from his children or to help them bear their own. He had depended utterly on Julia, emotionally and practically. Stella, as the eldest daughter, was chosen to replace her in the household. She became a surrogate mother to Leslie's children, and (the heavier burden) a surrogate wife to him, sympathizing with his stresses and strains and sharing his sorrow.

When Stella became engaged to her most ardent and persistent admirer, John (Jack) Waller Hills, in the summer of 1896, her chance for happiness relieved the gloom. But Leslie's possessiveness

*The Stephen family grave in Highgate Cemetery*

cast a shadow. He was reluctant to lose Stella. Selflessly, she agreed that she would live in a neighbouring house after her marriage. With this compromise, she married Jack in April 1897, and they went on honeymoon. But the couple's happiness was short-lived. Three months later Stella died, from peritonitis complicated by pregnancy. The shock to the family, and to Stella's new husband, was immense. A second blow had been delivered to Virginia's fragile mental health and to her conception of love and marriage.

A seven-year period of relative stability, if not happiness, now intervened. But Leslie, fifty when his youngest child was born, was ageing and his health failing. He was lonely and deaf, with a constant – though quite unjustified – fear of poverty. He was diagnosed with intestinal cancer in April 1902 but lived on for two more years. When he died in February 1904, Virginia was wracked with guilt to think how much more she might have done for him. While Vanessa, who as household manager after Stella had borne the brunt of Leslie's bad temper, briskly arranged the move to Bloomsbury, Virginia broke down under the strain of her father's death and made her first suicide attempt (see p. 177). From May to December she was under medical supervision. At last she was well, and the next two years were exciting, happy ones, brought to a sudden end by another, inexplicable death.

It was, impossibly, her beloved brother Thoby. The four siblings, plus family friend Violet Dickinson, had embarked on a trip to Greece and Turkey in the summer of 1906. On their return they found Thoby, who had gone home ahead of the others, being treated for malaria (a misdiagnosis, as it turned out – it was later discovered to be untreatable typhoid). Vanessa and Violet, too, fell ill. Virginia managed remarkably well under the strain, seemingly confident of the recovery of all three. Vanessa grew stronger. But three days after an operation for perforation of the bowel, Thoby died.

This time, perhaps surprisingly, Virginia did not break down. Thoby's death was a terrible shock, but somehow it was not the solid wall separating her from the future that the other deaths had been. Julia's and Stella's deaths had come upon an unwary and vulnerable teenager; Leslie's brought with it an unbearable confusion of feelings. Virginia's attitude towards Thoby had been more straightforward; there was no guilt to contend with, only a wish that she had known him better.

Virginia Woolf wrote about all four deaths in her novels. Julia's is commemorated in *To the Lighthouse*, probably the most autobiographical of Woolf's works. In *The Voyage Out*, Rachel's sudden death as she was on the brink of a new life can be traced back to Stella. Leslie's protracted illness is fictionalized as Rose Pargiter's long, drawn-out dying in *The Years*. Jacob Flanders' life, curtailed by war in *Jacob's Room*, is an echo of Thoby's death at twenty-six. Plain too, in *The Voyage Out* and *Mrs Dalloway*, are the author's doubts about the doctor's ability to save life – or sanity. (See later chapters for more in-depth treatments of these books.)

# Beginnings of Bloomsbury

. . . . . . . . . . .

### Kensington to Bloomsbury

Without Thoby Stephen, Bloomsbury might never have existed. His life was short, but it shaped the future for his sisters and brother. It began in 1905 when, after the death of their father, Vanessa, Thoby, Virginia and Adrian moved from the house where they had been born and grown up. For the young Stephens, the move from 22 Hyde Park Gate in wealthy Kensington to 46 Gordon Square in bohemian Bloomsbury was more than geographical. It was a shift from the Victorian age to the Edwardian, a rebellion against their parents' world and the creation of their own. Where 22 Hyde Park Gate had been all heavy drapes and black paint with raspberry edgings, Vanessa saw to it that 46 Gordon Square was furnished in light, modern fabrics with walls of plain white distemper. The clutter of Victoriana was replaced with a few carefully placed objects, which took on a completely different appearance in their new, airy surroundings. The Stephens' lives were transformed along with their interior decorations – for Virginia and Vanessa especially. They each had a sitting-room instead of just a bedroom for entertaining, and there was additionally a large shared drawing-room and study. Instead of endless tea-table duties on behalf of grieving relatives and elderly friends of their parents, they intended to write (Virginia) and paint (Vanessa), and make lots of new friends.

### How the Bloomsbury Group Started

The two years from late 1904 to late 1906 were a relatively happy period for the Stephen siblings. Their father's death had been a blow, but it left them free to lead their lives as they wished. Even Virginia realized in later life that Leslie's death had been the price for their freedom. It was fairly unusual then for young unmarried people to have their own establishment, without parents

## Bloomsbury Geography

Bloomsbury is a residential district of west-central London that includes a number of Georgian garden squares, the British Museum and parts of the University of London. Geographically speaking, it is the area bounded at the north by Euston Road, at the south by High Holborn, and west and east by Tottenham Court Road and Gray's Inn Road respectively. West of Bloomsbury, between Tottenham Court Road and Great Portland Street, is Fitzrovia.

*Map of Bloomsbury, west and central. Shaded areas and marginal arrows indicate positions of Bloomsbury residential squares*

*The gatehouse of Trinity College, Cambridge*

or older relatives, and the Stephens' social lives were packed with visits and visitors. To begin with there was a variety of guests, but gradually relatives and friends of the family were shed and Thoby's Trinity College friends assumed a prominent place in the lives of all four Stephens. Virginia and Vanessa had already met some of them during visits to Cambridge, but it was when the friends began to drop round to Gordon Square for Thoby's Thursday 'at home' evenings that the sisters really began to know them. The first gathering, on 16 March 1905, was not a great success – the taciturn Saxon Sydney-Turner was the only non-family visitor. But the following week there were nine guests,

and the talk continued until 1.00 a.m. – Bloomsbury had taken its first faltering steps.

For Thoby's friends, his Thursday evenings were a continuation of their Cambridge gatherings – most of them had belonged to at least one 'secret' society. Foremost among these was the Cambridge Conversazione Society, known as the Apostles, an exclusive debating club founded by twelve undergraduates in 1820, which had numbered Tennyson among its early members. It was a great honour to be asked to join, and membership was secret. Clive Bell, who had not been elected to the Apostles, formed the Midnight Society, whose members (Clive, Lytton Strachey,

Saxon Sydney-Turner, Leonard Woolf and Thoby) met at midnight on Saturdays to read from classic works of literature. It was from these two societies that Bloomsbury evolved.

### G.E. Moore

The intellectual mentor of Thoby and his friends was G.E. Moore, an unworldly, prodigiously intelligent, thirty-something don whose influence had spread widely among Cambridge undergraduates. Moore's philosophy, or the part of it adopted by Bloomsbury, was that things are intrinsically good (or not) and that truth and friendship were among the 'highest goods'. Truth was pursued to the minutest detail: 'What exactly do you *mean* by that?' was a typical Mooreish phrase taken up by his followers, and often repeated at the Thursday evenings.

---

### TRUE OR FALSE?

'All Cretans are liars.'

*Epimenides the Cretan, 6th century BC*

In making this claim, Epimenides must be lying – mustn't he?

---

### Who Was in the Original Group?

As demonstrated in the Preface, the composition of 'Old Bloomsbury' is not easy to define: there is much disagreement even among its members. Virginia Woolf saw 'Old Bloomsbury' as

that group which evolved from Thoby's 'at homes'. Leonard Woolf dates its beginnings to a dinner party that he attended on the evening of 3 July 1911, shortly after his return to England from Ceylon. Clive Bell claimed that his Cambridge Midnight Society had been at the heart of the real Bloomsbury, and in terms of the central friendships that propelled Bloomsbury into being, he was probably right.

### What Did They Talk about?

The talk at the earliest of Thoby's 'at homes' was high-minded, intellectual and philosophical – what it was *not* about was love and marriage, the staple of Hyde Park Gate conversations. Virginia and Vanessa had been used to lengthy discussions about the affairs and engagements of relatives and friends. Among Thoby's friends they were treated according to their contribution to the discussion in hand, and complimented on their grasp of the argument rather than on a new dress or hairstyle. Both found this very refreshing after George Duckworth's attempts to mould them into social successes. Under discussion at 46 Gordon Square were abstract topics such as good, truth, beauty and reality. Although Virginia was largely self-educated, she was almost as widely read as the undergraduates, and could hold her own on the subject of books. One such conversation she remembered was with Ralph Hawtrey about 'atmosphere' in literature. Lytton Strachey noted

*46 Gordon Square, where the first meeting of 'Old Bloomsbury' took place in March 1905*

disapprovingly one evening that Hilton Young, the future cabinet minister, had insisted on talking about politics. Chit-chat and the usual after-dinner subjects were not acceptable to most Bloomsberries.

## How the Group Grew

By the time Leonard Woolf returned to England from Ceylon in 1911, Bloomsbury was in full swing. Lytton Strachey's cousin Duncan Grant and their mutual friend, future economist John Maynard Keynes, had been drawn into the group. As had Desmond MacCarthy, who had been at Cambridge a few years before the others and shared Bloomsbury's admiration for Moore, a

personal friend of his. His wife Molly felt less at ease with the rough-and-tumble of intellectual debate, and was slightly isolated by her deafness after 1915, but she had a quirky and original outlook, and her writing was praised by Virginia Woolf. It was Molly who coined the term 'Bloomsberry' to describe an individual Bloomsburyian. Roger Fry's opinions on modern art became highly influential within the group from 1910. Apart from Moore, who was never actually a 'member' of Bloomsbury, Fry was probably their most important intellectual influence.

The Bloomsberries had come together to discuss philosophical abstractions, but there were a few other distinguishing features. There was their rejection, or at least scepticism, of the accepted tenets of society and of Victorian mores and tastes; and their openness about sexuality and sex-related topics. They freed themselves from the bounds of propriety around 1908 – the watershed is generally dated to an occasion when Lytton pointed to a stain on Vanessa's dress said enquiringly, 'Semen?' But the groundwork had already been laid after the marriage of Clive and Vanessa in February 1907. Both enjoyed 'copulation', as it was sometimes rather clinically called, and liked to receive visitors from their Louis XV bed. Towards the end of that year, Clive set up the Play Reading Society, and the friends grew accustomed to speaking suggestive lines from Elizabethan and Restoration plays. By the summer of 1908, Vanessa was reading with delight Lytton's semi-pornographic poetry and making copies for Virginia, and the talk was all of sex and 'buggery'. The second phase of Bloomsbury was underway.

CAPSULE

# The Intellectual Scene

· · · · · · · · · · ·

Bloomsbury, of course, was not the only group of intellectual friends in London in the early part of the twentieth century.

## The Fabian Society

- Founded by Sidney and Beatrice Webb, George Bernard Shaw, H.G. Wells and others in 1884 to fight for social reform. The precursor of the Labour Party, to which it still has links. To the Fabians we owe the minimum wage and the National Health Service.
- Sidney Webb wrote much of the Labour Party's 1918 constitution. He and his wife Beatrice published books on trade unionism, communism, democracy, local government, capitalism and the poor law, and founded the London School of Economics and the *New Statesman*.
- Shaw and Wells used plays and novels to convey their socialist ideals, but Wells fell out with the Society for their lack of radicalism (he was an advocate of free love).

- The Young Fabians included future minister Hugh Dalton, poet Rupert Brooke, and Amber Reeves, the lover of H.G. Wells who later gave birth to his child. (Wells's novel *Ann Veronica* draws heavily on their affair.)

## The Neo-pagans

- Named by Virginia Woolf because of their love for the outdoor life, the Neo-pagans were led by Rupert Brooke. Their 'simple life' tenet of outdoor camping and nude bathing originated with Bedales School, which rated character formation above intellect.
- Included Virginia's friend Ka (Katherine) Cox, Gwen and Frances Darwin (granddaughters of Charles), Frenchman Jacques Raverat, Brooke Bond tea heir Justin Brooke (no relation to Rupert), economics student Dudley Ward, Maynard Keynes's brother Geoffrey, and the Olivier sisters – Noel, Bryn, Margery and Daphne.
- More a summer recreation than an intellectual movement.

*44 Bedford Square, home of Ottoline Morrell*

Photographs of the Neo-pagans almost always show them at an outdoor camp, casually dressed in peasant-style clothes, barefoot, the girls in headscarves.

- Occasional crossover with Bloomsbury: David Garnett, childhood playmate of Noel Olivier, was one of the younger members; Virginia accompanied Ka on the 1911 summer camp; Vanessa joined the camp in 1913. Lytton's brother James Strachey, passionately in love with Rupert Brooke, hovered on the fringes. Lytton visited a summer camp, but stayed in a hotel nearby; for Maynard Keynes, the outdoor life was surprisingly agreeable.

## Ottoline Morrell and Garsington

- Lady Ottoline Morrell, who lived in Bloomsbury at 44 Bedford Square, was an extravagant character, with a romantic outlook and a high regard for anyone with an artistic talent (see also pp. 109–10).
- Ottoline moved into Garsington Manor in Oxfordshire in 1915. Friends flocked there as a haven from the war, and a place where conscientious objectors could do light farm work to appease the authorities.
- Guests included most of Bloomsbury, W.B. Yeats, Bertrand Russell (he and Ottoline had an affair), Henry Lamb (ditto), Mark Gertler, Dorothy Brett, Katherine Mansfield, John Middleton Murry, Siegfried Sassoon, Stanley Spencer, H.H. Asquith (the Prime Minister), Oscar Wilde's friend Robbie Ross.
- Fictional caricatures: Hermione Roddice in D.H. Lawrence's *Women in Love* (1920); Lady Septugesima Goodley in Osbert Sitwell's *Triple Fugue* (1924); Lady Rusholme in Gilbert Cannan's *Pugs and Peacocks* (1921); Priscilla Wimbush in Aldous Huxley's *Crome Yellow* (1921); Lady Sybilline Quarrell in Alan Bennett's play *Forty Years On* (1968) (see pp. 187–9 for books based on Bloomsbury).

### Sibyl Colefax and Chelsea

- Centred on the then unfashionable King's Road and environs. After the arrival of Sibyl Colefax, however, a loose-knit circle of friends sprang up.
- Society hostess Sibyl Colefax was co-founder of the decorating firm Colefax and Fowler, still going strong today and still based in Chelsea (110 Fulham Road). Her home, Argyll House on the King's Road, was nicknamed 'Lions' Corner House' (a pun on 'Lyons', a famous cafeteria in the Strand), after her habit of collecting celebrities. Bloomsbury and Chelsea visited each other's houses, although Virginia Woolf wrote to Logan Pearsall Smith that each group ridiculed the other behind its back (*Letters* 5, 6 Nov 1932).
- Another Chelsea resident was the sociable and easy-going Desmond MacCarthy, who metaphorically straddled Bloomsbury and Chelsea. He and his wife Molly lived in Wellington Square, off the King's Road, for three decades. Geographically he was a Chelsea resident, but intellectually he had much in common with his Bloomsbury friends.
- Neighbours were Desmond's old Cambridge friends Logan Pearsall Smith and Robert Trevelyan, Duncan Grant's friend the painter

*Argyll House, 211 King's Road, Chelsea, home of Sibyl Colefax*

Violet Hammersley, interior decorator Syrie Maugham, Osbert Sitwell, the American painter Ethel Sands and her partner Nan Hudson, and upcoming writer Cyril Connolly. Ellen Terry lived at 215 King's Road from 1904 to 1920.

### The Hampstead 'Thursdayers'

- Met on Thursday evenings in the early 1920s and consisted of: *Adelphi* editor John Middleton Murry; his wife, the New Zealand short-story writer, Katherine Mansfield (when she was not on the continent recuperating from tuberculosis); painters Dorothy

Brett and Mark Gertler; the Russian translator S.S. Koteliansky ('Kot'); D.H. and Frieda Lawrence (when they were in London); Sydney Waterlow, Virginia's old suitor and a cousin of Katherine Mansfield; Herbert J. Milne, assistant keeper of manuscripts in the British Museum; and J.W.N. Sullivan, an Irish scientist and journalist.

- The Hampstead set was inclined towards spiritual matters: Murry and Waterlow especially were constantly searching for 'truths' to guide their lives.
- Virginia Woolf thought them a misogynist bunch – the only women invited were Frieda Lawrence, Katherine Mansfield and D.H. Lawrence devotee Dorothy Brett, whose Hampstead house was used for meetings. The Woolfs were invited to join in 1922, but declined. Virginia had mixed feelings about Murry but on the whole disliked him, and she was not interested in spiritual salvation.
- The death knell came in 1924 after an acrimonious split between Murry and Kot over control of the *Adelphi*. Sydney Waterlow, failing to heal the rift, sided with Kot. The group was geographically scattered when Brett emigrated to New Mexico with the Lawrences and Murry, and Waterlow was appointed British Minister to Bangkok.

## Augustus John and Fitzrovia

- Named after Fitzroy Square and the Fitzroy Tavern, Fitzrovia can be described as the part of London immediately to the west of Bloomsbury, between Great Portland Street and Tottenham Court Road, and bounded by Euston Road and Oxford Street, where Fitzrovia borders on Soho.
- Fitzrovia had long been an artists' quarter – Constable lived and worked in Charlotte Street, and Pre-Raphaelite Ford Madox Brown in Fitzroy Square.
- The Fitzroy Tavern was the favourite watering hole of bohemian painter Augustus John, sculptor Jacob Epstein and 'Queen of Bohemia' Nina Hamnett, who had tried all the other pubs in the locale and pronounced this one the best. For a period from 1913 Nina worked at Roger Fry's Omega Workshops in Fitzroy Square (see pp. 84–5).
- Regulars at the Fitzroy Tavern were Kathleen Hale, best known as the creator of *Orlando the Marmalade Cat*, who had fled the provinces to seek adventure among the Fitzrovians, and took art lessons from Duncan Grant. George Bernard Shaw was another regular, as was his namesake George Orwell. Black magic practitioner Aleister Crowley sometimes dropped in, although he was not

wholeheartedly welcomed by the owner of the Fitzroy Tavern.

- In another Fitzrovia pub, The Wheatsheaf in Rathbone Place, Tenby-born Augustus John introduced fellow Welshman Dylan Thomas to his future wife, Caitlin Macnamara, in 1936.
- Augustus John, Epstein and Hamnett graduated to the smoky haze of Regent Street's francophile Café Royal, where they were joined by novelist Graham Greene and poet Cecil Day Lewis. Clive Bell was sometimes to be seen with one of his young ladies. Here poor artists had drunk downstairs and rich patrons dined upstairs since the days of Oscar Wilde.

# The Colonialist and the Novelist: Leonard and Virginia Woolf

. . . . . . . . . . .

## Leonard Woolf (1880–1969)

Absent from early Bloomsbury, Leonard Woolf became one of its most central members. He had, of course, been one of the Cambridge friends who were Bloomsbury's origin. Although he had much in common with them intellectually, in terms of class and money (of which they would all have been conscious) he was a rung lower down the ladder. He was also Jewish by descent, in an era of casual anti-Semitism, so he had good reason to think of himself as an outsider.

*Leonard Woolf*

Leonard's father, a successful lawyer, died at forty-seven. Mrs Woolf and her nine children were forced to live more frugally after his death, moving from their large house in fashionable Kensington to a smaller one in Putney. Their poverty was relative, but it felt like poverty nevertheless. The only way that the boys could be educated properly (the education of daughters was not viewed as essential or even desirable) was to win a scholarship, which several of them did. Scholarships enabled Leonard to attend St Paul's School in London and Trinity College, Cambridge.

### Cambridge

Cambridge was a new and exciting world for the young Leonard Woolf. He made many interesting and stimulating friends, beginning with Saxon Sydney-Turner, then Lytton Strachey, Thoby Stephen and Clive Bell. He, Saxon and Lytton became great admirers of the novels of Henry James and the philosophy of G.E. Moore, both of which influenced their conversation and their behaviour. They were elected to the Apostles debating society, in which Moore was by this time a leading light.

It was at Cambridge that Leonard met the elderly Leslie Stephen, and was impressed by his dignity and distinguished bearing. Later, Vanessa and Virginia visited, wearing white dresses and picture hats. Leonard Woolf observed that almost every man fell in love with them at first sight, but that they were so beautiful and so aloof that it was like falling in love with a work of art (*Sowing*, p. 186).

Though he had initially hoped to become a barrister like his father, Leonard decided instead to stay on at Trinity for a fifth year and take the civil service examination. But performing badly in the exam limited his career choices, and he applied for a post in the colonial service. He was accepted, and at the end of 1904 sailed for Ceylon.

### Ceylon

Leonard spent 1904 to 1911 in Ceylon as a hard-working but sceptical colonial administrator, beginning as a cadet and ending as Assistant Government Agent of Hambantota, a sprawling jungle district on the south coast. Hambantota and its inhabitants fascinated him, and they inspired his first novel, *The Village in the Jungle*. Leonard was responsible for sorting out local disputes as a magis-

trate, managing the salt farms and a large game sanctuary, carrying out the district census, and disease control among the livestock. He also had the grim task of presiding over judicial hangings.

The British colonials did not appeal to Leonard, and he hardly ever socialized with them. He was sometimes depressed, occasionally suicidal. Losing his virginity to a local woman only served to increase his self-loathing, as did several short-lived romances. Leonard had never meant to make a permanent life as a colonial civil servant, and after six years began to wonder where his future lay. In 1911 he was belatedly awarded a year's leave and left for England. He was never to return.

## Marriage

While Leonard was in Ceylon, Thoby Stephen had died, Vanessa Stephen had married Clive Bell, and Lytton had begun a campaign to persuade Leonard to return to England and marry Virginia. For Virginia, the return of her brother's friend was quite an event. She was immediately attracted to him, seeing off rival suitors Walter Lamb and Sydney Waterlow (see Hall 2006), and inviting Leonard to concerts and the ballet. He advised her on the purchase of Asheham House in Sussex, and on the tricky subject of earth closets (an unsophisticated type of lavatory). In the autumn she invited Leonard to join a cooperative housing scheme at 38 Brunswick Square (see pp. 148–9). By January 1912, Leonard had fallen in

love with Virginia and proposed. Like Julia, Stella and Vanessa, Virginia refused the first proposal, but by May had changed her mind. She announced rather sensationally to her friends that she was marrying an impoverished Jew who had ruled India, shot tigers and had men hanged. The wedding, in typical Bloomsbury style, was a low-key affair at St Pancras Registry Office on 10 August 1912, followed by two months of honeymoon. On their return the Woolfs went to live at 13 Clifford's Inn, just off London's Fleet Street (see p. 149).

Chapters of biographies and entire books have been devoted to the subject of the Woolfs' marriage, biographers' views of Leonard ranging from Saint to

*Clifford's Inn, off London's Fleet Street, where Virginia and Leonard lived after their marriage*

**Read On ...**

*The Village in the Jungle*, by Leonard Woolf, London: Edward Arnold, 1913; Oxford: Oxford University Press, 1981

*The Wise Virgins*, by Leonard Woolf, London: Edward Arnold, 1914; London: Persephone Books, 2003

*Autobiography*, by Leonard Woolf, London: Hogarth Press (5 vols: *Sowing*, 1960; *Growing*, 1961; *Beginning Again*, 1964; *Downhill All the Way*, 1967; *The Journey Not the Arrival Matters*, 1969)

*The Letters of Leonard Woolf*, ed. Frederic Spotts, San Diego: Harcourt, Brace, Jovanovich, 1989

*Leonard Woolf: A Biography*, by Victoria Glendinning, London: Simon and Schuster/ New York: Free Press, 2006

Svengali. He was in many ways just what Virginia needed: a practical, rational, highly ethical husband, whose ideas of hard work chimed with hers. Many lesser men would have run a mile when confronted, as Leonard was, with the fact that his new wife was mentally unstable and attempted suicide after thirteen months of marriage. But Leonard, as well as being deeply in love, had learned in Ceylon to be tough, self-disciplined and resilient.

**Work and Writing**

Leonard wrote only two novels, *The Village in the Jungle* (1913) and *The Wise Virgins* (1914), before giving way to his wife's primacy in that field. The first, much better known in Sri Lanka than it

is here, is based on Leonard's experience of Ceylonese village life, with all its superstitions and vendettas. *The Wise Virgins* is quite different. It is the story of what might have befallen Leonard if he had undergone his rites of passage in middle-class Putney instead of far from home.

Leonard's other books concern political matters: he wrote on imperialism, foreign policy, labour, industry and other associated subjects. Apart from the books, he wrote hundreds of articles, studied cooperative societies throughout the country, fought for workers' rights and reform of the divorce law, and worked on Fabian Society and Labour Party advisory committees. His book *International Government* (1916) laid the foundations for the League

There are thirty works by Virginia Woolf here — how long does it take you to find them? As an extra challenge, a few of them read backwards!

## Woolfwords

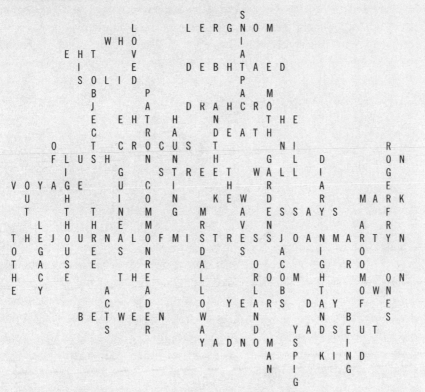

| 1 | A Room of One's Own | 16 | Monday or Tuesday |
|---|---|---|---|
| 2 | Between the Acts | 17 | Mrs Dalloway |
| 3 | Captain's Death Bed | 18 | Night and Day |
| 4 | Common Reader | 19 | On Being Ill |
| 5 | Death of the Moth | 20 | Orlando |
| 6 | Diary | 21 | Patron and the Crocus |
| 7 | Essays | 22 | Roger Fry |
| 8 | Flush | 23 | Solid Objects |
| 9 | Gipsy, the Mongrel | 24 | Street Haunting |
| 10 | In the Orchard | 25 | The Journal of Mistress Joan Martyn |
| 11 | Jacob's Room | 26 | Three Guineas |
| 12 | Kew Gardens | 27 | To the Lighthouse |
| 13 | Legacy | 28 | Waves |
| 14 | Man Who Loved His Kind | 29 | Voyage Out |
| 15 | Mark on the Wall | 30 | Years |

of Nations (today's United Nations). Despite the deep respect with which he was regarded by his contemporaries Leonard wrote in his autobiography, with characteristic matter-of-factness, that his 200,000 hours of political work had amounted to almost nothing. But additionally he co-founded the Hogarth Press, so enabling Virginia a free rein with her writing, and publishing a new generation of poets and authors. If this had been his only accomplishment, it would be an admirable one.

CAPSULE

# *The Voyage Out* (1915)

. . . . . . . . . . .

## Origins

Virginia began writing her first novel, the story of a young girl's voyage into maturity, in 1907, finally publishing it in 1915. Before this, she had written mainly articles and book reviews, with a shot at fictional biography ('Memoirs of a Novelist') that was rejected by *Cornhill Magazine*. She had also written, but not published, a few other short stories.

Originally calling it 'Melymbrosia' (a compound word suggesting a 'land of milk and honey'), she wrote and rewrote, trying to perfect her novel. She showed a draft to her brother-in-law Clive Bell. While in no doubt of her genius, he made some robust criticisms, which she took in good part. The novel was completed just before her wedding to Leonard Woolf in 1912, and accepted for publication by her half-brother Gerald Duckworth's firm in April 1913. But that summer, Virginia had a breakdown – perhaps significantly, she had recently been correcting proofs of her book. Proof-correcting was a torture for her; it was a period during which she reassessed her work and almost always found it severely wanting. She took an overdose of a sleeping drug, and it was only through the swift actions of doctors that her life was saved (see p. 178). Leonard delayed publication, and it was 26 March 1915 before *The Voyage Out* appeared in print. It was a moderate, though not a runaway, success: Leonard Woolf reported that a few of the 2,000 copies printed remained unsold even by 1929 (*Beginning Again*, p. 87).

## Plot Summary

Helen and Ridley Ambrose board the *Euphrosyne*, a cargo steamer leaving London for the Amazon. The other travellers are the ship's captain Willoughby Vinrace, who is a widower and Ridley's brother-in-law; his naïve young daughter Rachel; and the scholarly William Pepper. Richard and Clarissa Dalloway, worldly but conventional, board the ship at Lisbon. After Richard kisses Rachel on impulse, she has horrifying nightmares. The Dalloways disembark, and Rachel tells Helen about the kiss.

The ship docks in Santa Marina, in an unnamed South American country, and Rachel stays with the Ambroses in their villa. One night, Helen and Rachel spy on the hotel guests through a window but are spotted by St John Hirst. Hirst's friend Terence Hewet arranges a picnic so that the villa's inhabitants and the hotel guests may become acquainted. Arthur Venning and Susan Warrington, just engaged, are seen embracing by Terence and Rachel, and she recoils from the sight. There is a dance to celebrate the engagement. St John confides his hopes and fears to Helen and offers to educate Rachel. The lively and reckless Evelyn Murgatroyd, a counterpoint to Rachel, asks Terence's advice about dealing with two proposals of marriage.

Terence and Rachel grow closer. Mr and Mrs Flushing, an intrepid couple, arrange a camping trip downriver; Rachel, Helen, Terence and St John accompany them. Rachel

> 'We're off,' said Ridley.
>
> A slight but perceptible wave seemed to roll beneath the floor; then it sank; then another came, more perceptible. Lights slid right across the uncurtained window. The ship gave a loud melancholy moan.
>
> (*The Voyage Out*, ch. 1)

and Terence realize they are in love and plan their life together. Back at Santa Marina, Hughling Elliot has fallen ill and is tended by Dr Rodriguez, whose medical skills are called into doubt.

Soon Rachel takes to her bed with a headache, then becomes delirious and hallucinates. St John fetches a French doctor, who takes Rachel's condition more seriously than does Dr Rodriguez. Rachel rallies a little, but Dr Lesage warns that her life is in danger. Terence sees Rachel for the last time, and she dies while holding his hand. Momentarily he feels at peace, then reality hits him and he cries out her name in agony.

The final two chapters focus on reactions to Rachel's death. Miss Allan feels old and useless; Mrs Thornbury comforts a sobbing Evelyn. Mrs Flushing blames herself for organising the expedition, but her husband insists that unwashed vegetables caused Rachel's illness. Before long, their own lives take precedence. St John enters the lounge, exhausted and numb, but is unable to make conversation. He sits and watches, isolated by grief, as the others go up to bed.

## Sources

For a first novel, *The Voyage Out* is a mature and considered work. The title was probably suggested to Woolf by the lengthy sea journeys under- taken by her great-aunt Julia Margaret Cameron, Leonard Woolf and several members of the Strachey family to the British colonies in India and Ceylon. The voyage of the *Euphrosyne* is ostensibly for trading purposes, but the metaphorical voyage is Rachel's coming-of-age. However, it is an incomplete journey – Rachel is never to reach her land of milk and honey.

Virginia Woolf drew on several acquaintances for her characters. Rachel is partly a self-portrait, but her early death on the brink of a new life echoes Stella Duckworth's. Terence is based on Clive Bell. Helen and Ridley are reminiscent of Julia and Leslie Stephen, but, in her friendship with the young people, Helen is more like Vanessa Bell. St John Hirst owes much to Lytton Strachey. Mr Pepper is an amalgam of clever but dry and fussy Cambridge scholars, and Miss Allan bears the hallmarks of Violet Dickinson. Clarissa Dalloway has the more superficial aspects of glamorous family friend Kitty Maxse, while Richard's character was probably suggested by George Duckworth – both were connected in Virginia's mind with the Hyde Park Gate years.

## Themes

### Death

As in many of Virginia Woolf's subse- quent novels, death is a major theme.

There are more presentiments of it in this novel than in any of the others: small boys think Ridley Ambrose looks like Bluebeard, a notorious wife-murderer; he and Helen remark that the ship's steps could be fatal on a dark night; and with Mr Pepper Ridley discusses the death of a scholarly colleague. Rachel tells Helen that her aunts live in fear of the piano falling through the ceiling and killing them; the flowers of broom remind her of funerals.

The Dalloways are stranded in Lisbon because of an outbreak of cholera in Russia, and the death of pets is discussed at the breakfast table. Ariel's song from *The Tempest*, about a drowned father, and Shelley's 'Adonais', an elegy for a poet who died of tuberculosis (Keats) by a poet who later drowned, are quoted. Warships are seen in the distance. William Pepper, on leaving the Ambroses' villa for the hotel, prefigures Rachel's death by warning them against typhoid. Helen remembers one day that it is the 15th of March – the Ides of March, when Julius Caesar was murdered. Hewet quotes from a Thomas Hardy poem, 'He Abjures Love', in which death follows hard upon the heels of love, and tries (but fails) to persuade his fellow guests

that there is nothing horrible about death.

A number of dead relatives are recalled: Rachel's mother; Evelyn Murgatroyd's parents; old Mrs Paley's brother, and her deceased friend. Helen worries that her children will be in an omnibus accident. At the hotel, a chicken is beheaded by an old woman. There is talk of a famous explorer who died of fever ten years earlier. St John's mother writes to him of the suicide of her parlour-maid, and one of Evelyn's rejected lovers threatens to kill himself. By the time Hughling Elliot falls ill, the reader has probably absorbed a great many allusions to death and illness.

## Marriage

When she was writing *The Voyage Out*, Virginia was considering marriage to Leonard Woolf, and the novel portrays several couples and types of marriage. Helen and Ridley Ambrose have contrasting characters, and Helen experiences much that Ridley cannot share. But their marriage works chiefly because they allow each other freedom. The Dalloways are well matched because Clarissa is content to be purely 'feminine' while Richard

> [Helen's] mind left the scene and occupied itself with anxieties for Ridley, for her children, for far-off things, such as old age and poverty and death.
>
> (*The Voyage Out*, ch. 21)

is almost wholly 'masculine'. They also share a deep conservatism that drives Richard's ambitions and provides Clarissa with a sense of security.

Arthur Venning and Susan Warrington are a conventional young couple whose marriage, we are led to believe, will be run-of-the-mill. The Flushings share a sense of adventure and a refreshing bluntness of speech that contrasts with the others' measured tones. Terence and Rachel wonder what married life has in store for them. They plan that Terence will write and Rachel will concentrate on her music. Rachel feels that love has, paradoxically, made her more independent – Virginia's hope for her own marriage.

### Women

The 'woman question' is often referred to in the novel. Ideas of women's suffrage are given a thorough airing by Richard Dalloway, whose sense of manhood depends on women's subservience. Both he and Clarissa oppose giving women the vote, and Richard thinks Jane Austen the best female writer because she does not try to write like a man. Politics he sees purely as man's work.

Miss Allan has a profession (writing a brief history of English literature) only because she is unmarried – it is therefore acceptable for her to earn money. But her writing is not taken as seriously as is the work of Ridley Ambrose, William Pepper or Hughling Elliot, all of whom deal with more abstruse matters of learning. A capable and likeable woman, she wears a suffrage badge but does not force her views on others.

Terence Hewet is generally the mouthpiece for feminist sentiments. He wonders why women respect men so much, and tells Rachel it will be a long time before women take up the law or business. No one really knows about women's lives, he says, because their point of view is never represented. He uses St John as an example of the discrepancy between the education of sons and daughters: while St John's future is considered of great importance by his family, his sister's is ignored. It is a theme Woolf returned to in *Three Guineas* (see pp. 141–2).

# Bloomsbury Publisher: The
# Hogarth Press

. . . . . . . . . . .

### Beginnings

In March 1917 Virginia and Leonard
Woolf made a decision that would
change both their lives and influence
the future of publishing. They ordered
a handpress, together with type and
a booklet of instructions, from the
Excelsior Printers' Supply Company at
41 Farringdon Street, in the centre of
London's printing industry. Arriving a few
weeks later, it was set up on the dining

The typeface the Woolfs chose for
the Hogarth Press was Caslon Old
Face, created by William Caslon
in 1734. A standard face for many
years, its popularity declined in
the mid-nineteenth century but
rose again in the early twentieth,
coinciding with the revival in hand-
printing (of which the Woolfs were
a part) and the advent of hot-metal
typesetting.

table. During the following months the
Woolfs taught themselves how to operate
the press and advertised for subscribers
for their first publication. They named
the new venture the Hogarth Press,
after Hogarth House, where they lived
in Richmond.

The project, Leonard thought, would
divert Virginia from working too hard on
her writing. With a congenital trembling
of the hands that earned him an
exemption from wartime conscription,
he was ill-suited to the intricate manoeu-
vring of type, so this task was carried out
by Virginia or by an assistant, while
Leonard did the printing, one page at a
time. Virginia stitched on the covers by
hand. It was hard work, but engrossing,
and they both immediately saw that it
would be addictive.

### The Woolfs as Printers

'Publication No. 1' appeared in July 1917.
It was *Two Stories*, containing 'Three Jews'
by Leonard and 'The Mark on the Wall'

by Virginia, and was illustrated with four woodcuts by Carrington. Virginia wrote to her well-connected friend Ottoline Morrell, asking her to supply the names of potential subscribers, and sent advertising notices to Violet Dickinson for distribution to her acquaintances. The first sixty orders, Virginia told Vanessa, came from old ladies and Northern poets – none from friends. Only 150 copies were printed but these had become collectors' items within five years.

Carrington's friend Alix Sargant-Florence was offered the job of assistant at the Press in October 1917. On the first day she decided the job was too boring, and never came back. The following month another of the 'cropheads', former Slade student Barbara Hiles, was taken on to help with the second Hogarth

*Hogarth House, where the Hogarth Press was founded in 1917*

Press publication, Katherine Mansfield's *Prelude*. Barbara later laid claim to setting the title page after seeing that Leonard had not done a satisfactory job.

The Press went from strength to strength. The first edition of Virginia's story *Kew Gardens* sold out after a good review in *The Times Literary Supplement*, necessitating a reprint. But it wasn't all plain sailing: Vanessa complained about the reproduction of her woodcuts, so Virginia asked her to instruct the printer personally for the second edition. When reprinting *The Mark on the Wall* as a solo publication the Woolfs were forced to omit Carrington's woodcuts, which had caused the new printer some problems.

## Expansion and Success – Vita's Role

Business was brisk, and Lytton's friend Ralph Partridge was taken on as manager, with a salary of £100 plus a 50 per cent share of the profits. In October 1921 the Woolfs finally upgraded their printing press to a second-hand Minerva platen machine, operated by a treadle. This one was given to Vita Sackville-West in 1930 (when the Woolfs again upgraded to a better treadle press), and is now on public display at Sissinghurst Castle.

By 1928 profits had topped £200 (worth about £8,000 today), but the biggest money-spinners were the novels of Vita Sackville-West. In 1930 *The Edwardians* sold 20,000 copies in the first two months. A year later *All Passion Spent* secured 4,000 pre-publication orders. For *Family History* there were

## First Ten Publications of the Hogarth Press

*Two Stories* ('Three Jews' by Leonard Woolf and 'The Mark on the Wall' by Virginia Woolf, with four woodcuts by Carrington), July 1917 (*c.*150 copies; 1,000-copy reprint of Virginia's story in June 1919)

*Prelude*, by Katherine Mansfield, July 1918 (*c.*300 copies)

*Poems*, by C.N. Sidney Woolf, May/June 1918 (private edition; number of copies unknown)

*Poems*, by T.S. Eliot, May 1919 (*c.*250 copies)

*The Critic in Judgment or Belshazzar of Baronscourt*, by John Middleton Murry, May 1919 (*c.*200 copies)

*Kew Gardens*, by Virginia Woolf (with woodcuts by Vanessa Bell), May 1919 (*c.*150–70 copies, with June reprint of 500 copies)

*Paris: A Poem*, by Hope Mirrlees, May 1920 (dated 1919; *c.*175 copies)

*The Story of the Siren*, by E.M. Forster, July 1920 (*c.*500 copies; hand-set by Virginia)

*Stories from the Old Testament*, by Logan Pearsall Smith, May 1920 (number of copies unknown)

*Reminiscences of Leo Nicolayevitch Tolstoi* by Maxim Gorky (trans. S.S. Koteliansky and Leonard Woolf), July 1920 (*c.*1,000 copies, with 1,000-copy reprint in January 1921)

so many advance orders (6,000) that Virginia's fingers were worn raw from doing up the parcels. Vita's books far outsold Virginia's own, and boosted the Hogarth Press accounts considerably. She was fiercely loyal to the Press, declining lucrative offers from other publishers, even though, at times, she could have done with the money.

### Changes at the Press

By 1930 Virginia was complaining that the Press took up all their time. To combat this, Leonard took on John Lehmann, a young poet and friend of Julian Bell, and brother of novelist Rosamond and

actress Beatrice. But even with John's help the labour was wearying and time-consuming, and in 1932 Leonard and Virginia stopped setting the books by hand – the last was Dorothy Wellesley's *Jupiter and the Nun*, now a valuable collector's item because of its significance in the history of the Press. Virginia began to take a back seat, and in March 1938 John Lehmann purchased her share of the Press and became Leonard's partner. An advisory panel was formed including Virginia, along with some of the new generation of younger writers: Rosamond Lehmann, Stephen Spender, Christopher Isherwood and W.H. Auden. The new arrangement left Leonard and

Virginia with more time, but there were frequent disagreements with John, who often felt that Leonard was disregarding his opinions.

The Woolfs moved to 37 Mecklenburgh Square (see p. 150) in 1940, during the Second World War. That September the Square suffered an air attack, and the Press was moved to the premises of one of the Woolfs' printers, the Garden City Press in Letchworth, where it stayed until the end of the war. In 1946 the problems between Leonard and John Lehmann came to a head (Virginia had died in 1941), and the Press was sold to Chatto and Windus, who bought John out and made Leonard a director. Chatto was later absorbed into Random House. The Hogarth Press imprint survives today, reprinting the works of Virginia Woolf and occasionally publishing other titles of note in the Bloomsbury canon.

## Legacy of the Press

Although it began as an amateur activity, the significance of the Hogarth Press is enormous. In its early days it published translations of Russian works by Tolstoy, Gorky, Chekhov and Dostoevsky, Katherine Mansfield's *Prelude*, T.S. Eliot's *Poems* and later *The Waste Land*, and E.M. Forster's *Story of the Siren*. The Woolfs got friends and family to supply them with high-quality manuscripts: Clive Bell, Julian Bell, Adrian Stephen, Roger Fry, John Maynard Keynes, Marjorie Strachey, Julia Strachey and Harold Nicolson all contributed works,

as did writers of the calibre of Rose Macaulay, Edith Sitwell, Robert Graves, Gertrude Stein, C. Day Lewis, William Plomer, Stephen Spender, W.H. Auden, Christopher Isherwood, Rebecca West, H.G. Wells and John Betjeman. In 1924, the Press began publishing the International Psycho-Analytical Library of the Institute of Psycho-Analysis, including English translations of the works of Sigmund Freud. Other series included The Hogarth Essays (with cover designs by Vanessa Bell), The Hogarth Lectures on Literature, Merttens Lectures on War and Peace, Hogarth Living Poets and many more. The New Hogarth Library included titles by Rainer Maria Rilke, Herman Melville, Arthur Rimbaud and Federico García Lorca. For Virginia, the impact of being able to write what she liked was immeasurable. Her first two novels had

### Read On ...

*Thrown to the Woolfs*, by John Lehmann, London: Weidenfeld and Nicolson, 1978

*A Boy at the Hogarth Press*, by Richard Kennedy, London: Penguin, 1978

*A Checklist of the Hogarth Press, 1917–1946*, comp. by J. Howard Woolmer, Winchester: St Paul's Bibliographies, 1986

The University of Delaware has a website for its 'Seventy Years at the Hogarth Press' exhibition, held in 1987: www.lib.udel.edu/ud/spec/exhibits/hogarth

been published by her brother-in-law Gerald Duckworth's publishing firm, but her subsequent novels were produced by her own Press and it was only then that she was able fully to explore her own unique style.

# Night and Day (1919)

. . . . . . . . . . .

## Origins

Virginia had thought as early as 1902 about writing a play in which a man and a woman almost meet but keep missing one another. The idea came to fruition in *Night and Day,* in which the protagonists meet

> She would not have cared to confess how infinitely she preferred the exactitude, the star-like impersonality, of figures to the confusion, agitation, and vagueness of the finest prose.
>
> (*Night and Day,* ch. 3)

and feel a mutual attraction, but follow a convoluted path to true love. The concept of separateness and opposition survives in the title. Katharine, the would-be astronomer and elusive dreamer, is obviously Night, while the practical Ralph, dealing (as a solicitor)

with man-made law, represents the cold light of Day.

Woolf's second novel was intended to be the story of Vanessa. Begun in early 1917, it was finished by November of the following year. Duckworth's had published *The Voyage Out*, and according to the terms of their contract were entitled to first refusal on *Night and Day*. Gerald assured his half-sister that his company would publish it – frustrating her hopes that she would be freed from the contract and able to publish the novel under the Hogarth Press imprint. She had found it much less stressful to write than *The Voyage Out*, and was confident of its success. Not yet having discovered her modernist style, she thought it compared well with most contemporary novels, although it is now considered one of the most traditional of her works – a kind of updated Jane Austen.

## Plot Summary

Katharine Hilbery is from a literary family but has a secret yearning to study mathematics and astronomy. Ralph Denham, a solicitor's clerk, lives with his widowed mother and boisterous siblings. He visits the Hilberys and meets Katharine.

Ralph's friend Mary Datchet works for a suffrage society. Unknown to Ralph, she is in love with him, but he is increasingly attracted to Katharine.

At Mary's house, Katharine's friend William Rodney, an intelligent, highly strung young man, gives an informal lecture on Elizabethan poetry. He confides to Ralph his frustration with the elusive Katharine.

Katharine visits Mary's office, but is disinclined to join the suffrage cause. She agrees to marry William. Ralph is dismayed, proposes to Mary on the rebound, and she declines. She has guessed his feelings for Katharine, and tells Katharine, who decides to break with William and is relieved when he admits his attraction to her cousin Cassandra. They agree to tell no one about the broken engagement while Katharine acts as go-between for William and Cassandra.

Believing Katharine to be engaged, Ralph confesses his complex feelings to her. Determined to free himself of his idealization of Katharine, Ralph takes her to meet his family, expecting her to be out of place. Instead he loves her more than ever.

Katharine is forced to reveal news of the broken engagement to Cassandra. Later she calms William's fears of gossip and he declares his love for Cassandra, who overhears his assertion, and they are engaged. Ralph, wandering the street outside the Hilberys' house, is brought in and told of the new engagement.

Mr Hilbery is apprised of the situation but is baffled by the non-engagement of Katharine and Ralph.

Mrs Hilbery sees directly to the heart of the situation, and peace is established over the tea-table. Katharine and Ralph go for a walk, wondering at the simplicity and complexity of love. The book ends in a minor key, with the couple wishing each other good night on the doorstep of Katharine's home.

## Sources

Katharine Hilbery is a thinly disguised version of Vanessa Bell, with astronomy substituting for painting. Katharine's elusiveness, abstractedness and unsentimental approach to life are pure Vanessa, as Virginia saw her. The name Katharine she borrowed from the Vanessa-based character in Leonard's novel, *The Wise Virgins*. Ralph Denham, the serious, hard-working outsider, has similarities to Leonard Woolf. William Rodney possesses Lytton Strachey's tastes coupled with George Duckworth's conventionality and a dash of Walter Headlam, a classical schola and Virginia's first suitor. The incompatibility of the 'Virginia' character with the 'Lytton' character is firmly established, and William's eventual partner is an admiring but practical younger woman. In character, Cassandra is not Carrington, but the similarity in their names is perhaps significant. William encourages the affair between Katharine and Ralph; a remodelling of the triangular relationship between Lytton, Leonard and Virginia (see p. 60).

The suffragist Mary Datchet is drawn from political activists such as Margaret Llewelyn Davies. Leonard, who worked closely with Margaret studying cooperative societies, found her a stalwart and reliable colleague; Virginia admired her as a forceful and persuasive woman. Mrs Hilbery is based on 'Aunt' Anny Thackeray, daughter of the novelist William Makepeace Thackeray and sister of Leslie Stephen's first wife Minny. Likeable, quirky and romantic, with an irrational streak, Anny was a novelist in her own right, although her books never made her as famous as her father. The spirit of the poet Richard Alardyce hovers over Mrs Hilbery as W.M. Thackeray's reputation did over Anny.

Mr Hilbery, usually placid and urbane, shows a sprinkling of Leslie

Stephen's temper. He tries to ignore the emotional upsets in his house, and when they are forced upon him takes refuge in literature. He sees Ralph as a rival and feels jealous and possessive, resenting this annexation of his daughter. The attentive reader may be reminded at this point of Leslie's reaction to Stella Duckworth's engagement.

## Themes

### The Love Affair

Virginia Woolf's first and second novels can be seen primarily as love stories, though both have unconventional endings. They are thematically connected by a subtle but highly symbolic image. When Mrs Hilbery tells Katharine of her own first memories of love, she remembers travelling on a ship with her husband

> [T]he world, so far, had shown very little desire to take the boons which Mary's society for woman's suffrage had offered it.
>
> (*Night and Day*, ch. 6)

– her literal and metaphorical 'voyage out'. Katharine is more mature than Rachel and has some experience of love, but her affair with William Rodney is sterile. Only marriage to Ralph will allow her the psychological independence she needs. By the time Woolf had finished her second book, she had written out her interest in courtship and marriage – subsequent novels would relegate the love affair to a sub-plot.

### The Role of Women

The novel features several love stories, but not all are resolved. Katharine's cast-off lover finds a new partner, but why doesn't the deserving Mary get her man? Woolf's plot twist has a ring of authenticity: independent working women were viewed as distinctly unmarriageable a century ago. Even today, debate continues about whether men feel threatened by women who want equality.

The woman's role is seen under several different spotlights. Mrs Hilbery, with an over-active imagination, reigns supreme in the realm of the heart but is ill-equipped for the world of work. Katharine tries to instil discipline, but cannot control her mother's waywardness. Ralph wonders why Katharine doesn't take

up something challenging, but does not know about her secret mathematical studies. While these are not of practical use, as is Mary Datchet's work, they give Katharine's life meaning and structure. She considers Mary's work inappropriate for herself. Though never an activist, Virginia had a little experience of suffrage work. She helped to address envelopes for an Adult Suffrage League mailing, attended a conference of the Women's Co-operative Guild, and ran the Richmond branch of the Guild for four years (see pp. 135–6).

### Theatrical Qualities

Cassandra, in Greek mythology a prophetess doomed to have her predictions disbelieved, is here a symbol of hope. She is eccentric – in that she breeds silkworms in her bedroom – but practical and sensible. She descends into the action fortui-

tously on two occasions, like a *deus ex machina* from an ancient Greek drama (as a last-ditch attempt to resolve a complex plot a 'god' was lowered over the stage using a 'machine').

Cassandra's timely interventions are not the only play-like features of the story. The second half of the book, with its aborted couplings and misapprehensions, feels particularly stage-managed. Shakespeare is a constant presence. His name is frequently mentioned; Mrs Hilbery visits his birthplace at a crucial point in the story; and his dramatic influence can be perceived in the plot twists. The tradition of Shakespearean plays is observed in the book's ending, when stability is re-established. But oddly, it is not the stalwarts of society (Ralph Denham, William Rodney, Mr Hilbery) who settle everything, but the Muse of Romance, the normally impractical Mrs Hilbery.

*Shakespeare's birthplace, Stratford-upon-Avon*

# Small But Perfectly Formed:
# Virginia Woolf's Short Fiction

· · · · · · · · · · ·

Of the forty-six stories Virginia Woolf wrote, only eighteen were published during her lifetime. Others were published in *A Haunted House and Other Short Stories* (1943), and the rest, fortunately for her readers, appeared in 1985 in a fully annotated edition, together with several unfinished stories and story fragments.

## Remarkable Range

The early stories, dating from 1906, demonstrate a literary maturity despite the fact that their author was in her mid-twenties. They include a semi-autobiographical account of the Stephen sisters ('Phyllis and Rosamond'); a sketch about a woman frequently seen but never quite known ('The Mysterious Case of Miss V.'); a mock-diary purportedly written in the fifteenth or sixteenth century ('The Journal of Mistress Joan Martyn'); and a semi-autobiographical, mystical piece based on the Stephens' trip to Greece ('A Dialogue Upon Mount

Pentelicus'). Two of the later stories, 'The Legacy' and 'The Symbol', feature death as a prominent theme, though they are far from gloomy in their outlook. Woolf's final story, 'The Watering Place', written a few weeks before her death and about a conversation between three unnamed young women in a ladies' lavatory, shows clear signs of her damaged state of mind. During the thirty-five years

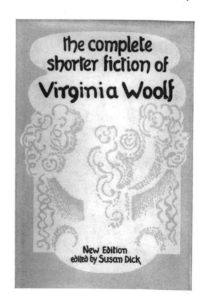

the complete
shorter fiction of
Virginia Woolf

New Edition
edited by Susan Dick

from first story to last, Virginia produced descriptive sketches, animals stories, party scenes, stories of revelation and misunderstanding, even an 'ode' in verse and prose inspired by a butcher's shop! The shortest piece, 'Blue & Green', is 264 words; the longest, 'The Journal of Mistress Joan Martyn', almost a novella at thirty printed pages.

## First Forays into Fiction

The first story Virginia submitted for publication was 'Memoirs of a Novelist', written in 1909 and masquerading as non-fiction. Unwary readers may feel they are reading a review of Miss Linsett's biography of her deceased friend, the writer Miss Willatt, but the two characters are pure invention. In this piece, as in 'An Unwritten Novel' and the later 'Portraits', Virginia is indulging her fondness for making up lives for 'ordinary' people. However, the mock-biographical style of 'Memoirs of a Novelist' was not to the taste of the editor of the *Cornhill Magazine*, and the story was rejected. Virginia never wrote

## Short Fiction Published During Woolf's Lifetime
(*details of first publication are given*)

'The Mark on the Wall', Hogarth Press, 1917

'Kew Gardens', Hogarth Press, 1919

'An Unwritten Novel', *London Mercury*, July 1920

'Solid Objects', *The Athenaeum*, 22 October 1920

'A Haunted House', *Monday or Tuesday*, Hogarth Press, 1921

'A Society', *Monday or Tuesday*, Hogarth Press, 1921

'Monday or Tuesday', *Monday or Tuesday*, Hogarth Press, 1921

'The String Quartet', *Monday or Tuesday*, Hogarth Press, 1921

'Blue & Green', *Monday or Tuesday*, Hogarth Press, 1921

'In the Orchard', *Criterion*, April 1923

'Mrs Dalloway in Bond Street', *Dial*, July 1923

'A Woman's College from Outside', anthologized in *Alalanta's Garland*, 1926

'The New Dress', *Forum* (US), May 1927

'Moments of Being: "Slater's Pins Have No Points"', *Forum* (US), January 1928 (published under subtitle only)

'The Lady in the Looking-Glass: A Reflection', *Harper's Magazine*, December 1929

'The Shooting Party', *Harper's Bazaar*, March 1938

'The Duchess and the Jeweller', *Harper's Bazaar*, April 1938

'Lappin and Lapinova', *Harper's Bazaar*, April 1939

for that journal again, but the technique was one she would return to for one of her best-loved novels, *Orlando*. After her snub by the *Cornhill* she did not attempt to publish her short fiction until 1917, when the Woolfs set up the Hogarth Press.

## Links between Stories and Novels

Given that the Woolfs had their own printing press, why did they publish so few of Virginia's stories? One reason was that she rated them less highly than the novels, seeing them as light relief from the strain of writing longer works. In a story she could explore a single idea and maintain a single mood throughout, rather than holding numerous threads together in a more complicated structure. Her short fiction is generally experimental: it was here that she tried out and refined new approaches and styles that might later form the basis of a novel.

Themes from the stories also resurfaced in the longer books. The train journey from 'An Unwritten Novel', during which the narrator imagines the life of a woman seated opposite, appears in *Jacob's Room*. This time we see from the perspective of the elderly woman, who tries to judge Jacob's character from his outward appearance. Like the narrator of 'An Unwritten Novel', she is quite wrong. Several stories fed into the writing of *Mrs Dalloway*: 'Mrs Dalloway in Bond Street', 'The New Dress', 'Happiness', 'Ancestors', 'The

Introduction', 'Together and Apart', 'The Man Who Loved His Kind' and 'A Summing Up'. These were collected as *Mrs Dalloway's Party* in 1973, with the exception of 'Happiness' (which does not feature the Dalloways, although it does contain a prototype of Peter Walsh). 'A Society' and 'A Woman's College from Outside' explore the theme of women's education, discussed in more depth in *A Room of One's Own* and *Three Guineas*.

## 'The Mark on the Wall' (1917)

*Two Stories* ('Three Jews' by Leonard and 'The Mark on the Wall' by Virginia) was the first publication of the Hogarth Press (see pp. 37–8). Surprisingly, Virginia seemed to be taking her responsibilities as a publisher more seriously than her writing – when the Woolfs began printing the booklet in May, Virginia hadn't even written her story. David ('Bunny') Garnett wrote to Virginia immediately after publication, praising the story. In Virginia's reply she compared the short burst of creation needed for a story to the constant toil of a novel. Roger Fry was another fan of Virginia's. In 1920 he, together with his poet and playwright friend Charles Vildrac, began to translate 'The Mark on the Wall' into French. But the translation was never completed.

> Why, if one wants to compare life to anything, one must liken it to being blown through the Tube at fifty miles an hour – landing at the other end without a single hairpin in one's hair!
>
> ('The Mark on the Wall')

The 'plot' of 'The Mark on the Wall' is almost non-existent, but Lytton Strachey thought the story a work of genius. The narrator's imagination is sparked by seeing a small round mark (it turns out to be a snail), and goes off at several tangents. The real interest lies in following the narrator's stream of consciousness, moving from thought to thought as the mind does in a state of daydream. We all do this, of course, but it takes the perceptiveness, imagination and humour of a writer such as Woolf to explore the full implications. Five years before the breakthrough of *Jacob's Room*, Woolf made a distinct departure from traditional, linear writing with this story.

## 'Kew Gardens' (1919)

In the summer of 1917 Virginia sent an early draft of her story to her friend and rival writer, Katherine Mansfield (the only writer she was jealous of, Virginia confessed), and received a gratifyingly positive response. It was another year before she sent a copy to Vanessa. Refining her work, Virginia examined her personal response to art. Was it possible she was developing an aesthetic instinct?, she humbly asked her sister. Keen to unite writing and art, she asked Vanessa for two woodcuts for 'Kew Gardens' and was very pleased with the result: the illustrations completely matched her vision, she said.

*Kew Gardens*

'Kew Gardens', like 'The Mark on the Wall', is not a story in the traditional sense: it is a series of impressions and conversations from a constantly shifting perspective. Virginia's new aesthetic awareness predominates as she describes the plants and flowers in terms of splashes of colour. This, together with 'Blue & Green' (see below), is her most painterly story. There are snatches from four dialogues, but humans have no precedence in the narrative over flowers, snail, butterflies or bird – each is an equal part of the whole scene. People often have the attributes of flora and fauna, and vice versa. At the end of the piece, distinct shapes become indistinct, merging into a kind of heat haze, with even man-made constructions and machines swept into the pattern of colour and sound.

> They walked on the past the flower-bed, now walking four abreast, and soon diminished in size among the trees and looked half transparent as the sunlight and shade swam over their backs in large trembling irregular patches.
>
> ('Kew Gardens')

## Monday or Tuesday (1921)

*Monday or Tuesday* was the only collection of Virginia's short stories that was published in her lifetime. At first she was disappointed with the book's reception in the press. Lytton Strachey's *Queen Victoria* was published at almost the same time, and was highly praised,

throwing into relief the lukewarm review for *Monday or Tuesday* that appeared in *The Times*. Virginia was not convinced that readers knew what she was trying to achieve, or were even interested. To make matters worse, an American publisher rejected the book. But the neglect soon turned to enthusiasm. A bookseller ordered more copies, Desmond MacCarthy wrote a glowing review in the *New Statesman*, and her other friends began to pass on their praise.

### Monday or Tuesday

'A Haunted House'
'A Society'
'Monday or Tuesday'
'An Unwritten Novel'
'The String Quartet'
'Blue & Green'
'Kew Gardens
'The Mark on the Wall'

The title story of *Monday or Tuesday* features an impressionistic version of an urban landscape, comparable to the end of 'Kew Gardens'. A heron flies over a town, while below it are the mechanical sounds of wheels, omnibuses and striking clocks. A scrap-metal dealer cries his wares as people discuss politics in a firelit room, an office worker takes her tea-break and someone – the narrator perhaps – daydreams by the fireside. The heron flies back across the night sky. And that is all. It is a deceptively simple sketch but the frequent repetition of the word 'truth' shows that there is more to it than meets the eye. Also arresting are the painterly glints of colour: white, gold, red, black, silver and blue. The two paragraphs of 'Blue & Green', Woolf's shortest story, have a similar quality. Here, a passage describing green objects is followed by one describing blue ones. This is the nearest of all the stories to poetry, requiring only the addition of line-breaks.

> Blue are the ribs of the wrecked rowing boat. A wave rolls beneath the blue bells. But the cathedral's different, cold, incense laden, faint blue with the veils of madonnas.
>
> ('Blue & Green')

Lytton Strachey's favourite story in the volume was 'The String Quartet'. This follows a group of people into a concert hall, reproduces snatches of their conversation and thoughts, and describes the music in a series of arresting images – of swirling water and leaping fish; of falling rose petals; of a gallant prince defending a lady's honour.

## A Haunted House and Other Short Stories (1943)

This volume, compiled by Leonard Woolf, was published by the Hogarth Press after Virginia's death. The fact that 'Short' is omitted from Vanessa Bell's cover design but included on the title page suggests that there was some confusion about the full title. It was first published on 31 January 1944 (but the book itself is dated 1943). Eighteen stories are included, only the final five of which had not been previously published. In a Foreword, Leonard stated that it had been Virginia's intention to publish

### A Haunted House and Other Short Stories

'A Haunted House'
'Monday or Tuesday'
'An Unwritten Novel'
'The String Quartet'
'Kew Gardens'
'The Mark on the Wall'
'The New Dress'
'The Shooting Party'
'Lappin and Lapinova'
'Solid Objects'
'The Lady in the Looking-Glass'
'The Duchess and the Jeweller'
'Moments of Being: "Slater's Pins Have No Points"'
'The Man Who Loved His Kind'
'The Searchlight'
'The Legacy'
'Together and Apart'
'A Summing Up'

a new collection, including six of the eight stories from *Monday or Tuesday* (she had decided to omit 'A Society' and would, in his opinion, have left out 'Blue & Green' as well).

Presumably this collection was intended to include the best and most accomplished of Virginia's stories. The title story, which she at first feared was sentimental, was inspired by Asheham House in Sussex, the house that Virginia 'time-shared' with Vanessa from 1911 and later occupied with Leonard until 1919. Situated in a shaded spot, it was dark and romantic but cold and damp in the winter, and reputed to be haunted. In Virginia's story, two ghosts wander around a house that they once lived in and which is now inhabited by another couple. The ghosts revisit scenes of past happiness, which still dwells in the house and is sensed by the living couple. The story is a celebration of the

Woolfs' marriage as well as a farewell to Asheham.

A less rosy view of marriage appears in 'Lappin and Lapinova'. This couple are not so well-matched and retreat into a fantasy world of rabbits and hares; the only way in which the sensitive wife can cope with her robust and unsympathetic in-laws. But when her husband tires of the game and cruelly puts an end to it, she realizes it was only within the fantasy that she loved him. In 'The Shooting Party' also, the upper-class family is extremely unpleasant. The squire shoots pheasants, while his elderly sisters devour a bird that is served for lunch and reminisce about deaths caused by hunting, and their brother's illegitimate and unacknowledged son by the house-keeper. The house, as decrepit as the family is decadent, disintegrates around them. The squire enters with his three enormous dogs, which attack a small spaniel to steal the pheasant carcass

it is eating. The squire raises his whip to them but knocks his sister into the fireplace, where she is buried by the family coat of arms hanging over the fireplace. We leave the scene of chaos to see the housekeeper making her escape by train, carrying a brace of pheasants.

Several of the Mrs Dalloway stories are featured in the collection. 'The New Dress' reflects Virginia's own self-consciousness about new clothes. Mabel, at Clarissa Dalloway's party (the same character appears in *Mrs Dalloway* as Ellie Henderson), feels out of place and ridiculous, like a fly trying to crawl out of a saucer of milk – a homage, perhaps, to Katherine Mansfield's 1922 story, 'The Fly', which uses the image of a fly struggling in ink. (Which, in turn, was a reference to a similar image in Chekhov's 'The Duel'.)

Virginia referred to 'Moments of Being: "Slater's Pins Have No Points"' as 'Sapphist' in a letter to Vita Sackville-West (14 October 1927). She was writing *Orlando*, another work with 'Sapphic' content, as a tribute to Vita. The lesbianism in the story is subtle, if passionate. A rose (later in the story it has become a carnation) falls from Fanny Wilmot's dress and her music teacher Julia Craye utters the remark of the subtitle, setting Fanny off on a series of ruminations about Julia's solitary life while she searches for the pin. She finds it and turns to Julia, who embraces her. Fanny is moved by a sudden vision of the passion underlying Julia's cool exterior and trembles as she replaces the flower.

## Other Notable Stories

### 'Solid Objects'

'Solid Objects' is one of Woolf's most intriguing stories. She began writing it in November 1918, inspired both by a visit from the self-absorbed painter Mark Gertler and by her own desire to possess paintings, pottery and sculpture. She recognized that this desire sprang from something more primitive than an artistic appreciation of the works. Uniting it with the passion for 'form' that she detected in Gertler, she used it as the basis of a story about a man named John who neglects a promising political career when he becomes an obsessive collector of pieces of glass and metal – things that most people would regard as rubbish.

### 'Ode Written Partly in Prose ...'

Despite the lyrical nature of her prose (or perhaps because of it), Woolf rarely made forays into verse. On one occasion she vented her anger at an over-zealous newspaper reporter, whom she compared to a bloodsucking flea (see Bell 1996, Appendix B). The only other 'poem' she wrote bore the cumbersome title of 'Ode Written Partly in Prose on Seeing the Name of Cutbush Above a Butcher's Shop in Pentonville' (written 1934), but is actually more prose-like than some of the earlier stories. By defining the piece as an 'ode', Woolf suggests that it will convey exalted emotions about a noble subject, in the manner of the ancient Greeks or the Romantic poets. And why should Byron, Herodotus and the mandarins of China not feature in a description of the life of a butcher? This unlikely combination of the lofty and the mundane allows Woolf to contrast the dreams of youth with the reality of working-class married life.

**Read On ...**

*The Complete Shorter Fiction of Virginia Woolf*, by Virginia Woolf, ed. Susan Dick, London: Hogarth Press, 1985 (includes notes on first publication dates, which I have followed above)

*Virginia Woolf: A Study of the Short Fiction*, by Dean Baldwin, New York: Twayne, 1989

*Wild Outbursts of Freedom: Reading the Short Fiction of Virginia Woolf*, by Nena Skrbic, Westport, CT: Greenwood Press, 2004

*Trespassing Boundaries: Virginia Woolf's Short Fiction*, ed. Kathryn N. Benzel and Ruth Hoberman, Basingstoke: Macmillan, 2004

# Virginia's Friend and Rival:
# Lytton Strachey

. . . . . . . . . . .

Lytton Strachey (1880–1932) was one of Virginia's closest friends – and rivals – from the beginnings of their friendship until his death. She first met him in 1900 or 1901, probably through Thoby or on a family holiday, and they got to know one another in 1905, when Thoby Stephen began to hold his Thursday evenings at 46 Gordon Square. Thoby looked upon his friend as a great eccentric, whose homosexuality was just one of his eccentricities. He brought home from Cambridge anecdotes about Lytton's exceptional intelligence, his physical fragility and his extreme sensitivity; Virginia was intrigued, and continued to be so, using Lytton as the model for two major characters in her first two novels.

## The Strachey Family

Lytton's family bore some similarities to Virginia's. He himself noted that both families were headed by old men, and had numerous branches and networks. The Stracheys were a dynasty of lawmakers

and colonial administrators. Lytton's father, Richard, and uncle, John, were prominent Anglo-Indians (as the white ruling class of India was referred to). Two of Lytton's older brothers went to India, but a few years later scepticism about the role of the British Empire set in. Lytton had nine siblings – Elinor, Richard (Dick), Dorothy, Ralph, Philippa (Pippa), Oliver, Pernel, Marjorie and James. The age gap between oldest and youngest was twenty-seven years – James, born in 1887, was younger than some of Elinor's children.

## Bloomsbury Connections

The younger children were brought up at 69 Lancaster Gate, opposite Kensington Gardens, but later many of the Stracheys would live in Gordon Square (see pp. 151–2). Not only did several of Lytton's siblings have geographical connections with Bloomsbury, they also had personal ties. Dorothy married the Swiss-French painter Simon Bussy. They and their daughter Janie were well known in the Bloomsbury circle, although they were not of it. The redoubtable Pippa was closely involved with the Suffrage movement, and it was at her suggestion that Virginia wrote the paper that evolved into *Three Guineas* (see pp. 141–2). Pernel became Principal of Newnham College, Cambridge, a post formerly held by Virginia's cousin Katharine. At her request Virginia wrote the lecture that became *A Room of One's Own* (see pp. 138–9). Oliver's daughter by his first marriage, Julia, was a great friend of Frances Marshall, later Partridge, Bloomsbury's renowned diarist. After Oliver's marriage broke up he courted Virginia for a brief spell in 1911, before marrying as his second wife Rachel (Ray) Costelloe, another Suffrage supporter

and the sister of Karin, who later married Adrian Stephen.

The idiosyncratic Marjorie, born in the same year as Virginia, was a close friend of hers before she married Leonard Woolf, and Virginia greatly appreciated her eccentricity and offbeat sense of humour. James, later a psychoanalyst and with his wife Alix the English translator of the works of Freud (a translation still in common use today), was of Lytton's siblings the closest to Bloomsbury; indeed some would classify him as one of them. Like Lytton (and Virginia, of course) he was a great gossip – the correspondence between the brothers shows plainly how they would try to top one another's scandalous tales. James is also known for his friendship with Rupert Brooke, whom he idolized from boyhood until a fierce quarrel in 1912.

## Cambridge and Early Writing

Lytton went up to Trinity College, Cambridge, in 1899 and enjoyed a limited fame – even notoriety – among the undergraduates, dons and professors before he had published a word. His lanky appearance and eccentric manner ensured that he did not go unnoticed, and he was never diffident about expressing a sensational opinion. Some of the more conservative of his fellow students found his irreverent attitude shocking. A confirmed atheist, he had no respect for religious feeling and mocked those who did, which earned him enemies at the same time that his humour and wit earned him friends. Among the latter

*Lytton Strachey by Henry Lamb, 1910*

were Leonard Woolf, Thoby Stephen, Saxon Sydney-Turner and Clive Bell – the core of Bloomsbury – and a little later John Maynard Keynes.

A writer from a young age, Lytton tried his hand at poetry, drama, parody and fiction, but his 'day job' was literary criticism. During 1907–9, while working for his cousin St Loe Strachey at the *Spectator*, Lytton contributed articles and reviews at the rate of one a week for a year and a half. But finding it took up all of his time, Lytton abandoned the only steady employment of his life to devote himself to his own writing. His first major publication was *Landmarks in French Literature* (1912), covering French literature from the Middle Ages to the late nineteenth century in less than 200 pages. It proved very successful, selling 12,000 copies within two years of publication.

But it was his next book for which he would be best remembered.

## Eminent Victorians, Queen Victoria and Elizabeth and Essex

*Eminent Victorians* (1918), was Lytton's breakthrough book, comprising four warts-and-all biographical essays. These concerned Henry Edward Manning (1808–92), the Anglican minister turned Catholic archbishop and cardinal; Florence Nightingale (1820–1910), the now-legendary nurse of the Crimea; Dr Thomas Arnold (1795–1842), a headmaster of Rugby School, famous for instilling his staff and pupils with stern

morals; and General Charles George Gordon (1833–85), the national military hero and veteran of China and Khartoum (Sudan). Readers had not seen this kind of biography before – they were used to prominent figures being treated with awe and reverence, and here was a young man telling his readers that heroes are much like the rest of us. The book was a runaway success. Virginia, having only published one moderately successful novel and still relatively unknown as a writer, could not help but feel his shadow looming over her.

Lytton followed up his success in 1921 with *Queen Victoria*, dedicated to 'Virginia Woolf'. By now the public knew to expect an irreverent, even disrespectful, account of the monarch's life. What they received was an intimate exploration of a romantic heroine and

*1872 statue of Queen Victoria, Victoria Gardens, Bombay*

hero, and a cast of supporting characters, whose motives and behaviour are often imputed to sexual drives. The view of Victoria that emerged was, surprisingly, largely sympathetic. The book was a bestseller in Britain and the US, and some critics thought that Lytton had surpassed himself. Virginia considered, however, that his fame had surpassed his merit.

Elizabeth and Essex (1928) was a very different affair. Its subtitle, *A Tragic History*, hints at Lytton's intention. He had first been inspired by the story of the Virgin Queen and her lover in 1909, when he wrote 'Essex: A Tragedy' in blank verse. *Elizabeth and Essex* reveals the legacy of that early, fictional work – the main criticism levelled against it was that it was too dramatic to be a true biography. Virginia's *Orlando* had been published the previous month, and the Elizabethan focus of both books meant that they were sometimes reviewed together. Both had been inspired by younger lovers – Roger Senhouse in Lytton's case, and Vita Sackville-West in Virginia's – and were a mix of fact and fiction. Sigmund Freud wrote to Lytton praising him on his psychoanalytic approach to examining Elizabeth's sexuality. But the modern consensus is that Lytton had taken his method too far, his dramatic flourishes throwing into doubt the accuracy of his story. However, in Lytton's lifetime the book sold record numbers of copies and made him a rich man.

## Major Works of Lytton Strachey

*Landmarks in French Literature*, London: Williams and Norgate/New York, Henry Holt and Company, 1912

*Eminent Victorians*, London: Chatto and Windus/New York: G.P. Putnam's Sons, 1918

*Queen Victoria*, London: Chatto and Windus/New York: Harcourt, Brace and Co., 1921

*Books and Characters*, London: Chatto and Windus/New York: Harcourt, Brace and Co., 1922

*Elizabeth and Essex: A Tragic History*, London: Chatto and Windus/New York: Harcourt, Brace and Co., 1928

*Portraits in Miniature and Other Essays*, London: Chatto and Windus/New York: Harcourt, Brace and Co., 1931

## Lytton and Virginia on Each Other's Work

On reading *Two Stories*, the first publication of the Hogarth Press, Lytton told Leonard Woolf that he thought 'The Mark on the Wall' a work of genius. His opinion was one of those that really mattered to Virginia, and she was on tenterhooks until he had delivered it.

Virginia read an early draft of the Cardinal Manning chapter of *Eminent Victorians* and pronounced it 'superb'. When *Eminent Victorians* was published

in its entirety, she made a joke of her envy, saying that his current health problems had been sent as a plague by God, and he would get no sympathy from her. Lytton was very complimentary about the solidity and characterization of *The Voyage Out*, with one reservation about the lack of overarching meaning, which Virginia accepted gracefully. He liked *Night and Day*, and she wrote to say how 'magnificent' she considered *Queen Victoria* when it was published in the spring of 1921. Virginia noted that he did not mention *Monday or Tuesday*, published during the same season, but was thrilled when she heard that he greatly admired 'The String Quartet'.

When *Jacob's Room* appeared, Lytton found numerous features to admire, including the lyricism of the narrative, the detail of the outdoor scenes and the

character of Jacob, with its similarities to Thoby Stephen. The *Common Reader* was 'divine'. But *Mrs Dalloway* he was less keen on; he was unconvinced by Clarissa and by her role in the story. In this he had touched upon Virginia's fear that Clarissa was too superficial and lacked depth. But her feeling that he was perceived as the better writer was finally quashed in 1928, with the publication of both *Elizabeth and Essex* and *Orlando*. Virginia disliked Lytton's book, thinking it all cheap surface gloss. She avoided saying anything about the book to him, knowing that he would understand the meaning of her omission. The narrative style of *Portraits in Miniature*, Lytton's last book, was a great improvement, in her opinion. He did not live to read and deliver judgement on *The Waves*.

## Portraits of Lytton

### The Voyage Out

Lytton was the basis for characters in Virginia's first two novels. In *The Voyage Out* (see pp. 32–6), St John Hirst is a brilliant young graduate, anxious about his future, who takes a dim view of the uncultured and conventional holiday-makers who are his fellow guests at the hotel. The likeness is unmistakeable. St John tries to educate Rachel by recommending she read Gibbon (whose writing she dislikes), and their incongruity is clearly demonstrated when they fail to connect in conversation or on the dance-floor. She is repulsed by his ugliness, and he by her femaleness. The situation is an exaggeration of Virginia and Lytton's incompatibility for marriage.

## Night and Day

Into this novel Virginia places the triangular relationship between herself, Lytton and Leonard Woolf. While Leonard was in Ceylon, Lytton became anxious that someone outside their circle would marry Virginia. He urged Leonard in letters to return to England and make her his wife. Just as Leonard was coming round to the idea, Lytton proposed to Virginia himself. To his surprise, she accepted; but both saw the impossibility of the marriage and retracted. Lytton confessed to his friend, but Leonard's ardour cooled, and it was to be another two years before he returned home.

The true story leaves only a small role for Virginia; most of the significant action is played out by the two men. But in Night and Day it is Katharine's manoeuvrings that liberate her from the engagement to William, freeing her to pursue a relationship with Ralph. William pairs up with Katharine's young cousin, Cassandra, who is eager to be educated, and who takes William's tastes and opinions seriously, while Katharine is often tempted to laugh at him. In this Cassandra resembles Dora Carrington (see below).

## Other Portraits

Lytton saw himself reflected in Bonamy in Jacob's Room. He appears in spirit in Orlando, changing sex as he occasionally desired to do, and Leonard Woolf saw elements of his character in the sensitive homosexual Neville in The Waves.

## Carrington

Apart from Virginia and Vanessa, Lytton's closest female friend was Dora Carrington (1893–1932), with whom he spent the last fifteen years of his life in a very unorthodox relationship. A graduate of the Slade School of Art in Chelsea, Carrington (who preferred to be called by her surname) seemed at first an unlikely companion for Lytton. For a start she was female while he preferred boys, and she had had her fill of male attention. Her fellow painter Mark Gertler had been pursuing her for some time, without success, and other admirers fared no better. (One of them, Gilbert Cannan, poured his feelings for Carrington into a novel called Mendel, published in 1916.)

### The First Meeting

Lytton met Carrington in the winter of 1915 when both were staying at Asheham House as Vanessa Bell's guests. Finding her cropped hair and penchant for breeches charmingly boyish, he tried to kiss her during a walk on the South Downs. She was horrified, and planned her revenge – she would cut off his beard while he slept. She crept into his room early the next morning, but at the last moment he awoke. Face to face with her tormentor, she was unable to carry out her plan. Embarrassment would have been natural, but another, more unexpected emotion struck her as she looked into his eyes. A friendship developed, in which Lytton was teacher and Carrington pupil. She was instructed to study Gibbon's *Decline and Fall of the Roman Empire*, as Rachel is by St John Hirst in *The Voyage Out*, and Lytton taught her to understand his beloved French. His friends looked on, puzzled and amused. Virginia, feeling a pang of jealousy, sought Lytton's reassurance that she was his favourite, and got it.

Lytton, who had always had trouble dealing with the practicalities of life, was more than happy to have someone lift the burden from his shoulders. And Carrington was equally happy to do those things that he found onerous – find a new house, decorate it, arrange the move and supervise household matters. In some ways it was very much like an orthodox marriage. But in other ways it was very unorthodox. They experimented with heterosexual sex, and enjoyed it as a temporary measure, but most of their physical relationships were with other partners.

### Complications

When in 1918 a young officer, Rex Partridge (renamed Ralph by Lytton), became interested in Carrington, a triangular relationship developed. Lytton loved Ralph, Ralph loved Carrington, Carrington loved Lytton. For Lytton's sake Carrington accepted Ralph's proposal of marriage in 1921 and he came to live permanently at Tidmarsh.

Two months later, Carrington had an on-and-off affair with Gerald Brenan, a serious young friend of Ralph's. The following year Ralph himself started to have affairs – one was with Marjorie Joad, who was to replace him at the Hogarth Press – then he met and fell in love with Frances Marshall. It was not an ideal arrangement, but at least there was now a quartet comprising (on the face of it) two couples instead of a precarious trio.

## Final Years

In 1924 Carrington arranged the move to Ham Spray, near Hungerford, the house that would be Lytton's home for the

*Ham Spray in Wiltshire, where Lytton and Carrington lived from 1924*

rest of his life. An occasional visitor was handsome young Oxford graduate, Roger Senhouse, a new amour of Lytton's, who proved very elusive and caused him much hurt and frustration. Carrington took up with her last lover, Bernard Penrose, nicknamed Beacus, who reminded her of her beloved brother Teddy, killed in the First World War. Beacus, like Roger, was in his twenties; also like Roger, he was not in love. In November 1929 Carrington found she was pregnant and had a termination, paid for by Ralph. By the summer of 1931, Lytton's and Carrington's obsessions for their younger partners were exhausted.

## Death

During their last few months Lytton and Carrington spent much of their time in one another's company. Carrington took up painting again and Lytton began the first of an intended series of commentaries on Shakespeare's plays. In late 1931 he began to feel unwell, and assumed it was one of the bouts of illness that had plagued him since childhood. But it went on for two months, and was diagnosed variously as gastric flu, typhoid, colitis, paratyphoid and enteric fever (it was actually stomach cancer). When Virginia heard, she recalled their long friendship, and made plans for future visits, future conversations. All of Bloomsbury was anxious, but none more

than Carrington, who sat at his bedside almost continuously. On 21 January 1932, Lytton breathed his last.

Carrington was distraught. The last fifteen years of her life had been dedicated to Lytton, and her future meant nothing without him. She had made one failed suicide attempt when Lytton was dying. After his death, friends surrounded Carrington, meaning well, but merely delaying the inevitable. The Woolfs were among the last to see her alive on 10 March, and she confided her unbearable grief to Virginia. The next day she borrowed a gun and shot herself.

### Read On ...

*Lytton Strachey: The New Biography*, by Michael Holroyd, London: Chatto and Windus, 1994

*The Letters of Lytton Strachey*, ed. Paul Levy, London: Viking, 2005

*Bombay to Bloomsbury: A Biography of the Strachey Family*, by Barbara Caine, Oxford: Oxford University Press, 2005

*Carrington: Letters and Extracts from Her Diaries*, ed. David Garnett, New York: Holt, Rinehart and Winston, 1971

*Carrington: A Life of Dora Carrington, 1893–1932*, by Gretchen Gerzina, London: Pimlico, 1995

# Bloomsbury Memories: The Memoir Club

. . . . . . . . . . .

### Beginnings

Founded in 1920 by Molly MacCarthy, the Memoir Club grew out of her Novel Club, established two years earlier to encourage Desmond MacCarthy to write the novel that all of his friends believed was lurking under the surface. The novel was never written, but the Memoir Club initiated a number of autobiographical papers that otherwise may not have existed. Members dined at a restaurant (sometimes Olivelli's in London's Store Street, still there today) and then went on to a member's rooms, often Clive Bell's at 46 Gordon Square, Duncan Grant's studio at Taviton Street, or Saxon Sydney-Turner's old rooms in Percy Street, taken over and redecorated by Vanessa Bell and Duncan Grant.

Members included Virginia and Leonard Woolf, Vanessa and Clive Bell, Molly and Desmond MacCarthy, Lytton Strachey, Saxon Sydney-Turner, Maynard Keynes, Morgan Forster,

*Olivelli's restaurant (now one of a chain), where the Memoir Club sometimes dined before meetings*

63

Roger Fry, Duncan Grant and Adrian Stephen. Later members, replacing those who had died, included Quentin Bell, Frances Partridge and Julia Strachey. Newcomers were elected (or rejected) by secret ballot. The Club had a single rule – that no one could join without the approval of all the existing members. Because the papers were autobiographical, the audience had to consist of trusted friends.

The first meeting, on 4 March 1920, included Virginia's old suitor, Sydney Waterlow, who read, according to Virginia, a paper describing a dream he had had. Other readers that day were Clive, Vanessa, Duncan, Molly and Roger. There was some understandable nervousness, with Molly almost coming to a stop, and Vanessa actually doing so. Clive and Roger spoke disinterestedly; Virginia looked forward to a time when they would let slip confidences. But after the second meeting, she felt uncomfortable at having revealed *too* much.

At the meeting on 17 November Virginia read '22 Hyde Park Gate', which was a great success. On 2 February the following year, Maynard Keynes read 'Dr Melchior: A Defeated Enemy', about negotiations at the 1919 Paris Peace Conference, and Clive read a paper about his affair with Annie Raven-Hill, a (married) neighbour of his parents, responsible for his sexual initiation. But most of the papers were not so risqué as Clive's. Morgan Forster's offerings described, among other things, his experiences as a tutor in Germany to

the children of the author Elizabeth von Arnim, and his first encounters with 'Bloomsbury'.

## Virginia Woolf's Contributions

Virginia's surviving Memoir Club papers, '22 Hyde Park Gate', 'Old Bloomsbury' and 'Am I a Snob?', are collected with other autobiographical writings in *Moments of Being*. Much of the first concerns George Duckworth, and accounts for the adverse opinion many Woolf readers now hold of him. Maynard Keynes thought it was the best thing Virginia had ever written, which disappointed and amused her in equal measure. Virginia portrays her half-brother as handsome but sentimental, and a stickler for etiquette. Determined to get into 'society', he uses Vanessa and Virginia as trophies to show off at dances and dinners, while he appears the perfect brother, showering them with gifts and treats. She ends the paper with the sensational claim that George wanted nothing less than to be a lover to his half-sisters. But can he really have been so bad, or was she writing for effect? When George died, Virginia wrote only of the trips and treats, nothing about the alleged abuse (see *Diary* 4, 1 May 1934).

[O]ne felt like an unfortunate minnow shut up in the same tank with an unwieldy and turbulent whale.

('22 Hyde Park Gate')

In 'Old Bloomsbury' Virginia takes up the story again. She contrasts the dark, cramped life at Hyde Park Gate with the airy freedoms of 46 Gordon Square. If it is less comical than '22 Hyde Park Gate' it is a happier piece, focusing on the new lifestyle and new friendships of the Stephen siblings. Her old friends were no doubt amused to hear her first impressions of them, along with her account of gossip and sex entering the conversation for the first time. Rumours about Bloomsbury parties and behaviour spread like wildfire, she reminds them, and shocked their more conventional friends and relations. But this disapprobation did not affect the core friendships, Virginia concludes, as their presence confirms.

In 'Am I a Snob?', a much later paper from the 1930s, Virginia confesses her admiration for people with titles. She makes sure that a letter bearing a coronet is easily visible to visitors; she is fascinated by the free and natural ways of the aristocracy; she is thrilled to be asked to lunch with Lady Oxford. Flatteringly, society hostess Lady Sibyl Colefax pursues her. When Sibyl's husband dies suddenly she invites Virginia to tea. Expecting intimate confidences, Virginia is disappointed to find that she can only communicate with Sibyl by reminiscing about her past glories.

## Vanessa Bell's Contributions

Surprisingly for someone who prided herself more on the paintbrush than the pen, more of Vanessa's Memoir Club papers than Virginia's have survived. She is known to have written the following: 'Memoir Relating to Mrs Jackson' (her maternal grandmother), 'Notes on Virginia's Childhood', 'Life at Hyde Park Gate after 1897', 'My Sister-in-Law', 'Notes on Bloomsbury', 'Memories of Roger Fry', 'Old Bloomsbury', 'The Strange Story of Mary Elizabeth Wilson', 'Notes on the Death of Lytton Strachey' (unfinished), 'A Brother as Chaperone: A Visit to the Chamberlains' (fragment) and 'Introduction to Fourteen Letters from Leslie Stephen to Mary Fisher'.

Many of these cover the same ground as Virginia's memoirs, but from a different angle. However, they are less expressive of her emotions; Leslie's groans at the weekly accounts reduced

Virginia to a state of rage and frustration, but Vanessa treats the matter with objectivity and distance, even sympathizing in hindsight with Leslie in the face of her silence (see pp. 73–4). In 'Memories of Roger Fry', written only weeks after his death, she reveals a little of her earlier passion: her impression of his beauty; her relief at finding an understanding confidant about her maternal worries; her joy at their new friendship. It is the most personal of the memoirs, but even here the restraint is evident (for more on Roger Fry, see pp. 81–5).

## Memoir Club: Published Papers

Virginia Woolf, '22 Hyde Park Gate', 'Old Bloomsbury' and 'Am I a Snob?', in *Moments of Being*, ed. Jeanne Schulkind, London: Chatto and Windus, 1976

Vanessa Bell, 'Memoir Relating to Mrs Jackson', 'Notes on Virginia's Childhood', 'Life at Hyde Park Gate after 1897', 'My Sister-in-Law', 'Notes on Bloomsbury' and 'Memories of Roger Fry', in *Sketches in Pen and Ink: A Bloomsbury Notebook*, ed. Lia Giachero, London: Hogarth Press/Chatto and Windus, 1997

Vanessa Bell, 'The Strange Story of Mary Elizabeth Wilson', *Charleston Magazine*, Issue 3, Summer/Autumn 1991, pp. 5–15 (see pp. 156–7 for more)

Lytton Strachey, 'Lancaster Gate' and 'Monday June 26th 1916', in *The Shorter Strachey*, ed. Michael Holroyd and Paul Levy, London: Hogarth Press, 1989 (also in *Lytton Strachey by Himself: A Self-Portrait*, ed. Michael Holroyd, London: Heinemann, 1971)

John Maynard Keynes, 'Dr Melchior: A Defeated Enemy' and 'My Early Beliefs' in *Two Memoirs*, ed. David Garnett, London: Rupert Hart-Davis, 1949

Duncan Grant, 'I Tatti: A Question of Labels', *Charleston Magazine*, Issue 10, Autumn/Winter 1994, pp. 5–12

Julia Strachey, 'Animalia', printed as 'Can't You Get Me Out of Here?' in the *New Yorker*, 23 January 1960, and reprinted in *Stories from The New Yorker 1950–1960*, New York: Simon and Schuster, 1960/London: Penguin, 1965

Julia Strachey, 'The Bathrooms in My Life', printed as 'Harum-Scarum Life with Hester' in Frances Partridge, *Julia: A Portrait of Julia Strachey*, London: Penguin, 1984 (ch. 9)

## Expansion

In the 1940s and 1950s the Memoir Club expanded a little to embrace the younger generation. In late 1947 Frances Partridge joined. At her second meeting, in January 1948, she noted the attendance of Clive, Vanessa and Quentin Bell, Desmond MacCarthy and his son Dermod, Bunny Garnett, Oliver Strachey, Duncan Grant and Morgan Forster. Dermod MacCarthy had prepared a paper about his father, and Morgan one about his aunts, who played a large psychological role in his life. Some papers got a second airing for the younger members, including Clive's on Mrs Raven-Hill, re-run in September 1950. But expansion was slow, even though in Frances Partridge's opinion new blood was badly needed. She privately condemned the over-exacting demands of existing members, who were only prepared to elect their own offspring.

## The End of the Memoir Club

The Memoir Club survived for more than forty years, but by the mid-1960s the number of original members was sadly depleted with the deaths of Lytton Strachey, Roger Fry, Virginia Woolf, Maynard Keynes, Adrian Stephen, the MacCarthys, Vanessa Bell and Saxon Sydney-Turner. After Clive Bell's death in 1964, no one had the heart to go on any longer and the Club came to a natural end. Many of the papers written by members were later published as free-standing articles (see above) or were incorporated into the memoirs of Frances Partridge, David Garnett and others.

# Jacob's Room (1922)

. . . . . . . . . . . .

*Jacob's Room*, the story of the young Jacob Flanders, in which the hero is never quite in full focus, exemplifies Virginia Woolf's new style of writing fiction, a literary form based on hints and omissions. A good year for innovation, 1922 also saw the first publication of James Joyce's *Ulysses* and T.S. Eliot's *The Waste Land*, as well as the first non-commercial radio broadcast by the BBC. It has been suggested that readers tune in to and out of Jacob's life as they would to a radio programme.

## Origins

Woolf conceived of her third novel as a mix of her three stories, 'An Unwritten Novel', 'The Mark on the Wall' and 'Kew Gardens'. By September 1920 she was thinking of her book almost exclusively, but the following February nerves had set in. Social distractions, illness and work on *Monday or Tuesday* delayed the completion of the novel until November. Then came the long job of revision and copying, and Virginia's fears that readers would not understand the connections between scenes, and think the book bad – or even mad. Leonard's approval was a relief, and confirmed Virginia's opinion that at last she had found her own 'voice', but both were uncertain how the book would be received. Proof-correcting depressed Virginia as it always did – but she considered her work superior to that of James Joyce, whose *Ulysses* she had just read.

## Plot Summary

> It is no use trying to sum people up. One must follow hints, not exactly what is said, nor yet entirely what is done.
>
> (*Jacob's Room*, ch. 12)

Betty Flanders, a widow staying with her three young sons in Cornwall, writes to her friend Captain Barfoot in Scarborough. At their boarding house, a servant looks after the youngest child – an unweaned baby, though Betty's husband has been dead for two years. Several years pass: Betty Flanders is forty-five and living in Scarborough. Local clergyman Mr Floyd, with hopes of pleasing Betty, is teaching the boys Latin. He proposes to Betty but she declines. Captain Barfoot comes to visit, leaving his invalid wife in the care of Mr Dickens.

At Cambridge University, Jacob

looks critically on women, wives and picnic parties, but enjoys intellectual debate and boyish sparring with his new friend Timmy Durrant. Timmy's sister, Clara, and Richard Bonamy are among Jacob's many admirers, but everyone who meets him receives a different impression. His lover is a dim-witted girl of dubious reputation called Florinda; meanwhile Clara finds that no other man matches up to Jacob.

Jacob sees Florinda in a Soho street with another man. We are left to guess his feelings. Fanny Elmer, a painter's model, falls in love with Jacob. He goes to visit painter friends in Paris, where Jinny Carslake likewise falls in love with him, then to Greece where he is enamoured of a sophisticated married woman, Sandra Wentworth Williams. They arrange to meet in London.

Back in London, Bonamy guesses that Jacob is in love. Clara, Florinda and Fanny pine for him while he pines for the unattainable Sandra. The First World War begins, and Jacob's acquaintances catch their last glimpse of him. After his death, a grief-stricken Bonamy helps Mrs Flanders to sort out Jacob's papers and possessions. They come across a pair of his old shoes, a poignant reminder of his physical presence.

**Sources**

Jacob Flanders' life echoes that of Thoby Stephen, Virginia's older brother, dead at the age of twenty-six. Jacob's Cambridge experiences are based on the first meetings of 'Old Bloomsbury', and some of Thoby's friends are discernible: the man with the pipe is Saxon Sydney-Turner; the red-haired man, Clive Bell; Richard Bonamy, who loves Jacob and reads highbrow literature, is Lytton Strachey; Simeon, with the Old Testament name, Leonard Woolf.

Jacob's Paris visit also was based on the Stephens' in 1904, when Clive Bell introduced them to the artists' quarter. Like Jacob also, the Stephens went to Greece – the trip resulted in the typhoid that was to kill Thoby. The fictional Sandra Wentworth Williams is taken from the real-life Irene Noel, whose family the Stephens visited on the Greek island of Euboea. Thoby was a great admirer of hers, as was his friend Desmond MacCarthy.

Several details of Jacob's life and death associate Thoby Stephen with Rupert Brooke, who died during the First World War. Jacob is educated at Rugby, like Rupert, and Trinity College, like Thoby. He goes up to Cambridge in October 1906, like Rupert – a month before Thoby's death. Jacob is killed just after Greece enter the war, in 1915, making him about twenty-seven, the age at death of Rupert Brooke – the actual date is unstated, and perhaps deliberately kept ambiguous. But Jacob's death during the First World War has a broader significance. His first name hints at fraternal strife (the biblical Jacob was estranged from his brother Esau for many years), and his surname

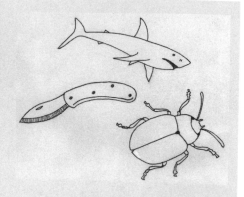

commemorates those who died on the battlefields of Flanders.

## Themes

### Death

The novel is an effort to put into perspective Thoby's death, and those of the young men who died during the First World War. At the end of the book, Jacob's room is empty, symbolizing the empty spaces left in the lives of all those whose fathers, brothers, lovers and sons died in the war.

There are frequent allusions to danger and death. Even an innocent-seeming description of a family holiday is full of hidden menaces: the young Jacob finds a sheep's skull on the beach; a neighbour loses an eye in an explosion; a crab trapped in a bucket is likely to perish there. Later there are references to invalids, tumours, widowhood, knives, a 'monster shark' and a dead beetle. A tree falls mysteriously in the night, sounding like pistol shots; Betty Flanders, waiting for Jacob, has unexplained misgivings. The peacock butterflies look beautiful and delicate but even they have their sinister side, feeding on carrion dropped by a hawk – a grisly foreshadowing of the war, when similar butterflies will perhaps feed on dead bodies in France and Belgium.

## Communication

Communication and the lack of it is a frequent motif. The book begins with Betty Flanders writing to Captain Barfoot. A letter from Scarborough, presumably from him, is in her front room. Apart from knowing that Betty is tearful while she writes, we know little about the contents of either letter. A little later Mr Floyd, a clergyman and her sons' tutor, proposes to her in writing. Betty reads his letter while thinking about the fish for dinner and scolding her youngest son. She is similarly distracted when she writes her reply. Meanwhile Captain Barfoot has been writing to Mr Polegate to ask his advice about sending Jacob to university; the reply settles Jacob's future.

> [M]others down at Scarborough ... can never, never say, whatever it may be – probably this – Don't go with bad women, do be a good boy; wear your thick shirts; and come back, come back to me.
>
> (*Jacob's Room*, ch. 8)

Betty writes to her son, passing on titbits of gossip rather than expressing her anxieties about him. Jacob's sight of a child at the pillar box should remind him to write to his mother, but he is too busy thinking of Virgil. Her letters are kept in an old box where he discards unnecessary objects. One is left unopened while Jacob goes to bed with Florinda. When he finally reads it, the narrator soliloquizes about the attempts to make contact embodied in letters, and how essential they are to civilized life. They bind friendships. But do we communicate through them? Jacob's letters are about abstract ideas; Betty hears nothing about his personal life, and a planned letter to Bonamy turns (in Jacob's imagination) into an essay on civilization in the style of Gibbon.

## Character

In Jacob Flanders, Woolf asks: Do we really know our friends and family better than we know complete strangers? When two buses pass in the street, the passengers get a momentary impression of one another, if any at all. They are locked into their own worlds, with their own tasks to carry out. Is it really any different with those we think we know?

People have different views of Jacob. Betty thinks her son clumsy and irritating, but he is Captain Barfoot's favourite. Clara Durrant thinks him unworldly and unpretentious. Fanny Elmer's first impressions are that he is slightly awkward but has a beautiful speaking voice. Mrs Durrant and her friends see him as distinguished; Julia Eliot thinks him too taciturn; Mr Sopwith is very fond of him. Timmy Durrant passes no judgement on his friend, but Richard Bonamy sees a mix of romance and recklessness in his character, with a little grumpiness. Sandra Wentworth Williams is reminded of Molière's Alceste, the Misanthrope. Her husband, though jealous, is reassured by Jacob's directness and predicts a future in politics for him.

Who we are, the narrator concludes, affects how we see others, and we probably read into them much that is not there. We must follow hints and glimpses, sometimes misleading; for instance the narrator observes that Jacob's interior monologue as he talks to Bonamy merely indicates his *possible* thoughts. But however indistinct and contradictory is our image of another person, we cannot resist trying to concoct one.

# Bloomsbury Art I: Vanessa Bell, Clive Bell and Duncan Grant

. . . . . . . . . . .

## Vanessa Bell (1879–1961)

### Vanessa and Virginia

From the nursery, Virginia and Vanessa had been close friends. Vanessa, nearly three years older, was maternal

*Vanessa Bell in 1932*

and dependable, but also enigmatic and mysterious. In Virginia's fruitful imagination Vanessa was goddess-like – beautiful, powerful and womanly. In adulthood Vanessa was statuesque and serene, with large, limpid, grey eyes and full lips, and Virginia, with her more delicate and ephemeral beauty, sometimes felt inferior. Fortunately the girls decided early on that Virginia would write and Vanessa would paint, and each conceded to the other in their chosen field. But Virginia frequently compared their lives and found her own wanting.

### Vanessa and Her Father

When Stella Duckworth died, Vanessa was expected to replace her half-sister as household manager, reporting to Leslie. Virginia and her father were close because of shared personality traits and a love of literature, but between Vanessa and Leslie there was no such tie. When she presented the household accounts to him each week, he would bellow and groan that they would be destitute before the month was out. Met with Vanessa's impassive silence, Leslie would groan all the louder at her lack of sympathy.

When in 1904 her father died, Vanessa did not feel as much guilt and grief as Virginia, who suffered a serious breakdown. Her dominant feeling was one of freedom. It was she who arranged the move from Hyde Park Gate to Gordon Square, and she was perhaps the most eager of the Stephen siblings to leave the old life behind, and begin a new one in Bloomsbury.

### Vanessa and Men

When the new life was cut short by the sudden death of Thoby, Vanessa accepted Clive's third proposal and married him in February 1907. But it was only a year later, after she had given birth to their first child, that Clive's attentions strayed to his then unmarried sister-in-law. For Clive it was one of his many flirtations, but for Virginia it was – to begin with – a way of sharing her sister's life. Vanessa was too reserved to show her grief and jealousy openly – besides, it was not the Bloomsbury way. Instead she wrote wistful letters to Virginia complaining that she only heard from her through Clive's reports.

A substantial crack appeared in the Bell marriage, and widened a couple of years later when Vanessa became friends with Roger Fry, who sympathized with her worries about her second son Quentin. When she, Clive, Roger and Harry Norton, a Cambridge friend, went to Turkey in April 1911, Vanessa was again pregnant. But she miscarried the child, and suffered a physical and mental breakdown. Clive was not a good nurse, but Roger had had plenty of practice nursing his wife, Helen, who was mentally unstable. His nursing 'methods' seemed to consist mainly of constant stimulation and great untidiness, but by sheer determination he helped Vanessa recover sufficiently to travel home.

They embarked on a two-year affair (see p. 83), but in 1913–14 Vanessa started becoming more intimate with Duncan Grant, the cousin and former lover of her friend Lytton Strachey (see p. 79), and Roger reluctantly but resignedly faded into the background. It is significant, however, that Vanessa's husband and lovers were all intimately connected with painting, and that the bond of friendship was strong enough to keep them within Bloomsbury when the passion had dwindled.

### Artistic Development

From a young age it was clear to Vanessa that she would be an artist. In 1896 she began to attend Arthur Cope's art school in South Kensington, then she was accepted for the Royal Academy School in 1901. Her first exhibited painting was a portrait of Violet Dickinson's friend Lady Robert Cecil, shown at the New Gallery in April 1905. Soon after this she started the Friday Club, an art society, inviting people she knew from the Royal Academy and the Slade, which she had attended for a few weeks the previous

winter. She arranged lectures by, among others, Clive Bell, Walter Lamb (whose brother Henry was a member) and Roger Fry (see pp. 81–5). She started sending pictures to the Allied Artists Exhibition and the New English Art Club. Roger Fry's Second Post-Impressionist Exhibition in 1912–13 featured two of her paintings, *Asheham* and *Nosegay*, and in 1919 she began exhibiting regularly with the London Group.

Vanessa Bell's works include portraits, domestic scenes, landscapes and still lives, some of them bordering on abstractionism, as well as fabric and rug designs for the Omega Workshops and Allan Walton, and book covers for her sister's novels and other Hogarth Press books. And despite her lifelong atheism, she and Duncan were asked to paint scenes for the interior of the little country church of Berwick, near Charleston. These did not receive the unanimous approval of worshippers, but can still be seen today. As can her own house, Charleston, decorated throughout

by herself, Duncan and their daughter Angelica. She and Duncan often worked side by side and such was their influence on one another that their styles are sometimes indistinguishable.

### Bloomsbury Painter

Vanessa painted portraits of Bloomsbury friends such as Roger Fry, Lytton Strachey, Leonard Woolf, Clive Bell, Duncan Grant, Saxon Sydney-Turner, E.M. Forster, Mary Hutchinson, David Garnett, Quentin Bell, Dorothy Bussy, and several pictures of Virginia Woolf. Despite their closeness – or perhaps because of it – Vanessa seems to have had trouble portraying her sister: two pictures, painted shortly before Virginia's marriage in 1912, show a sitter with blurred or no facial features. Another, painted in 1934, has recently been acquired by the Charleston Trust. This Virginia, seated in an armchair, has rather doll-like features. Perhaps surprisingly she painted very few portraits of Duncan – two, from 1912 and c.1920 show him at work, and another is unfinished.

Love for her subjects is not easily detectable in Vanessa's work, but personal antagonism occasionally intrudes. The portraits of Mary Hutchinson and Bunny Garnett, her husband's mistress and her lover's lover respectively, are far from flattering. But there is one picture that can be regarded as a tribute to Bloomsbury: *The Memoir Club* (1943), which shows a gathering of her friends. Those who could not be present in person – Lytton Strachey, Roger Fry

*Charleston Farmhouse, often known as Bloomsbury in Sussex, home of Vanessa Bell and her family*

and Virginia Woolf – are represented by portraits-within-the-portrait – paintings of them hang on the wall.

### Clive Bell (1881–1964)

Something of an anomaly among Thoby's Cambridge friends, Arthur Clive Heward Bell was the son of a coal industrialist, rather than of a colonial administrator (Lytton), a man of letters (Thoby) or a solicitor (Leonard). He was given as good an education as money could buy, attending a public school (Marlborough) and going up to study history at Trinity College, Cambridge, when he had just turned eighteen. His passion for art and literature made him the odd one out in his family: his parents, brother and sisters had fairly simple tastes, among which art did not number. In her letters Virginia characterized them, with much exaggeration, as barbarous country bumpkins.

### Clive, Vanessa and Virginia

Clive first became acquainted with the Stephen sisters in the early 1900s. He was sociable and genial, and – unlike Thoby's other Cambridge friends – quite at ease with young women. By 1905 he had fallen in love with Vanessa, much to the amusement of Lytton Strachey, who treated it as a great joke. In his opinion, Clive had no hope of winning her. Clive proposed to Vanessa three times in all, but it was not until November 1906 that he was accepted, thus depriving Virginia of a sister shortly after the death of her brother. In her state of emotional turmoil, Virginia's feelings towards Clive veered sharply between affection and revulsion; she knew that Vanessa was happy, but compared Clive with her handsome dead brother and wondered what Vanessa could see in his stocky frame and red curls.

Marriage to Vanessa Stephen ensured Clive's place at the heart of Bloomsbury. Despite his friends' numerous criticisms of him, Clive was an accomplished host, providing a warm, hospitable atmosphere in which good food and drink were always in plentiful supply and stimulating conversation was encouraged. His money ensured financial security for Vanessa, enabling her to concentrate on painting at her own pace and within her own tastes. It also meant, of course, that there was no need for either of them to earn their own money.

On the birth of Julian in 1908 Vanessa had little time for either husband or sister, who were thrown into one another's company. Virginia shyly showed Clive a draft of her novel, 'Melymbrosia' (which became *The Voyage Out*; see pp. 32–6), and noted his criticisms with gratitude. She later credited him with being the first person who thought she would be a successful writer. However, there were soon frequent tête-à-têtes, assiduous attentions, kisses and much mutual flattery – the flirtation was practically

*Clive Bell in 1933*

indistinguishable from an affair, except that there was no sex. Eventually, it petered out, but Vanessa never fully trusted Virginia afterwards. She kept her later relationships with Roger Fry and Duncan Grant secret from Virginia for as long as possible.

Clive, though, was an inveterate flirt. He continued to have affairs throughout his life, even with his friend Desmond's wife, Molly MacCarthy. The longest-lasting was with Mary Hutchinson, the wife of another friend. These were accepted with good grace, not because the Bloomsberries believed inherently in promiscuity, but because they believed in absolute honesty and the emotional freedom of the individual.

### Artistic Development

A reproduction of a Degas picture in his room at Cambridge marked Clive Bell out as an unusual young man. Very little was known in Britain about French painters at the turn of the twentieth century. On graduating he went to Paris to carry out historical research, but this was soon abandoned for the artists' quarter. In 1904 the Stephens visited and Vanessa was most impressed with Clive's knowledge of the contemporary art world.

The turning point in Clive's career was a meeting with Roger Fry in 1910 on a Cambridge railway platform. He, Vanessa and Roger talked about art for the duration of the journey to London and the seeds of friendship were sown. Clive was stimulated by the talk and Roger's ideas, among which was an exhibition of modern French art (see pp. 82–3). With his knowledge of the Parisian art world, Clive was well placed to become Roger's assistant, and helped to gather paintings for the exhibition.

### Bloomsbury Art Critic

Clive's ideas about art were heavily influenced by Roger Fry, although they were not identical to them, and when Roger found himself too busy to fulfil a commission to write a book on the new art movement he passed it to Clive. The result was *Art* (1914), Clive's first full-length book, in which he explores the qualities necessary to appreciate properly a work of art (aesthetic sensibility and intellectual ability) and the quality a work of art needs to possess in order to provoke an 'aesthetic emotion' in the beholder. This quality he identifies (following Roger Fry) as 'significant form', a theory that allows abstract art as much value as figurative art, because the value is inherent.

Clive wrote two further books about art, but this was his most influential. His writing style is very chatty and informal, as might be expected from someone with no formal art training. He speaks to the reader not about art as an academic discipline, but as an informative companion on a visit to the art gallery.

### Duncan Grant (1885–1978)

Born in Scotland, Duncan James Corrowr Grant was the only child of Major Bartle

*Duncan Grant in the garden of Charleston Farmhouse in the mid-1930s*

Grant and his wife Ethel. Bartle was the brother of Lytton Strachey's mother, Lady Jane, so he and Lytton were first cousins. Duncan's early childhood was spent in India and Burma, where he was educated by a governess. In 1894 he returned to England to attend Hillbrow Preparatory School, where James Strachey and Rupert Brooke, two years younger, were also pupils. After five years he moved to St Paul's School in London as a day boy, living with Lytton Strachey's family, except for holiday periods, which were spent abroad with his parents.

### Sex and Love

Both Duncan's parents had extramarital affairs, one of Bartle's resulting in a son, or so Duncan believed. But his father's broadmindedness about sexual matters did not extend to his son. When Bartle found out that the teenage Duncan had been reading sexually explicit literature, he took him to be assessed by the head of the Royal Bethlem Hospital for the mentally ill. Fortunately, the doctor was able to persuade Bartle that there was nothing to worry about.

Duncan was gentle, affable and charming (Virginia compared him to a soft, fluffy white owl), but he was a serial monogamist. His male Bloomsbury lovers included Lytton Strachey, Maynard Keynes, Adrian Stephen and Bunny Garnett. (It is a proof of his charm that he remained on good terms with all of these ex-partners.) Although he was almost exclusively homosexual, in 1913–14 he began a relationship with Vanessa Bell that was the most enduring of his life. They experimented with sex, lived together at Charleston Farmhouse with Vanessa's children, and even had a daughter together (Angelica Bell, born 1918), then they settled into a loving but non-sexual companionship.

While Clive was nominal head of the household, he mostly lived a bachelor's life in a London flat, from where he paid visits to Charleston. For the ever-impractical Duncan the partnership with Vanessa meant domestic comfort, security and the freedom to paint; for Vanessa it meant being near the person she loved best in the world, someone who shared her passion for painting as well as her relaxed approach to life. It seemed ideal for all three, but Duncan sometimes felt oppressed by the need to keep his homosexual affairs as low-key as possible, and Vanessa by her jealousy, which she did her best to hide. If Clive had any objections to the amiable Duncan, he kept them to himself. Angelica was brought up as Clive's daughter, and was not told about her real father until she was eighteen. In a final twist, she married in 1942 her father's former lover, Bunny Garnett, who had admired her in the cradle. It was a match vehemently opposed, understandably, by both parents.

## Artistic Development

Duncan was originally expected to follow his father into the army, but he proved an incompetent soldier and another career was sought. His aunt Lady Jane Strachey talked his parents into allowing him to study at the Westminster School of Art. He had already taken some lessons from Simon Bussy, the French painter who married Dorothy Strachey – years later Duncan claimed that Simon was the best teacher he had ever had. In February 1906 he realized his dream to live and work in Paris. He met Augustus and Gwen John, Henry Lamb and Boris Anrep, and was visited by the Bells and the Stephens. Through a friendship with art critic Bernard Berenson's step-daughters, Ray and Karin Costelloe (Ray became Bunny Garnett's first wife, Karin married Adrian Stephen), he stayed at the Berensons' villa in Florence, I Tatti, and learned at first-hand the politics of art-dealing.

Roger Fry admired Duncan's pictures and was a very useful friend to him. He encouraged Duncan to experiment,

*The tombstones of Vanessa Bell and Duncan Grant in Firle Churchyard*

to be more adventurous in his style and use of colour. When he heard of a commission to decorate the refectory walls of London's Borough Polytechnic in 1911, he made sure Duncan was one of the artists chosen, and the following year included his pictures in the Second Post-Impressionist Exhibition. Like Vanessa, Duncan designed for the Omega Workshops, and they collaborated on a number of projects, such as Maynard Keynes's rooms at Webb Court, King's College, Cambridge. Though their styles are often similar, some of Duncan's pictures – such as *The Queen of Sheba* (1912), or the murals for the Borough Polytechnic – are very distinctive.

### Bloomsbury Painter

Several of Duncan's early paintings feature Strachey cousins. In 1909, he painted portraits of Lytton, James and Marjorie (she is the figure with head in hands in *Le Crime et le Châtiment*, portrayed just after reading a French translation of Dostoevsky's *Crime and Punishment*). Early portraits of lovers are flattering – Maynard Keynes looks

out benignly from his 1908 picture, and a study of Bunny Garnett (1918), poses an interesting contrast to the one by Vanessa painted at the same time. A 1910 head-and-shoulders of Adrian Stephen is one of the few paintings of him. Virginia Woolf was also a rare model: in a 1911 picture, a three-quarter profile in hat and coat, she looks as though she is ready to dash out of the door. Painting the serene Vanessa was quite different. Two 1918 pictures show her, solid, calm and maternal, pregnant with Duncan's child. A more severe aspect of her character is evident in the 1942 painting of a magisterial Vanessa seated on a throne-like armchair, but both convey her rock-like quality.

Like Vanessa, Duncan was versatile, designing book covers, screens, textiles, ballet costumes and sets, and using a wide variety of subjects for his paintings – the male nude, domestic interiors, landscapes, abstracts and even Christian scenes in Berwick Church and Lincoln Cathedral, where he used family and friends as models for biblical figures.

**Read On ...**

*Vanessa Bell*, by Frances Spalding, Stroud, Glos: Tempus Publishing, 2006

*Art*, by Clive Bell, Oxford: Oxford University Press, 1987

*Duncan Grant: A Biography*, by Frances Spalding, London: Chatto and Windus, 1997

*The Art of Bloomsbury*, by Richard Shone, London: Tate Gallery, 1999

# Bloomsbury Art II: The Significant Roger Fry

· · · · · · · · · · ·

## Roger Fry (1866–1934)

### Artistic Development

Roger Eliot Fry, born to Quaker parents, was educated at Clifton College, Bristol, and studied science at King's College,

*Roger Fry in 1918, sitting in an armchair covered in an Omega Workshops fabric*

Cambridge. It wasn't until leaving Cambridge that Fry turned to art as a profession. A trip to Italy in 1891 inspired a love for the work of Raphael and Michelangelo, and the following year he studied at the Académie Julian in Paris and sent pictures to the New English Art Club. He began work as a lecturer, and quickly became successful, his natural energy and enthusiasm making him an invigorating speaker. But his painting did not flourish, and works submitted for exhibition were often rejected. His familiarity with the Old Masters led to work authenticating signatures and styles, and his reputation in this field grew. Then at last his own paintings – at this stage traditional watercolours – found financial success, and his first one-man show in 1903 was a triumph.

When the *Burlington Magazine*, which Roger had co-founded in 1903, ran into financial difficulties, he went to America to raise the funds to keep it afloat. A meeting with the influential millionaire businessman J. Pierpont

Morgan, president of the Metropolitan Museum of New York, led to a job as the Museum's Curator, then later as European adviser. But Roger's tastes were changing. In 1906 he saw a Cézanne painting for the first time, and his interest in the Old Masters gave way to a passion for contemporary art. By 1910, when he was introduced to Bloomsbury, he had fallen out with Morgan and was facing the fact that he would have to have his mentally ill wife Helen (née Coombe) permanently committed to an asylum. Roger had fallen in love with her wit, beauty and what he identified as a touch of genius, but within eighteen months of their marriage she suffered her first bout of paranoid schizophrenia. Though their life was subsequently overshadowed by her illness, it was not until Helen became violent that she was sent to The Priory psychiatric hospital in Roehampton. It was the greatest tragedy of Fry's life.

### Roger Fry and Bloomsbury

Roger Fry, thirteen years older than Vanessa, was known to her by sight before they had properly met. But it was not until the January 1910 meeting (see pp. 77–8) that a friendship began. While Clive was full of enthusiasm for his new friend's passionate views on art; Vanessa noted chiefly his beautiful speaking voice.

Hard-working and inspirational, Roger was described by Virginia Woolf as eager, clever, energetic, highly civilized, capable but somewhat naïve, with his pockets always full of useful and interesting objects, like a boy scout. He was a breath of fresh air to Bloomsbury. One of his ideas was for an exhibition of new French artists – not the Impressionists, who had shocked the previous generation, but those who had followed the path of Manet. These he called simply the 'Post-Impressionists'. The plan was shelved for several months until, impulsively, Roger decided that the time was right.

### The Post-Impressionist Exhibitions

In the autumn of 1910 Roger, Clive Bell and Desmond MacCarthy went to Paris to collect suitable works by Manet, Cézanne, Gauguin, Picasso, Seurat, Derain, van Gogh and others. The exhibition, put together in a matter of weeks, was held at London's Grafton Gallery from 8 November 1910 to 15 January 1911. Pressed for a title by a journalist, Roger had come up with the simple and direct 'Manet and the Post-Impressionists'. British art had reached an impasse, and these strange, colourful, expressive paintings looked as though they were from another world. The press heightened public interest by reporting sensationally that van Gogh was a madman and the other artists incompetent – or worse, pornographic – and that the future of European painting was in jeopardy.

The 'Second Post-Impressionist Exhibition' ran from 5 October 1912 to 31 January 1913. Covering the work of young French, British and Russian

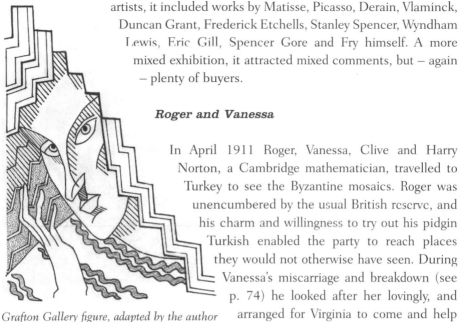

artists, it included works by Matisse, Picasso, Derain, Vlaminck, Duncan Grant, Frederick Etchells, Stanley Spencer, Wyndham Lewis, Eric Gill, Spencer Gore and Fry himself. A more mixed exhibition, it attracted mixed comments, but – again – plenty of buyers.

### Roger and Vanessa

In April 1911 Roger, Vanessa, Clive and Harry Norton, a Cambridge mathematician, travelled to Turkey to see the Byzantine mosaics. Roger was unencumbered by the usual British reserve, and his charm and willingness to try out his pidgin Turkish enabled the party to reach places they would not otherwise have seen. During Vanessa's miscarriage and breakdown (see p. 74) he looked after her lovingly, and arranged for Virginia to come and help

*Grafton Gallery figure, adapted by the author from the poster advertising the Second Post-Impressionist Exhibition*

her sister travel home. It was during her convalescence, in a cottage near to Roger's home, Durbins, in Guildford, that their relationship became intimate. Roger felt an attraction to Vanessa's earthiness and sensuality, and the more he saw of her the stronger his feelings grew. Over the next two years Vanessa regained her sexual and emotional self-confidence, but as she returned to health, she gradually fell out of love, discovering that Duncan Grant's relaxed attitude suited her better. The connection with Roger was not severed, however, and they remained friends. Roger continued to trust her judgement and went to her for sympathy and advice on many occasions, even on the subject of other women.

*Roger Fry's house, Durbins, near Guildford*

## *Legacy*

Though inexplicably omitted from Clive Bell's list of Bloomsbury members (see pp. 7–8), Roger Fry was certainly its most important artistic influence. The art historian Kenneth Clark described him as the most influential critic since Ruskin, seventy years earlier. The originator of 'significant form' and other radical theories of art, he introduced the Post-Impressionists to Britain. In 1913 he set up the Omega Workshops for young artists (see below). To Roger Fry also can be attributed the basis of Clive Bell's key theories of art.

## The Omega Workshops

The Omega Workshops were founded by Roger Fry, with Vanessa Bell and Duncan Grant as co-directors, in order to provide young artists with a reliable living. Situated on the ground floor of 33 Fitzroy Square in London, the Workshops opened on 8 July 1913. A legacy worth £1,000 a year from Roger's millionaire uncle, J.S. Fry, who had run a famous chocolate factory, made the whole enterprise possible, and kept it going through the lean times of the First World War. Artists working for the Omega were employed for half the week to design and make furniture and fabrics with a modern slant. The rest of the week they were encouraged to dedicate to their painting, financed by the sale of the goods. Because the Omega comprised fans of Post-Impressionism, patterns were bold and daring, looking modern

even today. Products included tables, chairs, sofas, cupboards, boxes, rugs, lamps, hangings, curtains, cushions, bed-linen, screens, hand-painted fabrics, dresses, scarves, fans, pots, tiles, trays, necklaces and wooden toys.

Roger Fry, Vanessa Bell, Duncan Grant, Mark Gertler, Simon Bussy, Frederick and Jessie Etchells, Nina Hamnett, Percy Wyndham Lewis, Henri Gaudier-Brzeska, Paul Nash and David Bomberg were among those who were employed by the Omega or sold their work there. Barbara Hiles (later Bagenal) and two other Slade graduates helped to run it. All regular workers were paid a flat rate of thirty shillings a week.

Ottoline Morrell, Lady Cunard, George Bernard Shaw, Augustus John, W.B. Yeats, Ezra Pound and Rupert Brooke all made purchases from the Omega, but its only publicity was the Bloomsbury grapevine. Despite this the Omega was asked to design a Post-Impressionist room for the 1914 Ideal Home Exhibition, and a number of exhibitions and interior design commissions followed.

The Omega Workshops started on a high but the energy soon ran down. Complaints by four of the Omega artists, who disliked the way Fry ran the Workshops, disagreed with his aesthetic values and felt they had been cheated out of commissions, led to their abrupt departure. The outbreak of the First World War in August 1914 meant that fewer people bought luxury goods. Duncan, as a pacifist, was forced to take up farm work in Suffolk to avoid conscription. When he and Vanessa moved to Charleston Farmhouse in Sussex in 1916, their role in the Omega dwindled and they began to accept private commissions. One of the leading Omega artists became ill with 'flu in early 1919, and an exhibition in March failed miserably. Roger was no longer enjoying running the Workshops and decided to close them in the summer of 1919, selling the last of the stock at half-price.

---

**Read On ...**

*A Roger Fry Reader*, ed. Christopher Reed, Chicago: University of Chicago Press, 1996

*Roger Fry: A Biography*, by Virginia Woolf, London: Hogarth Press, 1940

*Roger Fry: Art and Life*, by Frances Spalding, Norwich: Black Dog Books, 1999

*Letters*, by Roger Fry, ed. Denys Sutton, London: Chatto and Windus, 1972

*Omega and After: Bloomsbury and the Decorative Arts*, by Isabelle Anscombe and Howard Grey, London: Thames and Hudson, 1981

---

CAPSULE

# Mrs Dalloway (1925)

· · · · · · · · · · · ·

## Origins

*Mrs Dalloway* follows its heroine through twelve hours or so, as she prepares for her party then hosts it. The theme of the party intrigued Virginia and she explored it many times. She wrote a series of short stories on the theme of Clarissa Dalloway's party: 'Mrs Dalloway on Bond Street' (1923) was the first, and seven more were written around mid-1925 (see p. 48). An alternative version of 'Mrs Dalloway on Bond Street', 'The Prime Minister', features a character called 'Septimus Smith', who plans the premier's assas-sination and his own suicide. All of these fed into Virginia fourth novel. She had great ambitions for it: 'In this book I have almost too many ideas. I want to give life & death, sanity & insanity; I want to criticise the social system, & to show it at work, at its most intense' (*Diary* 2, 19 Jun 1923).

The structure and peripatetic nature of *Mrs Dalloway* (originally called 'The Hours') owe much to James Joyce's *Ulysses*, which Virginia Woolf read – and disliked – in August 1922. The novel had been brought to the Hogarth Press by Joyce's mentor Harriet Shaw Weaver in 1918. The

Woolfs declined to publish on the grounds of its length, and because they might have fallen foul of the obscenity laws. But Virginia was obviously intrigued by the novel's structure, and echoed it in her own book. As in *Ulysses*, the action of *Mrs Dalloway* takes place within a single day, and the city (Dublin in *Ulysses*, London in *Mrs Dalloway*) plays a significant and overarching role – buildings, landmarks, areas and streets are frequently named, locating the fictional characters in real, specific surroundings.

## Plot Summary

It is June 1923. Clarissa, wife of politician Richard Dalloway, walks through London to buy some flowers

*Big Ben*

for her party that evening. En route she meets Hugh Whitbread, a friend from childhood, now a polished civil servant. In a Bond Street florist's she hears a car backfire. Septimus Warren Smith, his mind unhinged by the war, imagines that the noise heralds some catastrophe. His Italian wife, Rezia, moves him along to Regent's Park to avoid the gaze of passers-by; meanwhile, Septimus is in a private hell.

Peter Walsh, who wanted to marry Clarissa in his youth, visits from India. He confides in Clarissa about his complex love life, and she invites him to the party. Clarissa's daughter, Elizabeth, arrives home and Peter leaves, and walks in Regent's Park. Septimus hallucinates about a friend killed in the war. His doctor, Sir William Bradshaw, ascertaining that Septimus has threatened suicide, advises 'proportion' and a spell in a rest home; he undertakes to arrange it with his colleague, Dr Holmes.

Richard Dalloway and Hugh Whitbread lunch with the elderly and indomitable Lady Bruton. Clarissa is not invited because the talk is of politics. Elizabeth and fervent Christian Doris Kilman, whom Clarissa dislikes, go out to tea. But both daughter and husband return feeling more empathetic towards Clarissa.

Rezia and Septimus have a briefly idyllic afternoon. He jokes about the hats she is making, as though he is completely well. Dr Holmes calls to take Septimus away. Septimus panics and, to escape him, leaps from the window and is killed on the railings below.

Clarissa's party begins. At first she thinks it a failure, but then rallies. Sally Seton, whom Clarissa loved as a girl for her daring and recklessness, has in the intervening years put on weight, married a lord and given birth to five sons. The Prime Minister arrives and stays a short while. Lady Bradshaw tells Clarissa of Septimus's suicide, and the news reveals to Clarissa her own attitude to life and death. Sally and Peter talk of Clarissa, who is busy with the other guests. The book ends as she approaches them.

> The strange thing, on looking back, was the purity, the integrity, of her feeling for Sally ... it had a quality which could only exist between women, between women just grown up.
>
> (*Mrs Dalloway*)

## Sources

A number of characters have been recycled from earlier works. Clarissa and Richard Dalloway were first seen in *The Voyage Out*, but they have mellowed over the years and it is difficult to discern the same characters. Clara Durrant and her mother originate from *Jacob's Room*, another book which features parties prominently; Mr Bowley, one of Mrs Durrant's guests, here sees the plane writing in the sky, an innovation first seen in Britain in 1922 when Virginia was working on *Mrs Dalloway*. Mrs

Hilbery, still dwelling in the past, was Katharine's mother in *Night and Day*.

Clarissa Dalloway was based on a Stephen family friend, Katherine Lushington (Kitty), who married *National Review* editor Leo Maxse. Kitty Maxse moved in 'society' circles and was horrified when the Stephens moved to Bloomsbury. But Virginia always believed there was something underlying Kitty's superficial glitter, and *Mrs Dalloway* is partly an effort to uncover it. On 4 October 1922 Kitty died after falling over a stair banister in mysterious circumstances. Virginia believed it was suicide and a similar incident was incorporated into her novel, but assigned to Septimus rather than Clarissa.

In Clarissa's passion for Sally Seton, later Lady Rosseter, Virginia recreates her own for Margaret (Madge) Symonds, who married Virginia's cousin Will Vaughan. Like Virginia's infatuation, Clarissa's is based on youth and inexperience – it fades when she finds her beloved has grown ordinary. Hugh Whitbread is a combination of the worst elements of George Duckworth and two of Virginia's former suitors, Walter Lamb and Sydney Waterlow. Clarissa likes him, but the reader is not necessarily intended to agree with her.

## Themes

### London

London is like another character in *Mrs Dalloway*, so well delineated that it is possible to trace Clarissa's route to Bond Street and the Warren Smiths' route to Harley Street (see p. 191). Clarissa meets Hugh Whitbread in St James's Park; the Warren Smiths and Peter Walsh walk in Regent's Park. Shops (Hatchard's bookshop, Mulberry's florist, the Army and Navy Stores), landmarks (Big Ben, St Paul's Cathedral, Trafalgar Square), street names (Cockspur Street, Dean's Yard, Piccadilly) and areas of London (Westminster, Kentish Town, Lincoln's Inn) are continually name-checked. All types of London society, from the monarch at Buckingham Palace and the Prime Minister to the poor mothers of Pimlico and the Piccadilly prostitutes, are represented. Clarissa is grounded in this world and observes all its details. Though he now lives in India, Peter Walsh, like Clarissa, looks on London as part of his heritage. But Septimus, significantly, is rootless and hardly notices his surroundings.

### The Party

Clarissa, uninterested in the politics that are her husband's profession, feels (like *To the Lighthouse*'s Mrs Ramsay) that her main contribution is to bring people together. Virginia knew several society hostesses, including Ottoline Morrell and Sibyl Colefax, whose parties were famous. She had mixed feelings about them, as she did about Kitty Maxse, but wondered what lay beneath their gloss. She was also interested in the party-going compulsion in her own character; the belief that to

*Piccadilly Circus*

*Trafalgar Square*

attend parties and talk to people was to achieve something. In *Mrs Dalloway*, Virginia explores the purposes and outcomes of three parties.

There are two minor 'parties' that rival Clarissa's. Lady Bruton holds a small lunch party for Richard Dalloway and Hugh Whitbread, in the hope of persuading them to join her in a campaign to persuade young Britons to emigrate to Canada. But although he admires Lady Bruton, Richard does not fall in with her idea and lets Hugh write the required letter to *The Times*. The other is a tea-party: Doris Kilman takes Elizabeth to the Army and Navy Stores in order to woo her away from her mother's decadent influence to a more ascetic path. But both rivals are vanquished – Richard and Elizabeth return to Clarissa, having resisted the temptations of Lady Bruton's politics and Miss Kilman's religion.

### Madness

Septimus Warren Smith is the counterpart to Clarissa Dalloway. together they embody the fine line between sanity and insanity. Both are hypersensitive, showing extreme reactions to external incidents: Septimus foresees disaster when the car backfires; Clarissa feels sick and humiliated when she thinks her party a failure.

While Clarissa's unspecified 'illness' hints at a mental breakdown, Septimus's condition has been brought on by his

> Then there were the visions. He was drowned, he used to say, and lying on a cliff with the gulls screaming over him. He would look over the edge of the sofa down into the sea.
>
> (*Mrs Dalloway*)

experiences in the First World War. It is a kind of shell shock, similar to that suffered by poets Siegfried Sassoon and Wilfred Owen. Sassoon was an acquaintance of Virginia's from early 1924, and it is quite probable that she knew of his war trauma while writing her novel.

Like Rachel's delirium in *The Voyage Out*, Septimus's madness is primarily based on Virginia's experiences of mental illness: the dissociation from reality; visual and auditory hallucinations; the sense of being on the edge of an abyss. Septimus's scorn of Dr Holmes and Sir William Bradshaw echoes Virginia's of her own doctors, who seemed to have a firm grip over her life (see pp. 176–7). As soon as Septimus threatens suicide, his life is forfeit to the authorities, as it was when he was a soldier. By his death, he escapes any further harm they can do him, as well as the internal horrors of his mind. 'Fear no more the heat o' the sun / Nor the furious winter's rages', lines from Shakespeare's *Cymbeline* which recur throughout the novel, are his epitaph.

# Stuck on Q: Saxon Sydney-Turner and Desmond MacCarthy

· · · · · · · · · · ·

## Saxon Sydney-Turner (1880–1962)

Very little is known about Saxon Sydney-Turner's roots for two reasons – because he did not come from a particularly notable family, and because he was very secretive about his background. The son of a Hove doctor and his wife, Saxon had one famous ancestor – Sharon Turner, an indefatigable historian and lawyer, who advised publisher John Murray on the publication of Byron's *Don Juan*.

The 'silent man' of Bloomsbury, Saxon is often omitted from lists of Bloomsbury members because his contribution was through his idiosyncratic personality rather than his achievements. Despite a

*Saxon Sydney-Turner with Barbara Bagenal's children*

wealth of interests and accomplishments, he lacked motivation and self-confidence and remained essentially a dabbler.

### Saxon and Old Bloomsbury

A natural scholar, Saxon did excellently at Westminster School and went up to Trinity College, Cambridge, in 1899, the same year as Leonard Woolf, Thoby Stephen, Clive Bell and Lytton Strachey. Leonard was his particular friend, while Lytton thought him very interesting as a psychological specimen, but in later years found him a depressingly taciturn companion. In appearance Saxon was undistinguished: not tall, with light brown hair and moustache, he was often to be seen with a pipe in his mouth.

Saxon was the only non-family guest at the first of Thoby Stephen's Thursday evening meetings in March 1905 (see pp. 19–21). Thoby, describing his friend to the eager young Virginia, told her that he didn't speak often, but when he did, it was always the Absolute Truth. In character he was modest, unassuming and kind, with an eccentric charm and tendency to mishaps that delighted Virginia, although she acknowledged that he was indecisive and lacked determination.

### Interests

Saxon's chief interest was music, especially opera, about which he knew a prodigious amount. He regularly went to Bayreuth for Wagner's *Ring* cycle, and in 1909 Virginia and Adrian Stephen

*42 Ventnor Villas in Hove, where Saxon Sydney-Turner grew up*

accompanied him. Virginia put the trip to good use by writing an article, 'Impressions at Bayreuth' (*Essays* 1). What does not appear in the article is her fascination with Saxon's odd habit of talking to himself and making up snatches of opera and silly songs. He seemed self-absorbed most of the day, but at midnight suddenly roused himself and would start a lengthy conversation – or monologue – that would go on for hours, while his listeners tried to fight off encroaching sleep.

Saxon's capacious mind contained a lot of facts about literature; his letters were strewn with literary allusions and he would copy out poems for friends. His encyclopedic knowledge proved very useful to Virginia for the wealth of factual information in *Orlando*, and the Preface contains a line of thanks to him. But Saxon's only published work consisted of a few poems in *Euphrosyne*, a privately funded collection of graduate verse. He loved puzzles: riddles, crosswords and acrostics (in which, for example, the first letter of each line of a verse spells out a word or phrase). It was his facility with words that helped to earn him a scholarship to Cambridge – part of the exam consisted of a Greek translation that contained a riddle, and he was the only candidate who solved it. What puzzled Virginia was why, with so much knowledge at his fingertips, Saxon was not a more interesting person.

Saxon spent his entire career working for the Treasury but, while Maynard Keynes forged ahead to make a name for himself, Saxon was content to shine less brilliantly in his London office. In his later life he developed a fondness for horse racing and began to gamble his meagre funds away, having to borrow money from friends to buy essentials.

### Love Life

It seemed impossible to his friends that Saxon would ever marry. They were right, but in 1916 he fell in love with Barbara Hiles, a former Slade student who was a friend of Carrington. Barbara was everything that Saxon was not – extrovert, bubbly, talkative and practical. But she also had a suitor, Nicholas Bagenal. After some vacillation, Barbara married Nick

in 1918, intending that she and Saxon should remain intimate friends, or even lovers. But Saxon wrote Barbara some very poignant letters, the gist of which was that he was unable to share her and would bow out gracefully. However, he eventually managed to come to terms with his loss and became a great friend to Barbara and to her children – their friendship lasted a good deal longer than the Bagenals' marriage.

## Desmond MacCarthy (1877–1952)

### Desmond and Bloomsbury

A quirk of character, which prevented both men from fulfilling their potential, links Desmond MacCarthy and Saxon Sydney-Turner. In personality they could

*Desmond MacCarthy, photographed by Ottoline Morrell in 1923*

not have been more different. Desmond was sociable, urbane, perceptive and genial (his *New Statesman* pseudonym was 'Affable Hawk'). A little older than most other Bloomsberries, he was born in 1877, and was a disciple and friend of G.E. Moore at Cambridge. He married Molly Warre-Cornish in 1906 and they lived in Suffolk for several years before moving to London. He was asked by Roger Fry to help prepare the Post-Impressionism exhibition in 1910, not because he was an infallible judge of paintings, but because he and Roger Fry were both members of the Cambridge Conversazione Society (the Apostles: see pp. 19–20) and knew and liked each other. Desmond and Molly lived in Wellington Square in Chelsea, but they knew most of the Bloomsberries, as Molly called them. She became a great friend of Virginia Woolf, who thought her writing – a novel called *A Pier and a Band* (1918) and a memoir published as *A 19th Century Childhood* (1924) – interesting and original.

*25 Wellington Square, Chelsea, home of Desmond and Molly MacCarthy*

### Love Life

Neither Desmond nor Molly was entirely faithful during their marriage. Molly was persuaded by Clive Bell into a brief liaison, although she was more interested in his friendship. Desmond had never completely got over his passion for Irene Noel (who had also been admired by Thoby Stephen). When Molly began to go deaf after 1915, she felt even more painfully her isolation from Desmond and there were some jealous scenes. Her affairs were largely discontinued; his were not. An eternal romantic, Desmond got on very well with women, and he fell in love at frequent intervals. The tension in the marriage was increased by Desmond's inability to hold down a well-paid job; the MacCarthys were eternally hard up. Eventually both sources of discord dried up: Desmond's last affair ended, and in 1928 he became chief literary critic for *The Sunday Times*; his long association with the paper continued until the end of his life in 1952.

## Work

The bulk of Desmond's writing was done for newspapers and magazines. A selection of his journalism, as well as two short stories, can be found in *Humanities* (1953). He also wrote a number of books on literary and dramatic criticism, plus a book on Leslie Stephen in 1937, though few of his works are known today. His wife and friends all believed that he would write a novel, and great efforts were expended in helping him, including Molly's creation of the Novel Club and the Memoir Club (see pp. 63–7).

Desmond's most prominent accomplishment was his ability to talk. Like Virginia, he could lead a conversation down witty and imaginative avenues and keep his friends entertained for hours. But though everyone agreed that this was his best asset, no record remains of the substance of his speech. Morgan Forster remembered that Desmond delivered a brilliant Memoir Club paper with his notes supposedly propped up inside an open case. It was only when the case tumbled over that his listeners realized it was empty – he had no notes at all. His talent and his love for speaking made Desmond much in demand as a broadcaster. In the late 1920s and early 1930s his radio talks were almost as prolific as his journalism. The purpose of these, as of much public service broadcasting of the time, was to bring culture – in this case, literature – to the masses.

Desmond led a full, active life and was a highly regarded literary critic, but he was conscious that he had not fulfilled his early potential – his journalism was prolific, but none of the books he had planned to write ever came to pass. It was his greatest regret.

---

**Read On ...**

*Sowing*, by Leonard Woolf, London: Hogarth Press, 1969 (see pp. 103–8, 113–19 for Saxon Sydney-Turner; pp. 143, 171–2 for Desmond MacCarthy)

*Before Leonard: The Early Suitors of Virginia Woolf*, by Sarah M. Hall, London: Peter Owen, 2006 (see ch. 4 for Saxon Sydney-Turner)

*Portraits*, by Desmond MacCarthy, London: MacGibbon and Kee, 1949

*Humanities*, by Desmond MacCarthy, London: MacGibbon and Kee, 1953

*Clever Hearts. Desmond and Molly MacCarthy: A Biography*, by Hugh and Mirabel Cecil, London: Victor Gollancz, 1990

CAPSULE

# To the Lighthouse (1927)

· · · · · · · · · · ·

## Origins

To the Lighthouse is the most autobiographical of Virginia Woolf's novels, based on her childhood summers in St Ives. In a diary entry of 17 October 1924 Virginia first referred to a character sketch called 'The Old Man', to be based on Leslie Stephen. By the following May she was planning a short novel called To the Lighthouse, with

> father's character done complete in it; & mothers; & St Ives; & childhood; & all the usual things I try to put in – life, death &c.
> (Diary 3, 14 May 1925).

The writing came more easily than had earlier novels, and by early 1926 Virginia was so absorbed by it that she found normal conversation difficult. By September, contemplating the novel as a whole, she felt that the method she had first used in Jacob's Room had triumphed, but still worried that the story might seem sentimental. The 'Time Passes' section gave her the most trouble, but, despite her doubts, a version of it was sent in October 1925 to Roger Fry's friend Charles

> Is it nonsense, is it brilliance?
> (Diary 3, 18 Apr 1926)

Mauron for translation into French ('Le Temps passe') for the winter issue of the journal Commerce.

## Plot Summary

Mr and Mrs Ramsay and their eight children are staying at their summer home on the Isle of Skye, a few years before the First World War. Other guests are Lily Briscoe, an unmarried painter; William Bankes, a scientist friend of Mr Ramsay; Augustus Carmichael, a failed poet addicted to opium; Charles Tansley, a young protégé of Mr Ramsay; and a courting couple, Minta Doyle and Paul Rayley. The Ramsays' youngest child, James, wants to sail to a nearby lighthouse, but is continually disappointed.

Lily is painting an abstract representing Mrs Ramsay and James. Mr Ramsay thinks of how he could have been a great philosopher, had it not been for the demands of family life. Tansley is not popular with the children, who are tired of scholars trailing after their father. Mr Carmichael sleeps most of the time and the children make fun of him. He is the only one not to respond to Mrs

Ramsay's beauty and charm – Lily, on the other hand, credits her with knowledge and wisdom.

Mrs Ramsay notices that Paul and Minta have not returned from a walk and assumes there has been a proposal. When she sees Lily and William together she decides they must marry too.

The centre of the book is a dinner party, which all the adult guests attend. The conversation is desultory at first, then the party livens up, the main course is paraded in and Mrs Ramsay is warmly congratulated for managing the household so magnificently. Mr and Mrs Ramsay read after dinner and achieve a moment of empathy.

In a short middle section we learn of the deaths of Mrs Ramsay and two of the Ramsay children – Andrew, killed during the war, and Prue, who dies in childbirth. The house is deserted for ten years before the remaining Ramsays visit again. The third part concerns this visit. Instead of William Bankes, Mrs Beckwith is one of the party. Charles Tansley, Minta Doyle and Paul Rayley are also missing. Mrs Ramsay's match-making has not worked as well as she would have hoped. Paul and Minta are married, but Paul has a mistress. Lily and William are still good friends, but are not romantically involved.

Lily sets up her easel to finish the painting she began a decade earlier. She watches as Mr Ramsay and the two youngest children, James and Cam, now teenagers, sail in a small boat to the lighthouse. Memories of Mrs Ramsay flood back, and Lily feels she understands many things about the past. The boat reaches the lighthouse, and Lily puts the finishing touch to her painting.

**Sources**

Mr and Mrs Ramsays' first names are never revealed, giving a sense of distance and suggesting a parent/child relationship. Mr Ramsay constantly feels, as Leslie Stephen did, that he is under-achieving; as though he is stuck on Q in an imagined alphabet of philosophical achievement. Mrs Ramsay, as Julia, is part goddess, part earth mother; a mixture of the practical and the ethereal. *To the Lighthouse* was published on the anniversary of Julia's death, confirming her place at the heart of the drama.

Cam and James represent Virginia and Adrian (the name Cam echoes the Virginia character, Camilla Lawrence, in Leonard Woolf's *The Wise Virgins*). Rose, the artistic daughter who makes costumes and table arrangements, is Vanessa. Prue, like Stella, is close to her mother and dies soon after marriage. Andrew, destined for a career in law, dies young in the First World War, sharing the fate of Jacob Flanders; both Andrew and Jacob are based on Thoby.

Lily Briscoe, though a painter, is not a replica of Vanessa Bell. Her silent worship for Mrs Ramsay reflects Virginia's for her mother. Lily's friend William Bankes has the same scholar's foible of fussing about vegetables as Mr Pepper in *The Voyage Out*, but is altogether more humane and sympathetic. A Mr Wolstenholme of whom Virginia writes in 'A Sketch of the Past' (*Moments of Being*) was the model for the soporific Augustus Carmichael; there is also something in him of Saxon Sydney-Turner. Charles Tansley is an amalgam of the earnest young students who followed in the wake of Leslie Stephen.

> Fifty pairs of eyes were not enough to get round that one woman with.
>
> (*To the Lighthouse*, Part III, ch. 11)

## Themes

### The Lighthouse

Virginia Woolf's claim that the lighthouse signified nothing in particular has not stopped speculation about its symbolism. It is undeniably the focus of the young James's desires and often of Mrs Ramsay's attention. The subject of whether or not James's longed-for expedition to the lighthouse will take place comes between Mr and Mrs Ramsay, becoming a struggle between his ruthless rationalism (it will rain) and her sympathy for her son (it may not). The expedition also becomes the hub of ill feeling between Lily Briscoe and Charles Tansley. Insisting that there will be no trip to the lighthouse is Tansley's way of aligning himself with Mr Ramsay and rationalism. Lily takes revenge by ignoring the comment and asking him innocently if she may come on the trip. The lighthouse is a constant presence; its torch-like form is echoed by the repeated images of Lily's paintbrush and the red-hot poker plants in the garden. Like the brief 'Time Passes' section of the novel, or the line down the centre of Lily's finished painting, the lighthouse can be seen either as a divisive or a unifying feature.

### Multiplicity

People's different viewpoints fascinated Virginia Woolf, and it is a theme made explicit in most of her novels. Here, Mrs Ramsay is the main focus. Lily Briscoe and William

Bankes both adore her, but know she is a complex being. She looks like a Greek goddess, thinks William, but is vital, not a statue; she can suddenly throw on an old hat and galoshes to chase one of her children. While conscious that he loves Mrs Ramsay, William sometimes feels nothing for her. Lily knows that although Mrs Ramsay devotes herself to the service of others, she is imperious and resolute.

Simultaneities in the plot are suggested by short or parenthetical sections. After Mrs Ramsay wonders whether her daughter Nancy is with the courting couple Minta and Paul, Nancy's point of view appears in a section of several pages which is completely enclosed by parentheses. The deaths of three characters are announced in brackets, as though subsidiary to the story. This is a comment on the incidental quality of death, which happens unexpectedly, while other people's lives go on. But it also echoes the novels of William Makepeace Thackeray (who was related to Virginia by marriage) – George Osborne's death in *Vanity Fair* is announced almost brutally, as an aside.

## Class

While Virginia was working on her novel, Clive Bell was propounding his masters-and-slaves theory in *Civilization* (1928). To Clive, the achievements of civilization depended on the masses serving an elite, but Virginia felt uncomfortable with this. She was often awkward in her dealings with servants, feeling the necessity for them, but unable to justify intellectually to herself why some people should serve others. This tension is explored in *To the Lighthouse*. We can't all be at the top of our professions, William Bankes tells Lily, and perhaps Titian and Darwin were only possible because of the lesser beings around them. Mr Ramsay is able to devote himself to philosophy because his wife takes care of all domestic matters, and Mrs Ramsay's dinner party is a great success only because she has a cook who can take three days over preparing the food. And the Ramsays depend on Mrs McNab and Mrs Bast to bring their holiday home back from the brink of ruin after a decade of neglect: the guests are ignorant of the hard work involved – to them the house is simply the same as ever.

> Possibly the greatest good requires the existence of a slave class ... The thought was distasteful to him.
>
> (*To the Lighthouse*, Part I, ch. 8)

# Bloomsbury Economist: John Maynard Keynes

· · · · · · · · · · ·

John Maynard Keynes (1883–1946), the son of a Cambridge economics lecturer and the grandson of a dahlia grower, was born at 6 Harvey Road, Cambridge, where he grew up with his parents, his sister Margaret and brother Geoffrey. Maynard was sent to Eton where he was considered a brilliant scholar, though his sporting prowess was below average. Because of his willingness to join in with most school activities, he was popular with pupils and teachers alike, but was privately critical of those he did not respect. A slight intellectual arrogance and impatience with

*6 Harvey Road, Cambridge*

lesser mortals was already evident to those who knew him well.

## Keynes and Cambridge

A few years younger than Thoby and co., Maynard Keynes went up to King's College, Cambridge, in 1902. That December he was invited by Lytton Strachey and Leonard Woolf to join the Apostles (see pp. 19–20). It was unusual for a student of mathematics to be asked, but his Eton reputation had preceded him. Maynard did not know Clive Bell or Thoby Stephen well (they were not Apostles) but he became a close friend of Lytton Strachey, and together they introduced a distinctly homosexual flavour to the Apostles. Occasionally their amorous tastes converged, usually causing heartache for Lytton.

Perhaps the unkindest cut of all was when Maynard 'stole' Duncan Grant from his friend. Lytton had adored his cousin for years. His passion was on the whole unequalled by Duncan's, but for a brief period in 1907 Lytton was quite satisfied with his response. He was keen for his lover and his best friend to meet, and engineered an encounter between Duncan and Maynard in late 1905. At that time they liked one another but nothing more. But in mid-1908 Lytton discovered they had been having an affair for some months. He controlled his bitterness and jealousy outwardly, but the betrayal created a rift between the friends that was never quite healed.

## Keynes and Bloomsbury

Maynard's affair with Duncan lasted for several years. From 1909 they shared a flat at 21 Fitzroy Square, and were frequent visitors to Virginia and Adrian Stephen at no. 29. Lytton's resentment over the appropriation of Duncan had perhaps hampered Maynard's approval by Bloomsbury, but as Duncan grew closer to the Bells and Roger Fry in 1910–11 through their shared artistic tastes, so his partner was gradually accepted. In 1911 he and Duncan were asked to participate in the experiment in cooperative living at 38 Brunswick Square with Virginia and Adrian Stephen and Leonard Woolf. Maynard's brilliance was rather daunting to newcomers, and Leonard Woolf found him overly self-assured and rather arrogant. He later worked for Maynard as literary editor of the *Nation & Athenaeum*, and saw no reason to change his opinion. Maynard was generally considered charismatic rather than handsome – although she appreciated his intelligence, Virginia

*John Maynard Keynes in 1911, the year he moved to the shared house at 38 Brunswick Square*

Woolf thought his penetrating eyes and full lips ugly – and he was occasionally disparaged by his Bloomsbury friends for his worldly success and his wealth. Maynard's great asset in Bloomsbury was that he encouraged plain speaking in sexual matters. His openness was greatly appreciated by Vanessa Bell, who had discovered the joys of sex, and of talking about sex, after her marriage.

Despite hobnobbing with the rich and famous, Keynes never lost touch with Bloomsbury. His geographical foothold there was secured when he bought 46 Gordon Square from Vanessa and Clive Bell in 1916. Clive took rooms at 50 Gordon Square and Vanessa moved to Charleston Farmhouse in Sussex, where Maynard was a welcome visitor and was given his own bedroom. It was here that

## Maynard Keynes on Virginia's Work

Maynard told Virginia in May 1921 that he thought her Memoir Club paper '22 Hyde Park Gate' (*Moments of Being*), with its entertaining portrait of George Duckworth, her best piece of writing to date. At that time her published works included numerous articles and reviews, *The Voyage Out*, *Night and Day* and the short stories in *Monday or Tuesday* (including 'The Mark on the Wall' and 'Kew Gardens').

Later, Maynard's favourite of Virginia's novels was *The Years* (1937). He preferred the linear approach to that of *The Waves* (1931), in which Virginia experiments more radically with form and symbolism.

Virginia expected him to censure *Three Guineas* (1938). Keynes's wife, Lydia, said that Maynard was critical but he himself remained silent on the subject, which, Virginia suspected, indicated that he strongly disapproved of the book.

he wrote *The Economic Consequences of the Peace* (1919). Later he bought his own country home, Tilton, very close to Charleston. In 1925 he married Russian ballerina Lydia Lopokova. His friends were surprised and a little dismayed – Lydia was by no means an intellectual and they didn't at all see how she would fit into their coterie. But for Maynard she was a breath of fresh air, a complete escape from his world. Through her and through Bloomsbury contacts such as Dadie Rylands, a second-generation Bloomsberry who lectured in English and produced plays at Cambridge, he became more involved with the arts, acting as treasurer for the Camargo Ballet Society, founding the Arts Theatre in Cambridge and chairing the Arts Council of Great Britain.

## Work

The most sophisticated of the Bloomsberries, Maynard was closely involved with the politics of the day. At Cambridge he spoke at the Union in favour of free trade and against protectionism, and was by inclination a liberal. He began his career after Cambridge in the India Office, a large civil service department, the function of which was chiefly administrative. Here he worked with great speed and efficiency while revealing his inability to suffer fools gladly. He left the India Office in summer 1908 to take up a lectureship in economics at Cambridge, and began to write journal articles on matters connected with India. He was made editor of the *Economic Journal*, was elected to the Political Economy Club, delivered lectures at the London School of Economics and took on private pupils for coaching.

Maynard's interest in mathematics, his degree subject, was not in the abstract theory but in the application to human problems, and he argued that the basis of economics was not in mathematical computations but in logic. He specialized in monetary policy, currency, finance and the stock exchange, and his first book, published in 1913, was *Indian Currency and Finance*. During the First World War, he was consulted for advice by the Treasury and left his Cambridge studies for a job at Whitehall. Making important contacts and impressing his superiors, he was moved into an advisory position at the heart of the Treasury, where he remained for the rest of the war. He frequently dined with politicians and returned to Bloomsbury with well-informed gossip about the political situation. Many of his pacifist friends were critical of his working for war aims. But as the war progressed and conscription was introduced, he was of great help to friends who were conscientious objectors, helping them in their applications for exemption. His own application emphasized that he had a conscientious objection to conscription, ignoring the fact that he was exempt in any case because he was engaged in important war work.

## Writing

After the war Maynard attended the 1919 Paris Peace Conference to represent the Treasury's position on how much and when the German government should be made to pay for the war. Six months later he left in disgust at the short-term views of his fellow negotiators, who seemed only to want to impose punitive financial measures on Germany, without an attempt to make the country economically viable. In the opinion of Keynes and others, what became known as the Treaty of Versailles could only result in catastrophe for Europe. He voiced his perspective in *The Economic Consequences of the Peace*, written at great speed, and published within months of the conference.

The book received a mixed reception, its greatest detractors being the French, who were perhaps the most disposed to see their former enemy, Germany, pay

*Palace of Versailles, where the Treaty of Versailles was signed*

for its treachery. After 1945 the book was under discussion again. Some commentators blamed Keynes for discrediting the Treaty of Versailles and so paving the way for the Second World War; others claimed that ignoring his advice resulted in the Depression of the 1930s and Hitler's consequent rise to power.

A Memoir Club paper, 'Dr Melchior: A Defeated Enemy', also dates from Maynard's experiences at the Paris Peace Conference, and depicts his impressions of the German-Jewish banker who helped negotiate peace terms. This was later published in *Two Memoirs* (1949) with 'My Early Beliefs', a reconsideration of the theories of G.E. Moore that so influenced Keynes and his friends at Cambridge. Their mistake, he says, was to absorb Moore's doctrine that the pursuit of 'good states of mind' (i.e. contemplation of love, beauty and truth) was the most essential part of life, but to disregard his belief that this should affect one's conduct. Hence

Moore's followers were ascetics on the one hand, despising money, power and success (or affecting to despise them), but decadents on the other, accepting no moral responsibility for their credo.

Keynes's *General Theory of Employment, Interest and Money* (1936) is a wide-ranging and influential book, which explores the role of the government in controlling a country's economy, and suggests among other things that unemployment is not always the fault of the unemployed – remarkably, this was a fairly radical concept in the 1930s. There were many other books on economics and politics, including three pamphlets for the Hogarth Press.

When people speak of Bloomsbury's greatest contributions, Virginia Woolf's fiction and Maynard Keynes's macroeconomic theories are generally among them. His role in the 1919 peace negotiations and his books are still known and discussed today.

**Read On ...**

*The Economic Consequences of the Peace*, by John Maynard Keynes, London: Macmillan, 1919

*Two Memoirs*, by John Maynard Keynes, London: Rupert Hart-Davis, 1949

*John Maynard Keynes*, by Robert Skidelsky, vol. 1, *Hopes Betrayed: 1883–1920*, 1983; vol. 2, *The Economist as Saviour*, *1920–1937*, 1992; vol. 3, *Fighting for Britain, 1937–1946*, 2000; all London: Macmillan

*The Life of John Maynard Keynes*, by R.F. Harrod, London: Macmillan, 1951

*Lydia and Maynard: The Letters of Lydia Lopokova and John Maynard Keynes*, ed. Polly Hill and Richard Keynes, London: André Deutsch, 1989

# Bloomsbury and Money

It is commonly supposed that all of the Bloomsberries had plenty of money inherited from their parents and lived a hedonistic lifestyle. While it is true that none of them was on the brink of starvation, most had to work for a living. Even those who did not were associated with a particular profession. Maynard Keynes, who had the least need to earn money by his own efforts, is one of the best known for his professional achievements.

**The Stephen sisters** were fairly self-sufficient from family legacies, including £2,500 left to Virginia from her Quaker aunt Caroline Emelia Stephen in 1909, in order that she need not feel forced to marry. By this time Vanessa was married to Clive Bell and was financially secure, able to paint for pleasure rather than for commercial reasons. Virginia was always conscious of what she could and could not afford, and neither she nor Leonard wished for expensive clothes or domestic luxuries. It was years before her novels started bringing in a substantial profit. Leonard Woolf reports that between 1919 and 1924 she made an annual average of £38 from her books and £132 from journalism (*Downhill All the Way*, p. 63; the two added together equate to about £6,500 today). It was only in 1926, on the strength of profits from *Mrs Dalloway* and *The Common Reader*, that the Woolfs were able to purchase flushing lavatories for Monk's House. Likewise, the sales of *Orlando* enabled them to build a new bedroom for Virginia and a new sitting room. In 1928, according to Leonard, she earned £1,434 from her books (*Downhill All the Way*, p. 144; worth about

£57,000 today), so at the age of forty-six she was finally making more money than she was spending.

**Leonard Woolf** saved some money from winning a sweepstake in Sri Lanka, but had to earn his living all his life, from political books, journalism, editorships and the Hogarth Press. Like Virginia he was always conscious of money, and kept meticulous notes on their income and expenditure throughout his life. For instance, we know that Virginia's £9,000-worth of stocks and shares provided her with nearly £400 annual income at the time of her marriage, but that her medical bills meant that the Woolfs needed to earn another £400 to £500 a year (*Beginning Again*, p. 90).

**Clive Bell**'s parents made their wealth from the coal industry and gave their son an allowance. On hearing of Clive's anti-war pamphlet *Peace at Once* (1915), burned by order of the Lord Mayor of London, his father threatened to stop the flow of money, but peace was soon restored in the Bell family, even if not in Europe. On Mr Bell's death in 1927, he left £271,303 to be shared out among his family. The shares that Clive inherited yielded dividends of about £1,200 annually, worth about £48,000 today.

**Lytton Strachey**'s family legacies had to be shared among Lytton and his nine siblings so there was not much to spare. For a couple of years Lytton reviewed books for his cousin St Loe on the *Spectator*, then gave it up to write his own books. The profits from *Eminent Victorians* (1918) left him comfortably off, then *Queen Victoria* (1921) and *Elizabeth and Essex* (1928) brought more financial gain. His wealth meant that his partner Carrington, like Vanessa Bell, could paint according to her own desires.

**Saxon Sydney-Turner** had little family money and won scholarships to school and university. On graduation he began working for the Treasury, where he stayed for the rest of his life. It has been suggested that the need to earn his living might have prevented him from turning his obvious talents into some concrete achievement, but it was more probably due to a lack of motivation. In old age he gambled his pension on horse racing and occasionally had to borrow money for groceries from Vanessa Bell.

**Duncan Grant** was always hard-up as a young man. One of Roger Fry's inspirations for creating the Omega Workshops was to provide Duncan and artists like him with a living wage. However, Duncan's friend and ex-lover Maynard Keynes was very generous to him (see below), and when he was living at Charleston with Vanessa many of his financial needs evaporated.

**Maynard Keynes** came from a wealthy family (his father inherited £17,000 in 1878, worth over £1 million today) and was never short of money. His annual income just before the First World War was about £800 (i.e. over £50,000; his age was about thirty); after it, he earned much more, working for the Treasury and writing books that made him world famous. He gambled on the stock market and the currency exchange, occasionally taking out bank loans to do so. Maynard was a generous benefactor to his friends, arranging allowances in 1937 for Duncan Grant, to enable him to live comfortably, and to Bunny Garnett for his sons' school fees.

**Roger Fry**'s money was tight, especially because medical fees for his wife's treatment for mental illness were expensive, but his behaviour was rarely driven by financial considerations. He made nothing from either of the Post-Impressionist exhibitions or from the Omega Workshops. He made some money from his job as adviser to the Metropolitan Museum of New York, and a little from art criticism, but he was never a rich man.

(N.B. To convert money from its original value to its modern value, see Lawrence H. Officer, 'Purchasing Power of British Pounds from 1264 to 2005', http://www.measuringworth.com/ppoweruk)

# On the Fringes

· · · · · · · · · · · ·

Many names have been identified with Bloomsbury because they were friendly with one or more Bloomsberries, or occasionally merely because they were in the right place at the right time. But they were not at the heart of the group of friends.

## E.M. Forster (1879–1970)

The most noteworthy fringe member is E.M. Forster, who, while he shared Bloomsbury's most significant precepts, was never at the core of Bloomsbury. Lytton Strachey nicknamed him 'the Taupe' (French for 'mole') because of his shy, blinking character and his habit of disappearing and reappearing unexpectedly. He went up to King's College, Cambridge in 1897, two years earlier than Thoby Stephen and his friends arrived at Trinity College, and was not one of Thoby's circle.

Morgan Forster is often classed with Virginia Woolf as a 'Bloomsbury novelist', and he published four major

E.M. Forster in 1915

novels before she had produced one: *Where Angels Fear to Tread* (1905), *The Longest Journey* (1907), *A Room with a View* (1908) and *Howards End* (1910). This last was the book that made his name, but it was his final work, *A Passage to India* (1924), that is generally considered his masterpiece and is still studied in schools and universities today. Another novel, *Maurice*, written in 1914 but not published until 1971, was based on a homosexual affair Forster had at Cambridge. He also wrote a number of short stories, one of the more unusual of which is 'The Machine Stops' (see below), a futuristic tale. All of the above, except for *The Longest Journey*, have subsequently been made into films and television plays (see p. 191).

### Forster and Woolf's Writings Compared

Forster's and Woolf's fictions have certain similarities of theme. Woolf's *The Voyage Out* sometimes reads like an alternative version of Forster's *A Room with a View*, with a tragic ending instead of a sunny one. In both, a young woman is on the verge of sexual awakening, and her lover holds avant-garde, feminist, socially subversive opinions. Both pairs of lovers are part of a group of British tourists abroad, and they become acquainted during a trip away from 'civilization'; that is, away from British influences. Lucy and Cecil's broken engagement is also echoed by that of Katharine and William in Woolf's *Night and Day*. Among the short stories, Forster's 'The Road from Colonus' and Woolf's 'A Dialogue Upon Mount Pentelicus' have in common the theme of the British transplanted to Greece (which Forster visited in 1903 and Woolf in 1906), a more 'primitive'

country, where characters in both stories have a revelation in a grove of plane trees.

Both novelists saw music as the trigger for imaginative scenes. In Forster's *Howards End*, while listening to Beethoven's Fifth Symphony, Helen hears shipwrecks, heroes, goblins and elephants represented. The unidentified narrator of Woolf's story 'The String Quartet', listening to Mozart, sees images of fountains, trees, fish. (For more on Bloomsbury and music, see pp. 113–14.)

They shared also an interest in the field of technology and innovation. Forster is often credited with predicting television, email and the internet in his 1909 story, 'The Machine Stops'. In *The Years*, Eleanor is keen to show off her shower bath – not a new invention, but still unusual in homes. Peggy imagines that one day it will be possible to 'see things' using the telephone – was Woolf anticipating videophones or perhaps, like Forster, the internet?

### Ottoline Morrell (1873–1938)

Ottoline Morrell was a flamboyant society hostess and patron of the arts, and friend to many Bloomsberries. Born Ottoline Violet Anne Cavendish Bentinck, she was half-sister to the 6th Duke of Portland. In 1902 she married Philip Morrell, later a Liberal member of parliament, and they began to open their house at 44 Bedford Square to illustrious visitors (see pp. 23, 151). When they bought a country house, Garsington Manor in Oxfordshire, she continued to invite writers, politicians, artists and philosophers. She also provided the conscientious objectors among them with farm work to satisfy the authorities during the First World War (see pp. 23, 149).

Ottoline was an extravagant character with a romantic outlook and a high regard for anyone with an artistic talent. She yearned to live life on a higher plane. She had affairs with Bertrand Russell, Henry Lamb and Roger Fry and counted Herbert Asquith (Prime Minister 1908–16) and his family as personal friends. It was Ottoline's misfortune to attract admiration and ridicule in equal measure. Virginia Woolf privately told exaggerated stories of Ottoline's appearance and behaviour. Lytton Strachey, who often stayed at Garsington for weeks on end, was scornful about his hostess in letters. But the most hurtful remarks were those made in print. In Dorothy Brett's memoir she described laughing at Ottoline with D.H. Lawrence. Lawrence himself caricatured Ottoline as Hermione Roddice in *Women in Love*. (For other fictional portraits see p. 23 and Seymour 1992, Appendix III.)

Ottoline gave up Garsington in 1928 and moved permanently into her London house at 10 Gower Street (see p. 152). She was in her mid-fifties and suffering from increasing deafness, She planned a more modest lifestyle with small tea-parties instead of weekend extravaganzas. While Virginia Woolf and T.S. Eliot welcomed the intimacy of these, Lytton Strachey missed the glamour and excitement of the larger gatherings and did not visit so frequently.

The affection of many of Ottoline's friends returned in 1928 when they saw with what dignity and courage she bore an operation for cancer of the jaw that left her face disfigured. Virginia, Lytton, Duncan Grant and Roger Fry wrote or visited, and Ottoline was always ready to forgive and forget their past misdemeanours. Even letters from D.H. Lawrence were welcomed and his betrayal pardoned.

Ottoline's chief talents were for love and friendship, but her most concrete contribution to Bloomsbury is a vast collection of 3,953 photographs of her friends. The twelve albums, covering 1907 to 1937, are now in the National Portrait Gallery. Many of the Bloomsbury pictures have been published in *Lady Ottoline's Album* (ed. Carolyn G. Heilbrun, London: Michael Joseph, 1976).

*Ottoline Morrell*

## Vita Sackville-West (1892–1962)

Clive Bell was Vita's first Bloomsbury friend, and he introduced her to Virginia Woolf in December 1922. It was the beginning of a long and sometimes intense friendship that inspired Virginia's most successful book to date, *Orlando* (1928) (see pp. 129–34). Vita came onto the scene too late to be considered part of Bloomsbury, and she was a conservative at heart – her traditional views sat uncomfortably with Bloomsbury radicalism.

The daughter of the 3rd Lord Sackville, Vita came from a long line of aristocrats. But she also had exotic forebears – her mother Victoria was the illegitimate daughter of the 2nd Lord Sackville and Spanish dancer Josefa Durán (called Pepita). Victoria married her cousin Lionel, who inherited the title because his uncle had no legitimate heirs. From an early age their daughter Vita wrote melodramatic, romantic plays and historical novels. Her first published works were verse, but she is best known for her novels, many of which were published, very lucratively, by the Hogarth Press (see pp. 38–9). She and Virginia, both novelists, were never truly rivals: Virginia envied Vita's sales but not her writing style.

Vita and her husband Harold Nicolson were not a great hit in Bloomsbury circles, seeming stiff and uncommunicative next to the friends who had known one another for two decades. Nevertheless, the Vita–Virginia friendship flourished. Vita invited Virginia to join the PEN Club, of which she was a committee member, but Virginia detested joining clubs and declined. She did accept invitations to stay with Vita at her home, Long Barn in Kent, despite knowing of Vita's 'Sapphic' tendencies, and their friendship developed into love. Vita claimed in a letter to Harold that she had been to bed with Virginia twice, but no such confession was made by Virginia, and its full implications are uncertain. *Orlando* was written as a tribute to Vita, with perhaps a touch of apology that she could not meet Vita's more passionate demands. Virginia still loved and depended upon Leonard, and they did not have the open relationship that Vita enjoyed with the bisexual Harold.

## T.S. Eliot (1888–1965)

The American poet Thomas Stearns Eliot was a close friend of the Woolfs, but not of Bloomsbury in general. His Anglo-Catholic beliefs were at odds with Bloomsbury's atheism, and his formal, restrained manner seemed rather old-fashioned. His poetry, however, was much more modern. It was highly regarded by the Woolfs, who published his *Poems* (1919) and *The Waste Land* (1923) under the Hogarth Press imprint, on the strength of having read and admired *Prufrock and Other Observations* (1917). In 1927–8 Virginia joined with Ottoline Morrell in an enterprise to raise enough money to enable Eliot to leave his job at Lloyd's Bank and concentrate on poetry full-time, but when it became evident that Eliot was not convinced this was a good idea, the money had to be returned to the donors.

Though puzzled by his belief in God, by the 1930s Virginia Woolf thought of Eliot as a close friend, on a par with Lytton Strachey and Roger Fry. The neat and precise Louis in *The Waves* (1931) is generally thought to be based on Eliot.

## D.H. Lawrence's Circle

The zealous novelist and poet D.H. Lawrence (1885–1930) met some of the Bloomsberries but their privileged backgrounds and the homosexuality of Lytton Strachey, Duncan Grant and Maynard Keynes made him feel uncomfortable and, he claimed, gave him nightmares.

Katherine Mansfield (1888–1923) was a New Zealand writer whom Virginia Woolf acknowledged as her nearest literary rival, although Mansfield wrote short stories (collected in *In a German Pension* (1911), *Bliss* (1920), *The Garden Party* (1922), *The Doves' Nest* (1923)), never a novel. Her story *Prelude* was the second publication of the Hogarth Press in 1918. Her tuberculosis meant that she spent much time abroad convalescing. She was further distanced from Bloomsbury by her relationship with (and eventual marriage to) the critic John Middleton Murry, whom Woolf disliked.

Dorothy Brett (1883–1976), a painter and friend of Carrington, liked to be known by her surname. She hosted meetings at her Hampstead home for the 'Thursdayers' (see pp. 24–5) and

fell in love with John Middleton Murry, Katherine Mansfield's husband. She was a friend of the Lawrences and emigrated with them to New Mexico in 1924.

Mark Gertler (1891–1939) was a talented painter and former lover of Carrington, who came from a poor immigrant Jewish family from Poland. His single-minded, almost obsessional character is reflected in Virginia Woolf's story 'Solid Objects' (see p. 53). Diagnosed with tuberculosis in 1920, Gertler suffered from continual ill-health and depression, and committed suicide in June 1939.

(For more on Lawrence and his circle, see pp. 24–5 and 169.)

### Read On ...

*E.M. Forster: A Life*, by P.N. Furbank, vol. 1, *The Growth of the Novelist 1879–1914*, vol. 2, *Polycrates' Ring 1914–1970*, London: Martin Secker and Warburg, 1977 and 1978

*Ottoline Morrell: Life on the Grand Scale*, by Miranda Seymour, London: Hodder and Stoughton, 1992

*Vita: The Life of Vita Sackville-West*, by Victoria Glendinning, Weidenfeld and Nicolson, 1983

*Eliot's Early Years* and *Eliot's New Life*, by Lyndall Gordon, Oxford: Oxford University Press, 1977 and 1988

*The Life of D.H. Lawrence: An Illustrated Biography*, by Keith Sagar, London: Methuen, 1982

# Bloomsbury and Music

## Were any of the group musical?

Most Bloomsberries were better at appreciating music than playing it. In the previous generation girls had been taught to play the piano as a part of their education. Stella Duckworth, Virginia and Vanessa's half-sister, could play to a high standard. The Stephen girls rebelled against these ladylike accomplishments, but Virginia, especially, continued to enjoy listening to music.

At Fitzroy Square, Adrian played Beethoven and Wagner on the pianola, a type of player piano invented in America in 1895. The player drew air into the instrument by means of foot pedals, and controlled the flow depending on the required volume and tempo. Perforated music rolls fed into the pianola moderated the pitch and created different melodies.

During the 1920s the Woolfs listened to music regularly in the evenings, often Beethoven and Mozart, and Leonard wrote record reviews for the *Nation and Athenaeum* between 1926 and 1929.

Saxon Sydney-Turner (see pp. 91–3) loved music. His opera mania took him many times to the Bayreuth Festival in Germany, sometimes with Adrian Stephen and once (1909) with Virginia too.

In Clive Bell's article 'Plus de Jazz' (*Since Cézanne*, 1922) he writes of the death of jazz, a musical form for which he had no love, but was precipitate in announcing its demise.

In the 1930s Virginia made a new friend: Ethel Smyth, composer of *The Wreckers*. Virginia knew the work, having attended the British première at Covent Garden in 1909. Ethel had been a suffragette and wrote the anthem 'The March of the Women' for the Women's Social and Political Union in 1911. Virginia said she made some discoveries about Ethel's character from listening to her music. In 1931 Virginia and Ethel spoke to the London National Society for Women's Service about 'Music and Literature'. (For more on Ethel Smyth, see pp. 159 and 172–3.)

## What part did music play in Virginia Woolf's work?

Although Virginia thought of herself as fairly ignorant where music was concerned, it had a prominent role in a number of her works, and was occasionally an inspiration for her writing. In a letter to a friend she said that she always thought of her books as music. In the essay 'Street Music' (1905) the narrator asserts the right of organ-grinders and solitary violinists to express themselves, even though their craft, like that of all artists, is considered unseemly. 'The Opera' (1909) looks at audience preferences either for Gluck or for Wagner. Wagner is also featured in 'Impressions at Bayreuth' (1909), which recalls Virginia's trip to the opera festival. She observes how inadequate words are to reproduce the experience of listening to music; interesting, seeing as her 1921 story 'The String Quartet' (in *Monday or Tuesday*) attempts to do just that. In a helter-skelter series of images she traces the emotions and thoughts evoked by listening to a concert, and the snatches of conversation in the intervals (see p. 51).

In *The Voyage Out*, music expresses the untamed side of Rachel's nature. She is an accomplished pianist and plans to indulge her passion for music after her marriage to Terence, who intends to write a novel. Music is superior to literature, Rachel argues. Her impromptu playing at the hotel dance brings out the guests' suppressed excitement and makes the party go with a swing.

*To the Lighthouse* can be compared to the sonata form in music, with exposition ('The Window', setting the scene and defining the characters), development ('Time Passes', a short middle passage during which we leap a decade ahead) and recapitulation ('The Lighthouse', with the characters against the same background, but changed).

Virginia listened to Beethoven while writing parts of *The Waves* (see *Diary* 3, 18 Jun 1927 and 22 Dec 1930). The rhythm of the novel seems influenced by music – each character, or 'voice', is like a different instrument. She explained to a friend who had admired the musical properties of *Roger Fry* how the themes of Roger's life are presented in the opening chapter of her biography, then developments and variations appear in later chapters and are brought to a symphonic climax at the end (*Letters* 6, p. 426).

# Virginia Woolf's Non-fiction

· · · · · · · · · · ·

As well as her nine novels (ten if we include *Flush*), Virginia Woolf wrote a prodigious amount of non-fiction, some of which remains unpublished in collected form (at time of writing). She worked extremely hard except when forced into inactivity by illness, and always had at least two projects on the go, fitting reviews and essays around the novels, and writing long letters and diary entries as light relief. Below is a brief account of her non-fiction activities. (See pp. 64–5 for *Moments of Being*, and pp. 138–42 for *A Room of One's Own* and *Three Guineas*.)

## Essays

The two volumes of *The Common Reader* (1925 and 1932) were the only collections of Woolf's non-fiction published during her lifetime. They consist mainly of reviews, from Defoe and Addison to Gissing and Hardy. After Virginia's death, Leonard published several more collections.

## The Death of the Moth (1942)

This includes a variety of genres, including review, story, sketch and general discourse. Those of note include the title piece, almost a story in its contemplation and symbolism. In 'Street Haunting: A London Adventure' the reader accompanies the imaginative and witty narrator on a journey through the city streets. 'Middlebrow', a letter written to the *New Statesman* but never sent, voices the author's support for the intellectual aristocracy and the uncultured alike against the aspirational and bourgeois. In 'A Letter to a Young Poet'

## Essay Collections

(Unless noted otherwise, titles were published in London by the Hogarth Press)

*The Common Reader*, First Series, 1925 and Second Series, 1932

*The Death of the Moth and Other Essays*, ed. Leonard Woolf, 1942

*The Moment and Other Essays*, ed. Leonard Woolf, 1947

*The Captain's Death Bed and Other Essays*, ed. Leonard Woolf, 1950

*Granite and Rainbow*, ed. Leonard Woolf, 1958

*Collected Essays*, ed. Leonard Woolf, 4 vols, 1966–7

*The Essays of Virginia Woolf*, ed. Andrew McNeillie, 4 vols of 6, 1986–94; vols 5 and 6, ed. Stuart N. Clarke, are forthcoming

Woolf conveys to John Lehmann, the Woolfs' assistant on the Hogarth Press, her views on modern poetry. Two of the pieces delivered orally by Woolf were: 'Professions for Women' to the London and National Society for Women's Service in 1931 (see pp. 139–40) and 'Craftsmanship', on the power of words, a radio talk broadcast in 1937.

### The Moment (1947)

'The Moment: Summer's Night' – fact or fiction? It is classed as an essay, but reads lyrically, like 'Kew Gardens' or 'The Mark on the Wall'. With a quite different approach, 'On Being Ill' queries why, since it has such a great effect on the mind, illness has not been a more popular subject in literature. In this volume are also 'Roger Fry', written as the opening address of a memorial exhibition of his work in 1935; 'The Art of Fiction', a 1927 review of Forster's *Aspects of the Novel*; and the much-quoted 'The Leaning Tower', read to the Workers' Educational Association of Brighton in 1940. This gives an overview of the changing British literary world, commenting on those factors – such as war, politics, class – that give the writer's once-stable tower a distinct tilt; and the narrator makes a plea for the 'common reader' (i.e. her audience) to take control of the literary world.

> Yet what composed the present moment? If you are young, the future lies upon the present, like a piece of glass, making it tremble and quiver. If you are old, the past lies upon the present, like a thick glass, making it waver, distorting it.
> ('The Moment: Summer's Night')

### The Captain's Death Bed (1950)

'Mr Bennett and Mrs Brown', which started life as a short essay, is reprinted

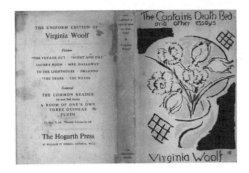

fifty pages, examines the different types of novelist: 'The Truth-Tellers', 'The Romantics', 'The Character-Mongers and Comedians', 'The Psychologists', 'The Satirists and Fantastics' and 'The Poets'. 'A Talk about Memoirs', less well known, is a fictional dialogue between two women (named Judith and Ann after Virginia's Stephen nieces) who discuss the odd and sometimes unexpected details in a biography that capture the imagination.

here in its longer form (beware: the long version is also published under the title 'Character in Fiction'). This is the well-known article in which Woolf, having been criticized by Arnold Bennett in print for her inability to create 'real' characters, points out that reality varies from person to person. 'The Sun and the Fish' concerns the solar eclipse that Virginia witnessed on 29 June 1927. 'Memories of a Working Women's Guild' was written as an Introduction to *Life As We Have Known It* (1931), Margaret Llewelyn Davies's collection of working women's memoirs.

### *Granite and Rainbow* (1958)

The book's title is a phrase used by Woolf in 'The New Biography' (a review of Harold Nicolson's book *Some People*) to define the contrast between the 'granite' of fact and the 'rainbow' of imagination. 'Women and Fiction' is a condensed version of *A Room of One's Own,* in which Woolf traces the obstacles and restrictions that have faced the female writer through history. 'Phases of Fiction', one of the longest of Woolf's essays at

> ... the biographer whose art is subtle and bold enough to present that queer amalgamation of dream and reality, that perpetual marriage of granite and rainbow.
>
> ('The New Biography')

### Diaries

When Leonard read extracts from Virginia's handwritten diary to the Memoir Club after her death, he had to censor some of her remarks on the grounds that she had exaggerated the truth. In 1953 Leonard published a selection of his wife's journals as *A Writer's Diary*. The entries start on 5 August 1918 and so omit references to Virginia's early development, but this slim volume also leaves out the more scurrilous comments about her acquaintances. It is a useful resource for learning about her writing process, but how much more interesting are the unabridged, warts-and-all diaries!

Virginia was not an obsessive diarist who noted at least one event each day and agonized over the long gaps. This she associates with the more conventional person such as Clara Durrant in *Jacob's Room*, who will not continue her diary entry for Tuesday into the space allotted for Wednesday. Virginia's diaries could more accurately be called journals – they were blank notebooks in which she recorded events, incidents and states of mind. She wrote swiftly, filling pages in the half-hour before tea or dinner, and always intended to use them to write her memoirs at a future date. In those few memoirs she did write (collected in *Moments of Being*), she occasionally quotes from her diaries or refers to them.

## Published Diaries

(All titles were published in London by the Hogarth Press)

*A Writer's Diary*, ed. Leonard Woolf, 1953

*The Diary of Virginia Woolf*, ed. Anne Olivier Bell, 5 vols, 1977–84

*A Moment's Liberty: The Shorter Diary*, ed. Anne Olivier Bell, 1990

*A Passionate Apprentice: The Early Journals 1897–1909*, ed. Mitchell A. Leaska, 1990

*Travels with Virginia Woolf*, ed. Jan Morris, 1993

### Letters

The first part of Virginia's correspondence to be published was that with Lytton Strachey, who was quite a match for her in terms of gossip. Some

of the people mentioned in the letters were still alive and editors Leonard Woolf and James Strachey felt obliged to substitute pseudonyms where remarks were especially malicious or scandalous. A complete edition of 3,767 of Virginia's surviving letters was published twenty years later, after most of those who might sue for libel or suffer hurt feelings had died. Several dozen more have subsequently come to light, and are published in various academic journals and in the *Virginia Woolf Bulletin* (see p. 199).

The letters are enormously entertaining, as they were intended to be. Virginia's correspondents are many and varied, and she tailors her writing to each, with hardly any repetition. The number and length of the letters, bearing in mind that she always had plenty of work waiting in the background, hints at the speed with which her mind worked. The language is informal, of course, but the quality is high, and occasionally those flights of fantasy that appear in her work are visible here too.

## Published Letters

(Unless noted otherwise, titles were published in London by the Hogarth Press)

*Virginia Woolf & Lytton Strachey: Letters*, ed. Leonard Woolf and James Strachey, 1956

*The Letters of Virginia Woolf*, ed. Nigel Nicolson and Joanne Trautmann, 6 vols, 1975–80

*Congenial Spirits: The Selected Letters of Virginia Woolf*, ed. Joanne Trautmann Banks, 1989

*Paper Darts: The Illustrated Letters*, ed. Frances Spalding, London: Collins and Brown, 1991

## Biography – *Roger Fry* (1940)

In 1940 Woolf published her only full-length biography, *Roger Fry*. Soon after Roger's death in 1934 Helen Anrep, wife of the Russian mosaicist, who had been Fry's lover since 1926, asked Virginia to write about him. Virginia wanted to pay this tribute to her friend, but found the work a slog. It was much more restrictive than writing novels, though not so taxing on her imagination, and though the lows were not so low, neither were the highs so high.

Virginia's special talent, for imagining characters and events and surrounding them with layers of meaning, was not needed for this undertaking, which demanded a marshalling of facts into a chronological sequence and a flair for euphemism. In *Jacob's Room*, she could allow the reader to construct the figure of Jacob from hints and glimpses. In *Orlando*, she could use the character of her friend Vita Sackville-West to create a colourful fantasy with details plucked at will from history. But here she was required to be precise and accurate – on neither point was she particularly strong. She often escaped the daunting responsibility by working on something else

– *The Years*, *Three Guineas*, *Between the Acts* or 'A Sketch of the Past'.

There were problems. How should she treat Vanessa Bell's affair with Roger? On this occasion the Bloomsbury code of frankness fell victim to Virginia's discretion on behalf of her sister. And how could she reconcile the Fry family view of Roger with those of his friends? One solution was to allow Roger to speak for himself, in generous chunks quoted from his autobiographical writings and letters, and to quote his friends and acquaintances. The result is that the biography chugs along at a vigorous pace, always in the present tense, with the occasional diversion into imagination. So Woolf accomplished her only biography while instilling something of her own style into the work. The laborious task was at last completed, and *Roger Fry* was published on 25 July 1940. It was Virginia's last major work to be published during her lifetime.

## Woolfs and Other Animals

Virginia grew up in a family in which animals were ever present – the Stephens kept pets, Julia invented animal stories for her children, and Leslie and Thoby drew birds and beasts with some skill (a few of Leslie's drawings are printed in *Julia Duckworth Stephen: Stories for Children, Essays for Adults*).

The Woolfs owned pets for most of their lives, usually dogs, although Leonard became very fond of cats in his later years. They frequently talked about their pets to each other, as well as to visitors and correspondents, and refer to them in diaries and autobiographies. Virginia's animal stories include 'Gipsy, the Mongrel', 'The Widow and the Parrot', 'Nurse Lugton's Curtain' and 'Lappin and Lapinova', but her most extensive is a fictional biography, *Flush*, based on Elizabeth Barrett Browning's spaniel.

### Flush (1933)

Although *Flush* is subtitled 'A Biography', Woolf takes liberties with the genre, using her fertile imagination to envisage human events

as seen from a spaniel's viewpoint. Begun as light relief from reading proofs of *The Waves* and writing *The Years*, the book gradually became a burden. But on publication it sold well immediately, enabling the Woolfs to build a new pond in the garden at Monk's House.

*Flush* is, surprisingly, a controversial item in Virginia Woolf's canon. While Desmond MacCarthy and David Garnett reviewed it favourably in the press and Morgan Forster thought it a perfect example of its kind, unsentimental and full of insights about animal behaviour and perspective, other readers and critics found it trifling and insignificant. Rebecca West thought it a family joke that should have been kept within the family. It is, perhaps, a book best appreciated by dog enthusiasts, but there is plenty of Woolfishness too. The mock-heroic opening in which Flush's pedigree is traced is surely a tribute to Lytton Strachey's *Eminent Victorians*, in which lofty reputations are punctured, and the Kennel Club hierarchy gives an accurate reflection of the British class system. The philosophical exploration of the significance of words and language, of which Flush is largely ignorant, is more pointed here than in several of Woolf's other works.

## The Woolfs' Dogs

- Shag – the Stephen family dog of the 1890s, part collie and part Skye terrier, according to Virginia, and the subject of her essay 'On a Faithful Friend' (1905), written after Shag's death. Shag is also mentioned as the dog of her childhood in 'A Sketch of the Past' (*Moments of Being*).
- Charles – the indefatigable fox terrier that Leonard bought from an advertiser in *Exchange and Mart*, and that accompanied him to Ceylon in 1904 but died the following year. Leonard tells in his autobiography (*Growing*) how Charles killed a large snake soon after arriving in Ceylon, thereby guaranteeing Leonard's prestige.
- Gurth – the sheepdog that replaced Shag at 46 Gordon Square; he and Hans (see below) escaped when Virginia took them on holiday with her to Wells, Somerset (see VW's letter to Saxon Sydney-Turner, 14 Aug 1908).
- Hans – the dog that Duncan Grant remembered snapping at lighted matches during his visits to Fitzroy Square; also famous for making a mess on the floor during a visit by Lytton's mother, Lady Strachey; both she and Virginia ignored the faux pas.
- Grizzle (also spelled Grizel) – a mixed-breed dog, part fox terrier,

owned by the Woolfs from 1922 to December 1926, when she was put down after having contracted eczema.

- Pinka (also spelled Pinker; originally called Fanny) – this black spaniel, given to Virginia and Leonard by Vita Sackville-West in the summer of 1926 (died 1935), was an inspiration for Virginia's book *Flush*.
- Sally – Pinka's successor, purchased in June 1935, a black and white spaniel devoted to Leonard; died summer 1943.
- Merle (originally called Flip) – an attractive black and white sheepdog bought by Leonard to replace Sally in November 1943; she was often a topic of conversation when Leonard travelled with her on trains.
- Nigg – a dog owned by Leonard in the 1950s. According to Leonard, Nigg fought with J.R. Ackerley's beloved German shepherd, Queenie, and thereby brought to a premature end the friendship between the two men, as Leonard described in a letter to William Plomer (Woolf 1989, p. 570).

## The Woolfs' Cats

- Peat – a cat acquired by the Woolfs in December 1940. Virginia told a young friend that she had seen Peat playing with one of her gloves, only to realize a moment later that it was a bat (see VW's letter to Elaine Robson, 10 Jan 1941).
- Blue Wave – a cat of Leonard's in the 1940s.
- Troy – a Siamese cat, one of his favourites, owned by Leonard in the 1950s; his sentiments on Troy's death are expressed in a letter to Sylvia Townsend Warner (Woolf 1989, p. 524).
- Bang – a black, half-Siamese cat of Leonard's in the 1950s. Like many cats, Bang disliked having his owner's attention distracted from him and swiped at Leonard's pen when he was writing letters.

## Mitz

Mitz, a marmoset (a small monkey with a long tail and tufts of fur around the head and ears) from Brazil, was the most unusual pet that the Woolfs owned. They first saw her when they 'marmoset-sat' for wealthy friends, who had bought her from a junk shop in 1934. Mitz took to the Woolfs' home so well that it was decided she should stay there. Leonard took advice from a zoo and due to his care she recovered from the variety of ailments from which she had been suffering. But Leonard was warned that the longest the zoo had been able to keep a marmoset alive was four years.

Having been told by the zookeeper that marmosets are extremely

it. Mitz was mischievous, prone to ear-splitting cries and somewhat gluttonous (partial to snails, worms and bird's eggs). She was often an irritant to the Woolfs' friends, but she came in very useful when they drove through Nazi-controlled Germany in 1935. She charmed everyone who saw her, and attracted smiles and cries of delight from passers-by and even from the military authorities. In Leonard's view, the Nazis refused to believe that anyone who owned such a lovable and amusing creature could possibly be a Jew. Mitz died during the particularly cold Christmas Eve of 1938, but had survived six months longer than most of her British counterparts. (See Leonard's account of Mitz in *Downhill All the Way*, pp. 186–95.)

sensitive to cold, Leonard got into the habit of carrying Mitz inside his jacket. She became very attached to him, and so possessive that Leonard could persuade her down from a tree by kissing Virginia underneath

**Read On ...**

*Julia Duckworth Stephen: Stories for Children, Essays for Adults*, ed. Diana F. Gillespie and Elizabeth Steele, New York: Syracuse University Press, 1987

*Complete Shorter Fiction*, by Virginia Woolf, ed. Susan Dick, revised edition, London: Hogarth Press, 1989

*Flush: A Biography*, by Virginia Woolf, London: Hogarth Press, 1933

*Letters of Leonard Woolf*, ed. Frederic Spotts, London: Harcourt, Brace, Jovanovich, 1989

*Mitz: The Marmoset of Bloomsbury*, by Sigrid Nunez, New York: HarperFlamingo, 1998

# Adventures and Escapades

· · · · · · · · · · ·

## Bloomsbury in France

Apart from Britain, France is the country most associated with Bloomsbury, because of its importance to the painters. British artists had long had a connection with France before Roger Fry studied at the Académie Julian in Paris in 1892, to be followed fourteen years later by Duncan Grant. Duncan later moved to a smaller school, La Palette, where his fellow students included Henry Lamb, and through him Duncan got to know Augustus John's circle, though he never felt quite at ease in their company.

Clive Bell, having abandoned the historical research for which he first went to Paris, was there in 1904 when Thoby, Vanessa, Virginia and Adrian Stephen visited. He was their guide to the artists' quarter and introduced them

*Roquebrune*

to Rodin. Paris was still thought of as the heart of artistic civilization when Roger Fry, Desmond MacCarthy and Clive Bell arrived there in late 1910 to collect paintings for Fry's exhibition, 'Manet and the Post-Impressionists'.

Dorothy Bussy, Lytton Strachey's elder sister, lived in Roquebrune with her Swiss-French painter husband Simon Bussy from October to April of each year. During a visit by Lytton in 1904 Bussy painted his portrait, seated at a desk and working on his fellowship dissertation. Roger Fry, visiting the Bussys in May 1915, painted several landscapes there.

Vanessa and Duncan went frequently to Paris until 1921, when, persuaded by Roger Fry that the south of France was much more conducive than England, not just to painting but also to the painter's way of life, Vanessa took up residence on the south coast for a few months of every year. First in St Tropez, where she was accompanied by the children and by Duncan Grant, while Clive continued his sociable pursuits in Paris. But soon another region was calling – Cassis.

### Vanessa in Cassis

Roger encouraged Vanessa to come to Cassis when he stayed there in 1923. Two years later Virginia Woolf visited the coastal town with Leonard. But when Vanessa finally went, it was in unexpected circumstances. In early 1927 Duncan, in Cassis with relatives, contracted pneumonia and Vanessa rushed to his aid. As his situation stabilized, Vanessa relaxed a little, painting, arranging French lessons for Angelica and getting to know the other artists in the area. Clive and the Woolfs joined them and the whole party revelled in the warmth, colour and peace of Cassis.

At the end of the year, Vanessa, with Roger's help, found a cottage to rent for the next three years – La Bergère. Angelica's friend, Barbara Bagenal's daughter Judith, often came to stay, and the Woolfs, Lytton and Carrington, and Desmond MacCarthy visited at various times, though Roger, as a fellow painter, was the most welcome guest. There was one disadvantage – the wind (mistral) characteristic to the south of France created havoc with the painters' easels, and occasionally made it impossible to paint out of doors. But to Vanessa it was still a haven, even if it did get rather crowded with visitors at times.

The autumn of 1930 was the last time Vanessa and Duncan stayed in Cassis until December 1937, but Roger continued to spend a lot of time in France, as did Clive Bell. Vanessa and Duncan's final visit to La Bergère was in 1938 – perhaps they knew that the anticipated war might make it difficult to return. They sorted out their possessions and left their sanctuary for the last time.

## Bloomsbury Escapades

Several scandalous exploits, involving one or more of the friends, made the name of Bloomsbury famous.

### The Zanzibar Hoax

This was the first of two hoaxes-by-impersonation involving Adrian Stephen, and organized by his friend Horace Cole. On 2 March 1905 a telegram was sent to the Mayor of Cambridge announcing the arrival that afternoon of the Sultan of Zanzibar. Adrian and three friends, in exotic-looking gowns and turbans, masqueraded as 'Prince Mukasa Ali', the Sultan's representative, and his entourage. The four men, accompanied by another in ordinary clothing, who was posing as their interpreter, boarded a train at Liverpool Street station. The Mayor and Town Clerk received the party and took them to King's College Chapel and Trinity College, at which they expressed much admiration. The 'interpreter' explained that the 'Prince' had to catch an early-evening train to London and the party was escorted to the railway station. As soon as their escort had gone, they got into two cabs and drove into the countryside, where they changed

and presumably had a hearty laugh at the Mayor's expense. (See VW, *A Passionate Apprentice*, pp. 246–7, 410–11.)

### The *Dreadnought* Hoax

A trick similar to the Zanzibar Hoax was perpetrated on a larger scale in 1910. A group led by Horace Cole, including Adrian, Duncan Grant and Virginia Stephen, boarded HMS *Dreadnought*, pride of Britain's Royal Navy, in disguise. Duncan and Virginia and two others were blacked up and turbaned to look like princes in the Emperor of Abyssinia's contingent; Adrian, the 'interpreter', did most the talking, using Swahili mixed with Greek and Latin. There was some unnerving scrutiny by William Fisher, one of the *Dreadnought*'s officers, who happened to be a very respectable cousin of Adrian and Virginia, but incredibly all the officers were taken in. As representatives of the Royal Navy, they were keen to convey politeness and efficiency; they may also have been convinced by the feeble disguises because Abyssinia (today's Ethiopia) was exotic and unfamiliar to the British at that time.

The fall-out was almost as extraordinary as the hoax itself. Horace Cole

> [O]bviously the work of foolish persons.
> (First Lord of the Admiralty on the *Dreadnought* Hoax, *Hansard*, 24 Feb 1910)

liked to publicize his pranks, and informed the newspapers. Reporters called at 29 Fitzroy Square, wanting a photograph of Virginia in evening dress. The Royal Navy was outraged. William Fisher insisted on an apology from Adrian and the names of the other hoaxers. Adrian and Duncan tried to apologize to the First Lord of the Admiralty, but were sent away. Duncan was kidnapped by several officers and taken to Hampstead Heath in his carpet slippers, where the officers, greatly puzzled at his passivity, gave him a symbolic beating. Despite the disapproval of her Stephen relatives, Virginia never regretted her part in the hoax, which she described (tongue-in-cheek) as a stand against the might of the establishment. She used the episode in her story 'A Society', in which

Rose is described as boarding a naval vessel in disguise as an Ethiopian prince, and the themes of masculine aggression and overweening pride are also present in *Three Guineas*.

## Carrington's Literary Hoaxes

Carrington was fond of ridiculing her acquaintances with practical jokes. In February 1922 she sent Clive Bell a letter purportedly from George Bernard Shaw, with a tart remark about his recent criticisms of Shaw's play series *Back to Methuselah* in the *New Republic*. Clive wrote apologizing for his comments, but Shaw replied that he had sent no such letter. Clive concluded that Shaw's mind was going. Carrington was highly amused and gleefully told Lytton that her new mission in life would be to ruin love affairs and incite animosities by forging letters. Another of her forgeries won her two guineas in a competition. In July 1931 the *Week-End Observer* offered a prize for a mock-obituary of a writer in that writer's style. Carrington, of course, wrote a pastiche of Lytton. Tragically, the piece was prophetic – Lytton died the following January (see p. 62).

## Bloomsbury Parties

There were occasionally outrageous parties in Bloomsbury. For a fancy-dress party at Crosby Hall in Chelsea in early 1911 Virginia, Vanessa, Clive, Duncan, Roger, Adrian and James Strachey made their own Gauguinesque costumes by draping themselves in African fabrics, flowers and beads, and exposing large areas of browned flesh. In the wake of these parties, scandalous rumours spread like wildfire, including one that Vanessa had fornicated with Maynard on a sofa. She did not, although, fired with exhilaration, she did dance naked to the waist. The parties sometimes incorporated amateur dramatic productions. In 1924 Marjorie and Alix Strachey threw a party at 50 Gordon Square during which Schnitzler's *La Ronde* was enacted in more than usually lurid detail, with some very convincing mock-sex. Two years later Maynard and Lydia Keynes performed a home-made play about a real-life sexual scandal, Duncan Grant starring as a wolfhound. Some of the most memorable of the 'am dram' evenings were devised by Virginia Woolf.

## *Freshwater* (written 1923/1935)

Virginia Woolf's only play was a comedy loosely based on the Isle of Wight household of her great-aunt, the photographer Julia Margaret Cameron. Two versions exist: one written in 1923 and another, revised and expanded into three acts, from 1935. It was the later version, complete with sexual puns and updated allusions, that was performed at 8 Fitzroy Street (Vanessa's studio) on Friday 18 January 1935 as part of a belated celebration of Angelica Bell's sixteenth birthday. A number of Bloomsbury denizens were persuaded to perform, including Vanessa Bell and Leonard Woolf as the eccentric Julia Margaret and her long-suffering husband Charles Hay Cameron, Angelica as a youthful and restless Ellen Terry, Duncan Grant as her husband, the elderly painter G.F. Watts, and Adrian Stephen as Alfred Tennyson, continually expecting a visit from Queen Victoria. Other parts were taken by Julian Bell, Ann and Judith Stephen, and Eve Younger, a friend of Angelica's. There was even a part for Mitz the marmoset.

## Skinny Dipping

Virginia was generally highly self-conscious about her body and hated even having to shop for clothes. But on one occasion she indulged in behaviour which would have been more characteristic of Vanessa – skinny dipping. Her only venture into naturism took place while she was staying with Rupert Brooke at Grantchester in August 1911. Feeling more adventurous than usual, she stripped off and joined him in the water, hidden by the night's darkness. It was a great step for her, and one that she made the most of, describing it to her sister whom she knew would pass it on. Vanessa obliged by writing an insinuating rhyme to Saxon Sydney-Turner about the escapade, but the 'Rupert romance' that Adrian often teased Virginia about did not materialize. (See Hall 2006 for more about Virginia and Rupert Brooks.)

# *Orlando* (1928)

· · · · · · · · · · ·

*Orlando*, a exuberant fantasy-adventure that capers through three centuries of history, was published at the mid-point of Virginia Woolf's novel-writing career. Leonard and Vanessa considered the book Virginia's best work to date. Vita Sackville-West was thrilled and confessed herself in love with Orlando, the gender-bending hero/heroine for whom she herself had been the model; her husband Harold Nicolson was almost equally delighted. Rebecca West, writing in the *New York Herald Tribune*, thought the book a masterpiece. In the first two months over 6,000 copies were sold.

## Origins

The seeds of *Orlando* were planted on March 1927, as Virginia later noted in her diary. The book she had in mind, 'The Jessamy Brides', was to include 'Sapphism' and Constantinople, and:

> Satire is to be the main note
> – satire & wildness ... My own
> lyric vein is to be satirised.
> Everything mocked ... For the
> truth is I feel the need of an
> escapade after these serious
> poetic experimental books
> whose form is always so closely
> considered. I want to kick up my
> heels & be off.
>
> (*Diary* 3, 14 Mar 1927)

*Knole, near Sevenoaks in Kent, Vita Sackville-West's childhood home*

Virginia had visited Knole, the grand estate which was home of Vita Sackville-West, in mid-January and the sense of history, stretching back to the sixteenth century, had left a deep impression. Vita's travels to Turkey, Egypt and Persia (present-day Iran) with her husband Harold Nicolson, a diplomat, added to the sense of colour and exoticism. *Orlando* soon took precedence over Virginia's other writing. By Christmas she had reached the third chapter; in January 1928 Vita's father died and Knole passed to her uncle. Two months later Virginia completed the novel, though in a less exuberant spirit than when she began it.

## Plot Summary

In the age of Elizabeth I, the Queen admires the physique of sixteen-year-old Orlando and makes him a Knight of the Garter. In King James's reign. The Russian court is stranded in the Thames by the Great Frost (in actuality, the winter of 1607–8), and Orlando is enchanted by Sasha, a Russian princess. But Sasha is elusive. The ice melts and the Russians sail away.

Orlando sleeps for seven days, then grieves over Sasha and becomes an avid reader and playwright. He invites Nick Greene, a famous writer, to visit, but they fall out on the subject of literature. Disillusioned, Orlando destroys all his work except for 'The

Oak Tree', which he changes from a play to a poem. He is pursued by the ardent Archduchess Harriet: to escape her, he becomes ambassador to Constantinople. It is the reign of King Charles II. Orlando marries a gypsy then falls into another deep sleep, and is intrigued to wake seven days later as a woman. He lives among the Turkish gypsies in Broussa, but pines for home.

Back in England, Orlando is embroiled in property inheritance lawsuits. The Archduchess reappears and explains that he is really a man, Archduke Harry. He proposes but still does not suit Orlando, who goes to London to find love and life and meets Pope, Addison and Swift; Queen Anne is now on the throne.

The nineteenth century is heralded by clouds and rain, and Orlando is unable to write. She meets Marmaduke Bonthrop Shelmerdine and they marry. Shelmerdine departs for Cape Horn. Nick Greene advises Orlando to publish her poem, 'The Oak Tree'. It is now the twentieth century. Orlando has four sons (three as a man; one as a woman); her house is a museum; she has won 200 guineas for her poem. Yearning for Shelmerdine, she is amazed to see him jump from a passing aeroplane – a wild goose flies overhead in the same moment. It is the present day.

## Sources

*Orlando* is a heady mix of Vita Sackville-West's character, fictionalized episodes from her life and a wealth of historical detail. Vita's 'Sapphic' tendencies are represented by a change of sex; her passionate affair with Violet Trefusis (the daughter of Alice Keppel, King Edward VII's mistress) is reflected by Orlando's with Sasha. Her love of literature appears in the plays and poetry Orlando writes and his/her continual brushes with literary figures. One of these, Nick Greene, represents the ubiquity of second-rate literature. He is partly based on Robert Greene, Shakespeare's rival, and reappears in *A Room of One's Own* (1929) as

the cad who gets Judith Shakespeare pregnant, precipitating her suicide.

*Orlando* was Virginia's way of making up to Vita for the loss of Knole, the estate where she had grown up and which – as a woman – she could not inherit. The same fate threatens to destroy the happiness of Orlando, as a woman in the eighteenth century, but the lawsuits are decided in her favour. Her marriage to Shelmerdine, as androgynous as Orlando herself, neatly reflects Vita's to the bisexual Harold Nicolson.

## Themes

### The Elasticity of Time

The events of *Orlando* ignore the usual constraints of time, stretching from the late Elizabethan era to the date of publication (11 October 1928). During these 300 years, Orlando matures from a sixteen-year-old boy to a woman of thirty-six (Vita's age at publication). Time is sometimes highly specific and at other times vague; most commonly the date is revealed but the year unstated. Orlando meets Sasha at 6 p.m. on 7 January. On Saturday 18 June he fails to wake from sleep and instead wakes at 7.45 a.m. seven days later.

Later, he awakes from another seven-day sleep on Thursday 10 May as a woman. Orlando's son is born at 3 a.m. on Thursday 20 March. The mixture of precision and vagueness mocks the factual details found in standard biographies such as those in the *Dictionary of National Biography*, edited by Woolf's father.

### The Literary World

One of the strands Virginia Woolf threaded through her novel was her ambivalent attitude towards literature. Each age, she observed, unsatisfied with itself, yearns for a 'golden age' in which literature was at its zenith. Only the writer of an earlier age is recognized as a genius. She and her friends, as she acknowledged, advocated the literature of the ancient Greeks.

Orlando's first view of a poet is of a fat man with a dirty ruff, writing at the servants' dinner table; later Orlando wonders whether it was Shakespeare. The discrepancy between literary reputations past and present is reinforced by the changing fortunes of Nick Greene. In the early seventeenth century, when writers were often poor and disreputable, he denounces the

> [H]ow many different people are there not – Heaven help us – all having lodgement at one time or another in the human spirit? Some say two thousand and fifty two.
> (*Orlando*)

current state of poetry and appeals to Orlando for a quarterly allowance. In the Victorian age, when literature was highly respected and had finally become commercial, he is the plump and prosperous Sir Nicholas, still lamenting his literary peers and yearning for those he once denigrated. In the novel's present day writers are rewarded and given cash awards: Orlando herself wins the Burdett Coutts Memorial Prize, named after a famous Victorian benefactress who gave away millions to good causes, for 'The Oak Tree' (Vita's 'The Land' won the Hawthornden prize in 1927).

### Scattered Selves

Biography, the narrator of *Orlando* claims, generally deals with six or seven selves, but a person may have thousands, controlled by a 'key' self. The different aspects of Orlando include Queen Eliza's favourite, Sasha's lover, courtier, ambassador, soldier, traveller, gypsy, lady, hermit, woman of letters, and the many Orlandos who are in love with Shelmerdine. Virginia Woolf also wrote about multiple selves in the essay 'Evening over Sussex: Reflections in a Motor Car' (*Death of the Moth*). As Orlando considers her selves, she too is in a car. When both the spirit of Queen Elizabeth and an aeroplane carrying Shelmerdine arrive at Orlando's ancestral home, past and present selves are reunited.

# A Vindication of the Rights of Women and Men: Feminism and War

· · · · · · · · · · ·

## The Woolfs and Feminism

Virginia's first activity on behalf of the suffragists was to address envelopes for the Adult Suffrage League. She remarked in a letter to Violet Dickinson (27 Feb 1910) that the suffrage office, full of earnest young men and women, was like a novel by H.G. Wells. She had mixed feelings about 'the woman question', aware of the unfairness of sexual inequality, but detesting the fact that it was necessary to fight for rights which should have been hers automatically. To her it was quite irrational that men should be favoured merely because they were men. She was not a political activist in the banner-waving sense, but her two 'feminist' books have had a great influence – in the United States they are considered among her best works.

Virginia and Leonard Woolf were acquainted with Margaret Llewelyn Davies, secretary of the Women's Co-operative Guild (instrumental in setting a minimum wage for women working

in retail) and a member of the National Union of Women's Suffrage Societies (NUWSS). Through Margaret, Leonard became deeply involved with the Women's Co-operative Guild, studying cooperative societies, attending meetings and writing pamphlets. Virginia hosted meetings of the Richmond branch for four years, inviting friends to speak and encouraging the dozen women who attended to discuss points raised.

Virginia was greatly impressed by Margaret's work, although she admitted in a letter to her (16 Nov 1919) that she would probably never completely understand it. *Night and Day*'s suffragist Mary Datchet was partly based on Margaret, but it was the comic portrayal of the suffrage office that Margaret noticed, and disliked. She worked tirelessly on a number of fronts, prompting Leonard Woolf to write later that if she had been a man, her activities would have occupied half a page in *Who's Who*. In 1931 she edited a book containing the memories of working women and asked Virginia to write an introduction. While normally of the opinion that a book should stand on its own merits, Virginia made an exception and provided Margaret with a lengthy letter that she could use for this purpose. (For more on Margaret Llewelyn Davies, see Leonard Woolf, *Beginning Again*, pp. 101–4.)

## Suffragists and Suffragettes

There is often confusion between suffragists and suffragettes. Both groups were fighting for women's right to vote, but roughly speaking the suffragists (such as the National Union of Women's Suffrage Societies, or NUWSS), were at the peaceful end of the spectrum while the Suffragettes (a derogatory term invented by a *Daily Mail* reporter in 1906) believed in direct action, such as assaulting policemen (often very mildly), chaining themselves to railings or committing criminal damage. The term 'suffragette' was soon appropriated by the activists, and was used as the title of a periodical edited by Christabel Pankhurst. The suffragettes were usually members of the Women's Social and Political Union (WSPU), founded by the Pankhursts

in 1903 as a breakaway faction of the non-militant NUWSS. Emily Davison, who was killed when she ran in front of King George V's horse at the 1913 Derby while trying to publicize the movement, is probably the most notorious suffragette and WSPU member. Many others were arrested as a result of their militant activities and underwent harsh and humiliating treatment in prison. When they went on hunger strike in protest, they were often painfully force-fed by their captors. It was not until after the First World War, when the government was forced to acknowledge the part women had played in the war effort, that they were allowed to vote.

Bloomsbury members believed in women's right to vote, but they wanted a lot more – equality. In this sense they were more like modern feminists than suffragists.

*2 Gower Street, where Millicent Fawcett lived and died*

## The Stracheys and Feminism

The Strachey women were feminists by descent: Jane Strachey had collected signatures for a petition in favour of women's votes as early as 1866. Her suffrage activities had brought her into contact with Millicent Fawcett, founder of Newnham College and president of the non-militant NUWSS, who became a good friend.

Philippa (Pippa) Strachey was extremely active in women's societies from 1907 until her retirement in 1959. At various times Pippa was secretary of the London Society for Women's Suffrage and of the Women's Service Bureau; she was also secretary and then honorary

secretary of the Women's Employment Federation. She helped the NUWSS to organize its first national demonstration on 9 February 1907, which, because of the bad weather that day became known as the 'Mud March'. She asked Virginia to speak to the London and National Society for Women's Service on 'Professions for Women', which she did in 1931 (see pp. 139–40). In 1953, this organization was renamed the Fawcett Society and Pippa was asked to be its honorary secretary.

Pippa's sister-in-law Ray, the second wife of Oliver Strachey, shared her interest in feminism. Ray studied mathematics at Newnham College, and in 1915 became parliamentary secretary for the London Society for Women's Suffrage. During the First World War she was chair of the Women's Service Bureau and throughout the 1930s the

### Votes for Women

Between 1869 and 1894 only unmarried, property-owning women were allowed to vote in Britain, and only in local elections; later the right was extended to include married women. In 1918 the right to vote in national elections was granted to upper- and middle-class women over thirty, but it was not until 1928 that women got parity with men and were entitled to vote at twenty-one, whatever their class.

In the United States woman were entitled to vote from 1920, due to an amendment to the constitution.

first chair of the Cambridge University Women's Employment Board. In 1935 she was a co-founder of the Women's Employment Federation. She was editor of the feminist newspaper *The Common Cause*. Her books include *The Cause* (1928) and *Careers and Openings for Women* (1935): the first is cited by Woolf in *A Room of One's Own* and became a feminist classic; both are cited in *Three Guineas*.

Pippa's younger sister, Pernel Strachey, was educated at Newnham College and later became its Principal (1923–41). Evidently she believed in the higher education of women, although she was not a campaigner like Pippa and Ray. She asked Virginia to speak on 'Women and Fiction' in 1928, and so was instrumental in inspiring the ideas behind *A Room of One's Own*.

---

# Feminist Writings

· · · · · · · · · · ·

### *A Room of One's Own* (1929)

Virginia Woolf wrote 'Women and Fiction' after being asked by Lytton's sister Pernel Strachey to deliver a paper to members of the Newnham Arts Society. She delivered a similar paper to Girton college six days later. They were revised and expanded into *A Room of One's Own* and published the following year.

The narrator has been asked to give a lecture on women and fiction at a university, 'Oxbridge', which stands for both Oxford and Cambridge. The rest of the book relates her observations of Cambridge and the findings of her later research: that women are under-represented in life, as in literature. That women have always been poorer than men. That their writing has traditionally attracted

derision from men and women alike. The greatest minds are androgynous, the narrator concludes, and exhorts her audience to write regardless of their gender.

Two phrases have accumulated much resonance since Woolf wrote *A Room of One's Own*. The first is an assertion: 'a woman must have money and a room of her own if she is to write fiction', which she sets out to prove in the course of the book. The second is a character, 'Shakespeare's sister', a purely imaginary construction that illustrates why so little writing by women survives from before the nineteenth century. Judith, the sister

of William, has as much talent as her brother, but none of his opportunities. Woolf exhorts her audience to think of the Shakespeare's sister who exists within each of them, and to fulfil their potential as she could not.

## 'Professions for Women' (1931)

On 20 January 1931 Virginia had a 'Eureka' moment in her bath: a new idea for a book occurred to her, to be called 'Professions for Women'. The inspiration came from a paper she had been asked by Pippa Strachey to read to the London and National Society for Women's Service. The book mutated into *The Years* and *Three Guineas*, and the title 'Professions for Women' was reserved for the paper delivered to Pippa's society and published in *The Death of the Moth* in 1942. The same work, with the same title, has also been published in *Killing the Angel in the House*.

The essay is a rejection by Woolf of the Victorian ideal of womanhood, which sought to deny women any position outside the domestic sphere. In the most vivid section the narrator describes how her first efforts of writing were hampered by a feminine spirit hovering over her shoulder, reminding her that she should defer to men; that she should try to be – and to write – what they would find acceptable. The Angel is, therefore, a symbol of female oppression by other females who act on behalf of men. In a violent twist, the narrator tells how she (metaphorically) stabbed the Angel to death with her pen and set herself free to write what she

> Like [William], she had a taste for the theatre. She stood at the stage door; she wanted to act, she said. Men laughed in her face. The manager – a fat, loose-lipped man – guffawed. He bellowed something about poodles dancing and women acting – no woman, he said, could possibly be an actress. He hinted – you can imagine what … At last – for she was very young, oddly like Shakespeare the poet in her face, with the same grey eyes and rounded brows – at last Nick Greene the actor-manager took pity on her; she found herself with child by that gentleman and so – who shall measure the heat and violence of the poet's heart when caught and tangled in a woman's body? – killed herself one winter's night and lies buried at some cross-roads where the omnibuses now stop outside the Elephant and Castle.
>
> (*A Room of One's Own*, ch. 3)

liked. This 'killing the angel' would, to Woolf's generation, have been a clear rebuff to the popular Victorian poem by Coventry Patmore, *The Angel in the House*, which pictured the married woman as simply the helpmeet of her husband and mother to his children, without a life of her own.

## *Three Guineas* (1938)

*Three Guineas* and *The Years* were originally conceived of as a single volume, 'The Pargiters', which had sprung from the idea of 'Professions for Women' (see above) in 1931. It was intended to be a 'novel-essay' on women and social history, but Virginia later decided to split the fiction from the non-fiction, and *Three Guineas* emerged.

The tripartite structure of the book is based upon the supposition that the narrator has been approached by three people: one asks her to join a society to help prevent war; another tries to enlist her support for a women's college; the third is from an organization that helps women gain entry to the professions. A guinea was in Woolf's time the standard subscription fee, and is required for each of the three causes which her narrator is asked to support. The guinea coin was named after the country in Africa from where its gold originated, and was traditionally worth one pound and one shilling. The coin itself had passed out of circulation by the early nineteenth century, but certain luxuries affordable only by the rich were still measured in guineas, as occasionally they are today.

The tone is cool and logical, vigorous rather than angry, but its anti-war and anti-sexist standpoints are forcefully argued. At times opposing perspectives are anticipated and shown to be self-contradictory. The book reveals an enormous amount of research: Woolf seems determined to back up her points with plenty of evidence and the end-notes are thorough and often lengthy, accounting for about one-fifth of the book's length.

The narrator asserts that she will only support the organizations if certain conditions are fulfilled that would make it possible to change society and ensure that their aims are met. These conditions are: that all official honours, including college degrees, should be declined, in order that they are not pursued for their own sake; that as much money should be spent on educating women as is spent on men, while making sure that women are not changed by wealth, as men have been; that before political dictatorships are abolished we must first overthrow those that prevail in the home – that is, the power of men over women.

Finally, the narrator suggests that to help stop war, women must take a different path to men: 'we can best help you to prevent war not by repeating your words and following your methods but by finding new words and creating new methods ... not by joining your society but by remaining outside your society but in co-operation with its aim.'

To this end, the narrator sends her guinea to each organization but will not join the men's anti-war society.

## Arthur's Education Fund

What is that congregation of buildings there, with a semi-monastic look, with chapels and halls and green playing-fields? To you it is your old school; Eton or Harrow; your old university, Oxford or Cambridge; the source of memories and of traditions innumerable. But to us, who see it through the shadow of Arthur's Education Fund, it is a schoolroom table; an omnibus going to a class; a little woman with a red nose who is not well educated herself but has an invalid mother to support; an allowance of £50 a year with which to buy clothes, give presents and take journeys on coming to maturity.

(*Three Guineas*, ch. 1)

'Arthur's Education Fund', the phrase made famous by *Three Guineas*, is not one Woolf invented but borrowed from William Makepeace Thackeray's novel *The History of Pendennis*. In Thackeray's novel, it refers to a sum of money put aside for the education of Arthur Pendennis, the son of the family. Into such funds, observes Woolf, goes all of a family's available money that might otherwise be shared with the mother and sisters for their comfort and education.

## Woolf Writing about Women

All of Virginia Woolf's novels concern the fortunes of women to some extent, but her specifically 'feminist' writings are:

'A Woman's College from Outside' (story, written 1920)

'A Society' (story, written 1920)

*A Room of One's Own* (1929)

'Professions for Women' (1931)

Introduction to *Life As We Have Known It*, ed. Margaret Llewelyn Davies (1931)

*Three Guineas* (1938)

## Bloomsbury and the First World War

To many in Bloomsbury the First World War seemed to be the end of civilization. With a number of causes rooted in European empire-building – German attempts to build a powerful navy; French distrust of Germany; and the popularity of nationalism across Europe – the last straw was the assassination of Archduke Franz Ferdinand, the heir to the Austrian throne. The assassin was a Serb nationalist, protesting against the Austrian takeover of Bosnia-Hercegovina in 1908. On one side were Austria-Hungary and Germany; on the other, Russia, France and Britain. Belgium tried to remain neutral but was invaded by Germany as a route to France.

Britain declared war on Germany on 4 August 1914, but only in 1916 was conscription introduced. The Military Service Act, as it was called, allowed for three types of exemption: ill-health, vital war work and conscientious objection on moral grounds. Most Bloomsberries were against the war – some were conscientious objectors – but they fell into each of the three exemption categories.

*Memorial to the fallen in the world wars, Hyde Park, London*

- **Leonard Woolf** was prepared to fight and attended a tribunal at Kingston barracks, but was exempted from service in the First World War because of a congenital tremor in his hands. He began work on *International Government*, the book that would set the tone for the future League of Nations. In 1917 his brother Cecil was killed and another brother, Philip, was seriously wounded.

- **Clive Bell**, a pacifist, took up farm work at Garsington Manor as an alternative to conscription; his anti-war pamphlet, *Peace at Once* (1915), was burned by order of the Lord Mayor of London.

- **Lytton Strachey** attended two military tribunals in Hampstead in 1916, prepared to go to prison rather than prolong the war even in a clerical capacity. Famously, his witty and suggestive answer to the question, What would you do if a German soldier tried to rape your sister? was that he would endeavour to get between them. He was exempted on health grounds and spent the war years proving that even heroes have feet of clay, in *Eminent Victorians*.

- **Duncan Grant** was a conscientious objector who worked as an agricultural labourer at Wissett Lodge, Suffolk, with David Garnett; when Vanessa Bell moved to Charleston, they worked for a local farmer, Mr Hecks, whose family still lives in the area.

- **Roger Fry**, at fifty, was too old to fight and spent the war running the Omega Workshops. In April 1915 he helped his sisters organize the Quaker relief fund in France, but the Quakers had to come to his rescue when he tried to get to the front to visit a friend and was arrested as a spy.
- **Maynard Keynes** was exempted from service because of his important Treasury work, although he also applied for exemption on the grounds that he was a conscientious objector (see pp. 103–4). He helped Duncan Grant and David Garnett secure exemption from conscription.
- **Saxon Sydney-Turner** was exempted because of his work for the Treasury.
- **Desmond MacCarthy** worked for the Red Cross in France in 1914 and later joined the War Office, then the Admiralty, working in naval intelligence for the rest of the war.
- **Adrian Stephen** considered joining up, but instead worked for the Union of Democratic Control and the National Council for Civil Liberties (anti-war bodies). **Karin Stephen**'s mother Mary Berenson threatened to stop their allowance

because of their pacifism. In August 1916 Adrian found work at Stud Farm, near Cheltenham, with Gerald and Fredegond Shove.

- **Oliver and Ray Strachey** supported the war; Oliver worked on code-breaking at the Foreign Office, and Ray worked for women's organizations (see pp. 137–8).
- **Ottoline and Philip Morrell** were both anti-war; Philip's pacifist speech in parliament (he was a Liberal MP) effectively finished his career.
- **Mark Gertler** was a pacifist and conscientious objector. One of his most famous paintings, *Merry-Go-Round* (1916), shows wartime figures on a fairground ride, in an endless and futile pursuit of one another.
- **Rupert Brooke**, a former friend of several Bloomsberries, turned against them after a crisis in his personal life in 1911. He became very nationalistic, perhaps partly in opposition to Bloomsbury, and during the First World War signed up for Winston Churchill's new Royal Naval Division. He died of septicaemia on a hospital ship en route to the Dardanelles on 23 April 1915, without having entered the battle. (For more on Rupert Brooke and Bloomsbury, see Hall 2006.)

**Read On ...**

*Bloomsbury*, by Quentin Bell, new edition, London: Weidenfeld and Nicolson, 1986 (see ch. 3, 'The War')

*Bloomsbury: A House of Lions*, by Leon Edel, London: Hogarth Press, 1979 (see chapter entitled 'The War' in Part IV)

*Virginia Woolf*, by Hermione Lee, London: Chatto and Windus, 1996 (see ch. 19, 'War')

# Upstairs, Downstairs: Bloomsbury Houses

· · · · · · · · · · ·

Bloomsbury had long been known as an artistic, bohemian area before Virginia Woolf and her friends moved there. The actress Sarah Siddons lived at 14 Gower Street in the 1780s, and Mary Wollstonecraft wrote *A Vindication of the Rights of Woman* while living in Store Street in 1792. Several of the Pre-Raphaelite painters lived in Red Lion Square in the 1850s and Ford Madox Brown lived with his family at 37 Fitzroy Square in the 1870s. Christina Rossetti spent the last eighteen years of her life at 30 Torrington Square and George Bernard Shaw was a tenant of 29 Fitzroy Square in the late nineteenth century (see p. 148). By Virginia Woolf's time, Bloomsbury's proximity to the University of London and the Slade School of Art – as well, of course, as its relative cheapness – had attracted numerous students.

According to the apocryphal saying, the Bloomsberries 'lived in squares but loved in triangles'. Many of their homes were situated in Bloomsbury squares,

with a few country houses when they became more affluent – both are listed below. The descriptions are in chronological order of residence within each section: the Stephens, Bells and Woolfs in London; Other Bloomsbury Houses; and Bloomsbury in the Country. Many of the houses are still standing today, several bearing blue or brown plaques dedicated to Bloomsbury figures (see: www.virginiawoolfsociety.co.uk/vw_res. london.htm). Only the significant residences are included here and a few more places of interest are listed on pp. 194–8.

## The Stephens, Bells and Woolfs in London

### 46 Gordon Square (photo on p. 21)

*Bloomsbury, west-central London;* ⊖ *Russell Square*

Vanessa, Thoby and Adrian Stephen moved here in late 1904; Virginia in January 1905. It was a rather bohemian

*A nineteenth-century engraving of Fitzroy Square*

student area, though its elegant terraces look highly reputable now. On the ground floor was the study, and on the first floor a spacious drawing-room, where Bloomsbury came into being in March 1905 (see pp. 19–21). Virginia's sitting-room was on the top floor. In March 1907, while Vanessa was on her honeymoon, Virginia and Adrian moved to 29 Fitzroy Square, leaving no. 46 to the married couple. Maynard Keynes took over the house in 1916 until his death in 1946 (see 47 Gordon Square on p. 152), but the Bells retained rooms here until August 1925 when Keynes married Lydia Lopokova. Sold to the University of London in 1946 and in 1974 to Birkbeck College, which now owns nos 42 to 47.

### 29 Fitzroy Square

*Fitzrovia, west of Bloomsbury;* ⊖ *Warren Street, Great Portland Street*
Virginia and Adrian Stephen lived here, from February 1907 to November 1911, when they moved to 38 Brunswick Square. From 1887 to 1898, it had another famous resident – George Bernard Shaw. Duncan Grant remarked that the Stephens were the only people to own an entire house in the Square; all the others had been divided into flats. Virginia's rooms were on the second floor. Adrian's study, where the pair held their Thursday 'at homes', was on the ground floor. Virginia was living here when she began her first novel, *The Voyage Out*. Now business premises.

### 38 Brunswick Square

*Bloomsbury;* ⊖ *Russell Square*
Virginia and Adrian Stephen, Duncan Grant and Maynard Keynes moved here in November 1911; they were joined in December by Leonard Woolf. Virginia and Leonard left on their marriage in August 1912. The others kept the house until October 1914, when they went their separate ways. The house was demolished in 1936 for the University of London School of Pharmacy at 29–39 Brunswick Square – aptly so, in the light

of the events here of 9 September 1913 (see p. 178).

### 13 Clifford's Inn (photo on p. 29)

*East-central London;* ⊖ *Chancery Lane*
Virginia and Leonard Woolf lived here from 30 October 1912 to September 1913. Samuel Butler lived at no. 15 from 1864 until his death in 1902. One of the original Inns of Chancery (smaller versions of the Inns of Court), it felt to Leonard like a Cambridge college. The Woolfs ate their meals at the Cock Tavern (alive and well) across the road. Clifford's Inn was demolished in 1934 and replaced by an eight-storey block of flats and offices; only a doorway bearing the name remains. Leonard lived in the new block briefly from November 1941 to April 1942, but hated it.

### 17 The Green

*Richmond upon Thames, Surrey;* ⊖ *and* 🚌 *Richmond*
After Virginia's severe mental illness of 1913, the Woolfs lived in Asheham House, Sussex (see below) for a year. Then they rented rooms at no. 17 The Green from 16 October 1914 to 25 March 1915, leaving the day before *The Voyage Out* was published. The Woolf's Belgian landlady, Mrs Le Grys, supplied material for Crosby in Virginia's later novel, *The Years* (see pp. 167–5). Now business premises.

### 50 Gordon Square

*Bloomsbury;* ⊖ *Russell Square*
Adrian Stephen and his wife Karin lived on the lower floors after their marriage in October 1914. Lydia Lopokova lived here from April to October 1922, while Maynard was at no. 46. Vanessa Bell had taken the top two floors in February 1920; Clive also had rooms here. Vanessa found Lydia an unsettling influence, and asked for her to be moved to no. 41 (see p. 151). It is now a part of the University of London.

### Hogarth House, Paradise Road (photo on p. 38)

*Richmond upon Thames, Surrey;* ⊖ *and* 🚌 *Richmond*
Virginia and Leonard Woolf lived here, 1915–24, during the period when Virginia wrote *Night and Day, Jacob's Room* and *Mrs Dalloway.* Built around 1720. The Woolfs originally took a five-year lease and in December 1919 bought the house, along with the adjacent Suffield House, for £1,950. Suffield was let until 1921, then sold to a solicitor. The Hogarth Press (see pp. 37–41) was founded here in April 1917, and the nearby Kew Gardens inspired one of Virginia's most famous stories. The Woolfs left on 13 March 1924, letting the house to Saxon Sydney-Turner's mother, then selling it in 1927. Now business premises.

*The Tavistock Hotel, which now occupies the former site of 52 Tavistock Square*

### 8 Fitzroy Street

*Fitzrovia;* ⊖ *Warren Street, Great Portland Street*
Duncan Grant took a studio at the back of the building in 1922, followed by Vanessa in 1929. Whistler, Augustus John and Walter Sickert had also painted here. Virginia Woolf's *Freshwater* was performed in Vanessa's studio on 18 January 1935 (see pp. 128–9), and in 1936 Angelica took a room at the front of the building. The studios were let in 1939 but were damaged by an incendiary bomb in September 1940; Duncan's was completely gutted. The building was later demolished and the site is now occupied by offices.

### 52 Tavistock Square

*Bloomsbury;* ⊖ *Russell Square*
Virginia and Leonard Woolf lived here from 15 March 1924 to August 1939, their longest time in a London house. Virginia wrote many of her books while living here, from *Mrs Dalloway* to *The Years* and *Three Guineas*. The house was bombed in 1940 and the Tavistock Hotel was built in 1951. In the Square garden there are memorials to both of the Woolfs. A monument dedicated to the memory of Virginia Woolf stands at the south-west corner, and a ginkgo tree on the northern side of the garden celebrates Leonard Woolf's arrival in Ceylon in 1904.

### 37 Gordon Square

*Bloomsbury;* ⊖ *Russell Square*
Vanessa Bell and Duncan Grant had rooms here 1925–9. Other inhabitants were George (Dadie) Rylands and his friend Angus Davidson. Virginia's friend Ka Arnold-Forster (née Cox), her husband Will and son Mark rented Vanessa's rooms in early 1928.

### 37 Mecklenburgh Square

*Bloomsbury;* ⊖ *Russell Square*
Virginia and Leonard Woolf lived here briefly, from 13 October 1939 to 27 August 1940. It was partially destroyed by bomb damage in September 1940, when the Hogarth Press was moved to Letchworth (see p. 40). In April 1942, after Virginia's death, Leonard camped in the ruined house in preference to the new flats at Clifford's Inn (see p. 149). In 1957 William Goodenough House, owned by the Goodenough College, was built on the site.

## Other Bloomsbury Houses

### 44 Bedford Square (photo on p. 23)

*Bloomsbury;* ⊖ *Tottenham Court Road, Goodge Street*
Lady Ottoline and Sir Philip Morrell lived here 1906–15. Ottoline (see pp. 23, 108–10) held 'at home' evenings here from 1907, and became known as a brilliant hostess. The Morrells let the house when they moved to Garsington, and sold it to their friends the Asquiths in 1919. Now business premises.

### 21 Fitzroy Square

*Fitzrovia;* ⊖ *Warren Street, Great Portland Street*
A few doors from Virginia and Adrian Stephen at no. 29, Maynard Keynes took two rooms on the second floor here in November 1909. One was a bedroom for him when he was in London, the other a studio for Duncan, who otherwise lived with his family in Hampstead. In October 1911 Rupert Brooke borrowed Duncan's room, but he decided it was too dirty and uncomfortable and went elsewhere after a few weeks. Now an embassy building.

### 33 Fitzroy Square

*Fitzrovia;* ⊖ *Warren Street, Great Portland Street*
The ground floor contained Roger Fry's Omega Workshops from summer 1913 to summer 1919 (see pp. 84–5) Now the London Foot Hospital and School of Podiatric Medicine.

*51 Gordon Square*

### 41 Gordon Square

*Bloomsbury;* ⊖ *Russell Square*
James and Alix Strachey lived on the top floor 1919–56 (they married in 1920), letting the lower floors. Lydia Lopokova took the ground floor 1922–5, then married Maynard Keynes. From 1926 to 1933 Frances Marshall and Ralph Partridge rented rooms, occasionally joined by Lytton Strachey. In 1956, the landlords, the University of London, put the annual rent up from £250 to £900 (worth £15,000 in 2005) and James and Alix moved to Lord's Wood in Marlow, Buckinghamshire. Nos 39–41 Gordon Square now house the University College London History of Art department.

### 51 Gordon Square

*Bloomsbury;* 🚇 *Russell Square*
Leased by Lady Jane Strachey for her family in September 1919. She lived here on a permanent basis with her unmarried daughters Pippa and Marjorie; the latter taught the children of several Bloomsberries at the house in the 1920s. Other family members, including Lytton, often came to stay and others drifted back in their old age. Pernel, leaving Cambridge on her retirement, took up residence in 1941, and died here a decade later. Oliver, after a severe heart attack, lived here from 1944. Dorothy Bussy, Lytton's elder sister, lived here in her nineties with her unmarried daughter, Janie Bussy. In a tragic accident, Janie died as the result of a gas leak in the bathroom in 1960. The house passed out of Strachey hands in 1963, when the last residents, Pippa and Marjorie, went into a nursing home. Nos 49–51 Gordon Square now house the University College London Careers Service.

### 47 Gordon Square

*Bloomsbury;* 🚇 *Russell Square*
Maynard Keynes bought this house, which adjoins no. 46, in the 1920s and added a door to connect the first-floor drawing-rooms. He let the rest of no. 47. The drawing-room of this house is now the Keynes Library, which contains three paintings by Vanessa Bell and Duncan Grant. Now owned by Birkbeck College.

*10 Gower Street*

### 10 Gower Street

*Bloomsbury;* 🚇 *Russell Square*
Ottoline Morrell lived here with her husband Philip from 1927 until her death in 1938. A smaller house than 44 Bedford Square due to the Morrells' financial situation, Ottoline could only invite friends to visit in much smaller numbers than formerly (see p. 110). Now the Birkbeck College School of Politics and Sociology.

## Bloomsbury in the Country

### Little Talland House

*Firle, East Sussex;* 🚌 *Glynde (1½ miles), Lewes (5 miles)*
Virginia Stephen rented this newly built

house from January 1911 to January 1912 at a cost of £19.10s. a year. She invited her friends and family, including Leonard Woolf and Rupert Brooke, to her country home for weekends and holidays. Now privately owned.

## Asheham House

*Beddingham, East Sussex*
Virginia Stephen and Vanessa Bell leased the house from October 1911, letting it to friends in their absence. The Woolfs spent their first night of married life here and it became their country house for the next seven years. Virginia thought the house very romantic, if a little dark and damp in the winter; her story 'A Haunted House' uses it as a model. The landlord gave the Woolfs notice to quit in March 1919 and they left for Monk's House on 1 September. Asheham fell into disrepair, abandoned because of the encroaching pollution of the nearby cement works, and it was demolished in 1994 by the council. It is now a landfill site, open to the public but with nothing to show its past.

## Garsington Manor

*Oxfordshire;* 🚌 *Oxford (5 miles)*
Ottoline and Philip Morrell lived here 1915–28. The house needed a great deal of work to make it habitable, but during the First World War and after, there were many Bloomsbury visitors. Sold summer 1928. The grounds are now a popular summer opera venue (box office: 01865 361636, or see www.garsingtonopera. org). (See pp. 23 and 109–10.)

## Charleston Farmhouse (photo on p. 76)

*Near Firle, East Sussex;* 🚌 *Berwick (2 miles), Lewes (6 miles)*
Vanessa Bell leased the house for herself, her children and Duncan Grant from 1916. Clive Bell lived mainly in London but paid frequent visits. This was 'Bloomsbury in Sussex', an unofficial gathering place for London-weary Bloomsberries. Vanessa, Duncan and Angelica decorated the interior in exuberant style. Maynard Keynes wrote *The Economic Consequences of the Peace* here in 1919. The house is now owned by the Charleston Trust and is open to the public (see p. 196)

## The Mill House

*Tidmarsh, Berkshire;* 🚌 *Pangbourne (1½ miles)*
Lytton Strachey and Carrington lived here 1917–24. Rent and maintenance costs were shared by fellow Bloomsberries Maynard Keynes, Saxon Sydney-Turner, Harry Norton and Lytton's brother Oliver, who each contributed £20 a year for the privilege of being able to spend weekends and holidays there. The six-bedroom house was attached to a water-mill and set in grounds of over an acre and a half. Now privately owned.

## The Round House

*Pipe Passage, Lewes;* 🚌 *Lewes (½ mile)*
Virginia Woolf bought this picturesque house, part of a windmill built in 1802,

*Monk's House, Rodmell*

on impulse in June 1919. Leonard was less enthusiastic about its merits, however, and the Woolfs never lived here, moving instead to Monk's House in Rodmell.

### Monk's House

*Rodmell, East Sussex;* 🚌 *Lewes (4 miles), Southease (1½ miles)*
Virginia and Leonard Woolf spent lengthy periods here from August 1919 until their deaths on 28 March 1941 and 14 August 1969 respectively. The house, contrary to popular belief, came by its name only when put on sale in 1919. Virginia often wrote here, in a writing lodge in the large back garden, and Leonard became a keen gardener.

Now owned by the National Trust (see p. 189).

### Ham Spray (photo on p. 61)

*Ham, Wiltshire;* 🚌 *Bedwyn (3 miles), Hungerford (4 miles)*
Lytton Strachey purchased the house for himself, Carrington and Ralph Partridge for £2,300 in the summer of 1924. There were many visitors from Bloomsbury, as well as the lovers of all three. Lytton and Carrington both died here in 1932 (see p. 62), after which Ralph Partridge and Frances Marshall married and lived here until Ralph's death in 1960. Frances sold the house the following year. Now privately owned.

## Bloomsbury Servants

All Bloomsberries depended on one or two live-in servants to cook and clean, though not a whole team to run their households as in the Victorian days. Nevertheless Virginia thought her life dominated by servant problems. She wrote numerous letters and diary entries about servants, complaining about their behaviour, planning how to get rid of them, looking for new ones or loaning them to Vanessa. In this era, the private life of the servant, formerly invisible, was beginning to encroach upon that of the employer. Virginia noticed, even if Duncan did not, that his cleaning-lady Mrs Filmer (a name later used in *Mrs Dalloway*) was often inebriated. It was beginning to be apparent to employers such as Woolf that servants had private lives and private emotions. They differed in only two ways from the 'upper classes': they were uneducated, and they were poor. In her 1929 diary Virginia recorded that Annie Thompsett, who became the Monk's House cook, kept herself and her toddler on barely more than Virginia spent on cigarettes, sweets and local bus fares.

That Virginia had some understanding of the servant's lot is demonstrated elsewhere in her writing. Crosby in *The Years* is her most sustained portrait of a servant of the late nineteenth and early twentieth century. Crosby has no real life of her own and is emotionally dependent on the Pargiter family as they are dependent on her for their physical well-being. *Flush* also features a servant prominently. In the notes to this book Woolf suggests that Elizabeth Barrett's maid, Lily Wilson, deserves a biography of her own if enough information can be found. (Margaret Forster took up this suggestion in her novel *Lady's Maid* nearly sixty years later.) Woolf recognized that children have a closer relation to servants than do adults: she remembers in 'A Sketch of the Past' how she and the other children used to lower a basket on a string from the night nursery to the kitchen window. The cook, Sophie Farrell, would load it up with leftovers if she was in a good mood; if not, she would cut the string. While talking about 'Character in Fiction' (*Essays* 3) Virginia highlights the difference between the Victorian and the Georgian servant. In her mother's era, the cook stayed in the dark basement, hardly ever to be seen above ground level. (At Hyde Park Gate, a maid once dared to complain to Julia Stephen that their quarters were like hell, and was sent back to them in disgrace.) In contrast, in the reign of George V the cook wanders freely through the house, asking for fashion advice.

## The Woolfs' Servants

Sophia Farrell, a cook, usually called Sophy or Sophie, had started working at a young age for Julia Stephen. After the deaths of Julia and Leslie she went to Gordon Square with her young charges. When Vanessa married she went to Fitzroy Square to look after Virginia and Adrian, judging that Virginia needed her more, then to Adrian at 50 Gordon Square, then to Vanessa at the same address. She also worked for George and Margaret Duckworth, and for Margaret's sister, Lady Victoria Herbert. The Pargiter family's attitude to Crosby in *The Years* reflects the mix of irritation, gratitude and compassion that the younger Stephens felt for Sophie.

Nelly Boxall and Lottie Hope were Roger Fry's servants, along with another maid, a governess for the children and a gardener, with his sister Joan as general housekeeper. Nelly and Lottie were employed by the Woolfs in February 1916 as cook and maid respectively. In 1917 they cost the Woolfs £76 1s 8d (Leonard Woolf, *Beginning Again*, p. 232). The servant–mistress relationship was anything but easy – over the years there were arguments, threats and tears; Virginia said that her dealings with Nelly would fill a book. Nelly was with the Woolfs until 1930, when, after handing in her notice (as she had done several times before), she

was finally let go, much to Virginia's relief. Later (1934) she worked for actor Charles Laughton. Lottie went to Adrian and Karin Stephen in 1924 until they sacked her for stealing in 1930. But two years later Clive Bell took her on as cook at 50 Gordon Square, and from there she went to Charleston in 1939.

## The Bells' Servants

Mary Wilson at first seemed the perfect housemaid for 50 Gordon Square – helpful, tolerant and good-natured, liked by everyone. Then a series of calamities befell her loved ones – telegrams and letters arrived with news of the deaths of her mother, father and sweetheart, and the serious

illness of her brother. Mary was taken to hospital suffering from stress. Two letters arrived, purportedly from Mary's mother, but, according to Mary, in her brother's handwriting. Correspondence with Wilson family friends confirmed that he had lost his mind under the stress of losing both parents. Mary became irrational and had tantrums, and Vanessa decided that she must leave. Another servant was sent to escort her to meet a friend, but Mary absconded. In her absence, the mystery was solved – the letters, telegrams and phone messages were all traced back to Mary. Her parents were alive and well – her story was the product of a fertile but disturbed mind.

Grace Germany came to the Bells soon after Mary's departure. She started as a rather inept housemaid at sixteen and by the time she retired fifty years later had become an invaluable cook and housekeeper at Charleston. An attractive and adaptable young woman, she accompanied Vanessa and the children to Cassis in the 1920s, and took French lessons with Angelica. In 1929, when Angelica went away to school, Vanessa moved into a London studio at 8 Fitzroy Street and Grace, living nearby at 50 Gordon Square, cooked her meals. In 1934 Grace married Walter Higgens and was made housekeeper at Charleston. Their son was born the following year. Walter was employed as the Charleston gardener, and was a great help in augmenting wartime rations of fruit and vegetables. Grace was regarded as of the Bell family: at Vanessa's burial in 1961, there were only four mourners: Duncan Grant, Quentin and Angelica Bell – and Grace.

## Read On ...

Virginia Woolf: Life and London: A Biography of Place, by Jean Moorcroft Wilson, London: Cecil Woolf, 1987

The Hidden Houses of Virginia Woolf and Vanessa Bell, by Vanessa Curtis, London: Robert Hale, 2005

'Where Virginia Woolf Lived in London' and 'Virginia Woolf's Holiday Homes in the Country' by Stuart N. Clarke, 2000–1, www.virginiawoolfsociety.co.uk/vw_res.london.htm and www.virginiawoolfsociety.co.uk/vw_res.holiday.htm

Mrs Woolf and the Servants, by Alison Light, London: Fig Tree, 2007 (Penguin)

'The Strange Story of Mary Elizabeth Wilson', by Vanessa Bell, Charleston Magazine, Issue 3, Summer/Autumn 1991, pp. 5–15

# The Setting Sun: Bloomsbury in the 1930s

· · · · · · · · · · · ·

## Virginia Woolf

Virginia Woolf's novels of the 1930s, *The Waves* (1931) and *The Years* (1937), were a quantum leap from the high-spirited *Orlando*, her previous novel. Both demonstrate the extent to which Woolf was still experimenting with her style. On the non-fiction side, the 1930s yielded the second collection of essays under the title of *The Common Reader* (1932), the anti-war feminist treatise, *Three Guineas* (1938), and Virginia's only biography, of her old friend and Vanessa's former lover, Roger Fry (1940). There were the more light-hearted writings as well, to

*Virginia Woolf and her niece Angelica Bell, aged thirteen, in 1932*

which she turned for amusement: *Flush* (1933), a 'biography' of Elizabeth Barrett Browning's spaniel, and a major revision of *Freshwater*, a comic play that she had first written in 1923.

In her private life, the heat had gone out of the 'affair' with Vita Sackville-West, but a new friend and admirer appeared – Ethel Smyth, the composer and suffragette, who had read and admired *A Room of One's Own*, and asked to meet its author. It was a late-flowering friendship – Virginia was forty-eight and Ethel seventy-one when they met in 1930.

But age had not dimmed Ethel's passions. In her fifties she had been a friend, perhaps lover, of Emmeline Pankhurst, and had written 'The March of the Women', which became the anthem of the Women's Social and Political Union. Ethel's love for Virginia was devoted, but a little heavy handed. Virginia's response was warm but with a touch of ridicule of this uncompromising and energetic elderly woman, who blundered into Virginia's home asking dozens of questions and relating at length the story of her musical career. With her frequent demands for love and sympathy, Ethel was not the easiest of friends, but her beliefs and her behaviour fired Virginia's feminist anger, and much of *Three Guineas* and *The Years* were influenced by her (for more on Ethel Smyth, see pp. 112 and 167).

Against this new friendship there were painful losses.

## Bloomsbury Deaths

By the early 1930s most Bloomsberries had reached their half-century. Virginia Woolf, fifty on 25 January 1932, had begun to talk of herself as middle-aged in her thirties – now she felt 'elderly'. But the loss of friends of her own age was entirely unexpected. The first was Lytton Strachey, who died of stomach cancer in 1932; close behind came the suicide of Carrington, aged thirty-eight (see p. 62). Two years later, Roger Fry had a fall and died of the complications. He was older than most Bloomsberries at sixty-eight, but still possessed a vigorous intellectual curiosity and continued to

be an inspiration to his friends. He and Vanessa Bell had remained good friends since the end of their love affair, and his death was a great loss to her. Then in July 1937 came a tragedy on a par with the deaths of Thoby Stephen and Rupert Brooke – Vanessa's elder son, Julian Bell, who had volunteered as an ambulance driver in the Spanish Civil War, was fatally wounded by shrapnel. He was twenty-nine. Vanessa was devastated and felt she would never be happy again. Julian had been her favourite child. He could do no wrong in her eyes (despite the moral ambiguity of his numerous love affairs) and he had confided to her the intimate details of his life. Virginia was a great solace to her sister, but such was Vanessa's reserve that her thanks had to be relayed to Virginia through Vita Sackville-West. In tribute to Julian, and in spite of their private opinion of the quality of his writing, the Woolfs'

published in 1938 *Julian Bell: Essays, Poems and Letters.*

Also during 1937 Ottoline Morrell had an incapacitating stroke. Despite Virginia's caricaturing of Ottoline's romantic view of life, she had a genuine affection for her. The two became closer after 1928 when Ottoline's Gower Street gatherings became smaller and more intimate, and she had an operation for cancer of the jaw. The onset of Ottoline's ill-health brought out Virginia's more sympathetic side. After Ottoline's death in April 1938 (according to her biographer Miranda Seymour, the result of her doctor wrongly prescribing a dangerous new drug), her husband Philip asked Virginia to write an obituary for *The Times.* Virginia disliked writing obituaries but agreed on this occasion, and described Ottoline's strange mixture of splendour and absurdity. (For more on Ottoline Morrell, see pp. 109–10.)

CAPSULE

# *The Waves* (1931)

· · · · · · · · · · ·

*The Waves* is considered by many critics to be Virginia Woolf's finest achievement, the peak of her experimental method. It is not an easy book to read and impossible to skim. It is a book about 'everything'; primarily Life (with a capital L) and with sub-themes including friendship, fear, love, loss and death.

Virginia considered calling her novels 'elegies', but this has a more elegiac quality than all the others. It is lyrical to the point of poetry, the passage of the sun across the sky accompanying the passing lives of seven individuals.

## Origins

Virginia decided that her novel would not be a story in the traditional sense: 'this appalling narrative business of the realist; getting on from lunch to dinner: it is false, unreal, merely conventional' (*Diary* 3, 28 Nov 1928). It was a difficult book to write, radical in form, and very vague in Virginia's mind to begin with. Originally called 'The Moths', the novel was suggested by a letter from Vanessa Bell in Cassis dated 3 May 1927, which told of moths besieging the house at night-time. The inter-connected episodes in the new novel were to be punctuated by the arrival of moths, but as it evolved the rhythm of the waves assumed primacy. Much redrafting and cutting was necessary before she was happy with the result. Perhaps a total of 2,000 copies would be sold, she thought – in fact 6,500 were sold in the first three weeks.

> Why admit any thing to literature that is not poetry?
> (*Diary* 3, 28 Nov 1928)

## Plot Summary

A description of the 'plot' of *The Waves* does not give an adequate idea of the

lyricism and structure that are its chief attributes. In common with many of Woolf's novels, the storyline is not of primary importance.

The sun rises over the sea. Bernard, Susan, Rhoda, Neville, Jinny and Louis are children; each makes different observations about his or her world. Bernard comforts Susan, who is upset at seeing Jinny kiss Louis. In the schoolroom, Louis feels self-conscious about his accent, Rhoda about her inability to do arithmetic. All except Rhoda, finishing her sums, and Neville, who is 'delicate', are taken for a walk. They are given a bath and put to bed.

The sun mounts higher. The girls are sent away to school, where they play tennis, think about their relation to one another and dream of home (Susan) or love (Jinny and Rhoda). The boys go to another school, where they listen to Bernard's inconclusive stories and watch Percival, the schoolboy hero, play cricket. The children leave school and travel home by train.

The sun is still rising. Bernard and Neville are at university. Bernard's stories are longer, more involved. Neville, who intends to be a great poet, is still in love with Percival. Louis, a city clerk, lunches alone in a restaurant. Susan, in the countryside, is in her element; Jinny too, at a smart London party. Rhoda, at the same party, tries to hide behind the curtain.

Midday approaches. The friends, in their mid-twenties, gather for dinner in London with Percival, who is going to India. Bernard is engaged. The friends think about their childhood, each other and Percival.

It is midday. Percival has been thrown from a horse and killed; Neville is distraught. Bernard wants to talk of Percival with Jinny. Rhoda is on the edge of breakdown.

The sun begins its descent. The friends are in their thirties. Louis appreciates the orderliness of business. He and Rhoda are lovers; Susan is a wife and mother.

Neville's fame grows; Jinny has a string of lovers.

The sun descends further. Bernard, in Rome, knows that he will not fulfil his potential. Susan, secure in family life, has fulfilled hers. Neville has mellowed. Louis is prosperous, but Rhoda has left him and gone to Andalusia.

The sun sinks lower. The friends, middle-aged, gather at Hampton Court. They compare their lives. Jinny lives for clothes and parties, Susan for her family, Neville for his poetry. Rhoda can hide her fear of life, but the fear is there.

It is evening. An elderly Bernard 'sums up' the friends' lives.

> For this is not one life; nor do I always know if I am man or woman, Bernard or Neville, Louis, Susan, Jinny, or Rhoda – so strange is the contact of one with another.
>
> (*The Waves*, final section)

*Waves, Porthminster beach*

## Sources

The 'speakers' in *The Waves* can be viewed as six different characters or as six aspects of the same character. All reflect a part of Virginia, even when they appear to be based on someone else.

Bernard is tolerant and inclusive, a unifying and reassuring presence, though far from practical. He is a mix of Roger Fry (who lived in Bernard Street in his later years) and Desmond MacCarthy, the wordsmith who could not bring his skill to full fruition. The storyteller in him is also, of course, Virginia herself.

The name 'Jinny' is a variant of 'Ginny', one of Virginia's childhood names, and represents her party-going, sociable side, with a dash of glitz from Clive Bell's lover Mary Hutchinson, or Kitty Maxse, the model for Clarissa Dalloway (see p. 87). The sensual Jinny lives in the body, daydreaming of pretty dresses and heads turned in her direction.

In contrast to her, the nervy and highly strung Neville lives in the intellect. He adores Percival as Lytton Strachey adored a string of handsome young men, and admires Catullus, to whose poetry Clive Bell compared Lytton's verse. In his mind an apple tree is linked with a dead man, an incident that echoes Virginia imbuing an apple tree with her feelings about a Mr Valpy's suicide in 'A Sketch of the Past'. Neville's name possibly derives from Neville Bulwer-Lytton, the son of Lord Lytton, after whom Lytton Strachey was named.

Nature-loving Susan has violent but hidden passions, and feels herself only at ease with her family. Her possessive love for her children, and touches such as her hatred of linoleum identify her with Vanessa Bell (Grace Higgens had to put up with a cold stone floor at Charleston!).

Rhoda is uncomfortable in the company of the others. There is a subtle lesbianism in her portrayal: she has a crush on her teacher, Miss Lambert, and her affair with Louis does not satisfy her. Unlike Neville's, her longings remain hidden and unfulfilled. She is associated with the sea and water in general; her inability to cross a puddle, like Neville's apple tree, is a Woolfian 'moment of being' (see *Diary* 3, 30 Sep 1926). Her suicide in the novel also identifies her with Virginia, who had already made two suicide attempts.

Louis, whose father is a Brisbane banker, is neat, orderly and precise, like the Woolfs' friend T.S. Eliot, whose work they admired and published. Louis feels foreign, isolated, and sees into the brutality that lies beneath the surface. He is the youngest and at one remove from the group; he shares these characteristics with Adrian Stephen.

A friend of the group, but never speaking, Percival is a shadowy Thoby

Stephen character, an extension of Jacob Flanders from *Jacob's Room*. He is the typical schoolboy hero: confident, handsome and good at sport. The epithet 'monolithic' is used, as it was used by Thoby's friends, to describe him. He dies at twenty-five; Thoby died at twenty-six. Percival would have been a judge, thinks Bernard, the same profession that Virginia imagined for her brother in 'A Sketch of the Past'.

## Themes

### Life

As suggested above, there is a single theme in this novel – life. The structure and content are simultaneously very simple and very complex. The stages of the characters' lives are symbolized by the position of the sun in the sky, and the tide going in and out. Each of the nine sections is preceded by a description of the changing view over the sea as the sun rises and sets.

The lives of the six speakers weave in and out, with Bernard – the storyteller, the phrasemaker – having the last word. All six can be regarded as a single being: they have, externally, distinct characteristics and behaviour, but inside they are all unsure of their place in the group and in the world. They echo one another's phrases and experiences. Only Percival, who is admired by all for his confident grasp of life, does not have a voice, and his inner life remains a mystery.

Rhoda is the embodiment of negativity and annihilation; with symbolic logic she kills herself. Bernard stands for the life force and for continuity; he observes everything, large or small, and imagines what he cannot see, making up stories. But by the end of the novel, he has run out of words, giving rise to one of the most exquisitely lyrical passages in the English language:

What is the phrase for the moon? And the phrase for love? By what name are we to call death? I do not know. I need a little language such as lovers use, words of one syllable such as children speak ... I need a howl; a cry.

(*The Waves*, final section)

## Bloomsbury and the Second World War

Bloomsbury's attitude to Adolf Hitler and the Nazis was very different from its response to the First World War (see pp. 143–6). It was clear to many that Europe was becoming dangerously unstable, despite the best efforts of the League of Nations. Leonard Woolf, in the introduction to *The Intelligent Man's Way to Prevent War* (1933) warned that Europe was descending into barbarism and that a crisis greater than the 1914–18 war was approaching. The Woolfs went to Europe to judge the situation for themselves in 1935.

The Bloomsberries that still lived (Lytton Strachey, Roger Fry and Ottoline Morrell had died in the 1930s) did not identify themselves as pacifists any longer, although they considered war a last resort. Hitler,

they acknowledged, was a megalo-maniac who posed a worldwide threat and had to be stopped. By 1939 most Bloomsberries were too old to be called up, but many had a response to the war, though it was much more complex this time.

- **Virginia Woolf** gives her anti-war opinions in *Three Guineas*. She committed suicide during a period of mental illness in 1941 (see pp. 179–80).
- **Leonard Woolf**'s name was on the Gestapo blacklist because he was a Jew, as was Virginia's, for being married to a Jew, and they made a suicide pact in the event of invasion by the Nazis. He considered joining the Home Guard in 1940, but instead acted as a fire-watcher.
- **Adrian Stephen** travelled to Berlin to rescue a German friend from the Nazis just before the war. Witnessing their brutality, he, like the Woolfs, planned to commit suicide if Britain was invaded.
- **Clive Bell** liaised with the British Council to arrange for valuable works of art to be sent abroad to avoid bomb damage. He joined the Home Guard night patrols, with Duncan Grant and Quentin Bell, watching for signs of invasion.
- **Quentin Bell** was rejected for war work because he had had tuberculosis, but he took on farm work at Tilton (where Maynard Keynes lived), and joined the Home Guard with his father.
- **Duncan Grant** worked on naval commissions for the War Artists' Advisory Committee from the end of 1939.
- **Bunny Garnett** worked in intelligence for the Air Ministry. In March 1940 his first wife, Ray, née Marshall, died of cancer; two years later he married Angelica Bell.
- **Saxon Sydney-Turner** was still working at the Treasury in London during the Second World War. He often spent weekends with Frances and Ralph Partridge at Ham Spray in Wiltshire, once arriving covered with dust from a bomb dropped near his flat.
- **Mark Gertler** committed suicide on 23 June 1939, but this was more to do with tuberculosis, depression and his lack of success selling paintings than with the impending war.

**Read On ...**

*Virginia Woolf*, by Hermione Lee, London: Chatto and Windus, 1996 (see ch. 39, 'War')

*The Journey Not the Arrival Matters*, by Leonard Woolf, London: Hogarth Press, 1969

# Outside Looking in: What Other People Thought of Bloomsbury

· · · · · · · · · · ·

## Admirers

Bloomsbury's admirers were often friends, therefore many of them are considered fringe members, such as Ottoline Morrell (who was perhaps Bloomsbury's greatest admirer), Vita Sackville-West or T.S. Eliot; or else they had their own 'set', such as the Neo-pagans and Sibyl Colefax's Chelsea friends (see pp. 22–6 and 108–12). Others are given below.

### The 'Cropheads'

Carrington and her daringly short-haired friends – Barbara Hiles, Dorothy Brett, Alix Sargant-Florence and Faith Henderson – kept Bloomsbury in touch with the younger generation. Virginia, who didn't take them entirely seriously, called them the 'cropheads' or the 'Bloomsbury bunnies'. Carrington became a junior Bloomsbery herself when she began an unconventional relationship with Lytton Strachey. The others were slightly in awe of the older Bloomsberries and emulated their behaviour and lifestyle. When Barbara Hiles married Faith's brother Nicholas Bagenal in 1918 she planned to keep Saxon Sydney-Turner as a lover, much as Vanessa had balanced her life with Clive Bell and Duncan Grant. But Vanessa's situation had come about by chance and she considered Barbara's plan extremely ill-judged. Still, Barbara and Saxon remained close friends for the rest of their lives.

Dorothy Brett parted company with Bloomsbury when she became a friend of D.H. Lawrence in the 1920s. Alix Sargant-Florence married Lytton's younger brother James Strachey. Faith Henderson's husband Hubert was the editor of the *Nation & Athenaeum*, for which Leonard Woolf was the literary editor and Maynard Keynes part owner, so Faith saw the Bloomsberries intermittently.

### The YMWs (Young Male Writers)

This group included John Lehmann, who bought Virginia's share of the Hogarth Press, and W.H. Auden's circle (Stephen Spender, Christopher Isherwood, Louis MacNeice and Cecil Day Lewis, all of whom had work published by the Hogarth Press). They admired Bloomsbury's literature and its politics. Most were left-wing, even more so than their predecessors, and supported the Republicans in the Spanish Civil War

Hugh Walpole, a bestselling novelist in his own right, was a great fan of Virginia Woolf's writing. He recognized that her experimental fiction was on a higher level, complaining that his chauffeur loved his books but intellectuals such as the Bloomsberries hated them. When Woolf won the Femina–Vie Heureuse prize for *To the Lighthouse* in 1928, Walpole presented it to her.

### Enemies

Many of those who were outside the Bloomsbury circle saw it as a self-serving clique, snobbish and elitist, supporting each other but criticizing everyone else. Though this was far from the truth (for example, Virginia Woolf had a public disagreement with Desmond MacCarthy through the pages of the *New Statesman* in October 1920, and was highly critical privately of Lytton Strachey's writing as well as Clive Bell's behaviour), this reputation stuck and still survives today.

### Percy Wyndham Lewis

The caricatures of Ottoline Morrell in novels by D.H. Lawrence, Osbert Sitwell, Gilbert Cannan and Aldous Huxley have already been mentioned (see p. 23). But there were crueller portrayals of Bloomsbury, such as Wyndham Lewis's satirical and venomous novel *The Apes of God* (1930), which presents a horrific version of the social pretensions of 1920s art and culture. Lewis, an artist who co-founded the Vorticists with Ezra Pound, had worked briefly for Roger Fry's Omega Workshops in 1913. He had conceived a powerful grudge against Fry after a commission that he thought belonged to him was fulfilled by the Omega. He was a passionate and persistent enemy, attacking Fry in his Vorticist journal *Blast*, and by the time he wrote *The Apes of God* his hostility had spread to include the rest of Bloomsbury. In 1934 he published a book of critical essays, *Men Without Art*,

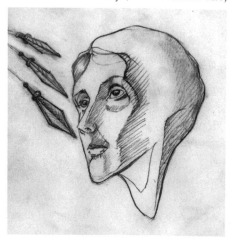

that devoted a chapter to condemning Virginia Woolf's writing as passé. Still grieving for the death of Roger Fry, and suffering from writer's block, Woolf agonized over his criticisms for two days. In her defence, poet Stephen Spender, in a review of Lewis's book in *The Spectator*, wrote that Lewis had allowed his literary criticism to become tainted by personal malice.

### Roy Campbell

Another attack appears in Lewis's friend Roy Campbell's long poem, *The Georgiad* (1931), written partly out of revenge on Vita Sackville-West for her affair with Roy's wife Mary. He disapproved of Bloomsbury's supposed promiscuity, its homosexuality, its atheistical outlook (Campbell was undergoing a spiritual crisis which ended four years later in his espousal of the Catholic faith) and its influence in literary circles. He made many enemies with his uncompromising satire – as in Lewis's works, the personal vindictiveness is plain to see.

### Rupert Brooke

Originally a friend of Lytton Strachey's brother James, who had idolized him since boyhood, Brooke turned against Bloomsbury after 1911, when he suspected Lytton Strachey of conspiring against him. He began to refer collectively to all Bloomsberries as 'the Jews', although only Leonard Woolf was Jewish. Brooke's friend Jacques Raverat was also anti-semitic but later grew out of it, and became a favourite correspondent of Virginia's in the 1920s.

### D.H. Lawrence

Lawrence, after a visit from David Garnett and Francis Birrell in 1915, complained that Garnett's homosexual Bloomsbury friends gave him nightmares of black beetles. Like Rupert Brooke he had a deeply ingrained fear of homosexuality, and his circle, including John Middleton Murry and Katherine Mansfield, remained at one remove from Bloomsbury. Though Katherine admired Virginia's writing, Murry did not. (For more on Lawrence's circle, see p. 112; for Lawrence's Bloomsbury caricatures in *Women in Love*, see pp. 187–8.)

### The Leavises

Influential literary critics F.R. and Queenie Leavis were among those who thought Bloomsbury snobbish, and propounded their views in their journal *Scrutiny*. Queenie Leavis, born a couple of social classes lower down the scale, was especially critical of Virginia Woolf, once joking that she was so undomesticated that she wouldn't know which end of the cradle to stir. In a hostile review of *Three Guineas* Queenie called Woolf's conclusions 'silly' and her attitudes 'nasty'.

# The Years (1937)

· · · · · · · · · · ·

## Origins

*The Years* sprang out of Woolf's 1931 talk, 'Professions for Women'. She planned a novel based on dated chapters punctuated with narrative essays about the lives of women during that era. Among the titles considered for the book were 'Here & Now' and 'The Pargiters', but it became *The Years* in 1935. As it grew sprawling and unmanageable, Virginia realized it would be better divided into fiction and non-fiction; the latter part became *Three Guineas* (for more on 'Professions for Women' and *Three Guineas*, see pp. 139–42).

## Plot Summary

The saga-like novel covers several generations of the Pargiter family and their friends. It is divided up into eleven sections, headed 1880, 1891, 1907, 1908, 1910, 1911, 1913, 1914, 1917, 1918 and Present Day. All begin with a description of the season or month – these were added at a fairly late stage in the writing and echo the 'prologue' sections in *The Waves*. Each chapter describes events in the lives of three related families: Colonel Abel Pargiter, his wife Rose, their children Eleanor, Morris, Edward, Milly, Delia, Martin and Rose, and the servant,

*Oxford seen from Magdalen Tower*

Crosby; Digby Pargiter, his wife Eugénie and daughters Magdalena (Maggie) and Sara; and the Malones, cousins of Mrs Rose Pargiter.

The novel opens in the spring of 1880. Colonel Pargiter visits his mistress, while at home his children make tea. Mrs Pargiter dies. Edward is at Oxford, where the Malone family entertains guests. The Malones hear of Rose Pargiter's death, and the funeral is held.

A decade later, Kitty is married to Lord Lasswade, and Milly to Edward's friend Hugh Gibbs. Edward is a scholar, Morris a lawyer. Eleanor runs the Pargiter household and is involved in social reform. Delia's hero, Parnell, dies. Abel visits Eugénie and her children.

It is the reign of Edward VII. Digby, Eugénie and Maggie are at a party. On her mother's arrival home Sara begs for romantic stories from her past, but Digby calls for his wife. A year later, Digby and Eugénie have died and their house is up for sale. Eleanor thinks how inaccurately Digby's obituary describes him. Martin and Rose recall a childhood quarrel.

Rose lunches with Maggie and Sara, now poor and living in a rented flat. Sara accompanies Rose to a meeting; also attending are Eleanor, Martin and Kitty. Sara describes the meeting to Maggie and they hear of the king's death.

Eleanor, back from a trip abroad, stays with Morris's family. Morris's children, North and Peggy, are there, and his wife Celia makes predictable remarks.

Abel Pargiter dies, and Eleanor sells the family home. Crosby goes into lodgings, taking the family dog, which dies soon afterwards. She

visits Martin, but he is impatient for her departure.

A few months before the outbreak of the First World War, Martin lunches with Sara and they meet Maggie, who has married a Frenchman and had a baby. While Sara sleeps Martin confides in Maggie about his love life. He goes on to Kitty Lasswade's party and talks to a young girl. After her guests depart, Kitty leaves for the country.

Eleanor dines with Maggie and Renny. Sara and her friend Nicholas are also there. There is an air raid and they take shelter in the cellar.

Crosby grumbles to herself about having to clean up after a 'dirty foreigner' in her retirement. Guns sound, although the Armistice has been announced.

Present day, summer. The family gathers for Delia's party. Eleanor is excited. Peggy is depressed and quarrels with North. Kitty arrives. The older people talk of Home Rule, war, women's suffrage. Thinking of how 'to live differently', North bumps into his uncle Edward. Nicholas makes a speech, and Rose and Martin, coming to listen, start up their old quarrel. The younger people dance upstairs, and Peggy and North resolve their differences. Kitty feels

> 'Look, Maggie,' [Sara] whispered, turning to her sister, 'Look!' She pointed at the Pargiters, standing in the window.
>
> The group in the window ... wore a statuesque air for a moment, as if they were carved in stone.
>
> (*The Years*, 'Present Day')

in need of Nicholas's wisdom, and North of Edward's. Two children sing an incomprehensible song. At sunrise, the guests prepare to depart. At the window, the older Pargiters are framed in a tableau for a moment. Eleanor sees a taxi draw up to a neighbouring house and a young couple get out. A new day dawns.

## Sources

Colonel Pargiter is not Leslie Stephen, but his reaction to his wife's death is based on Leslie's to Julia's death – he cries her name with arms outstretched, like Mr Ramsay in *To the Lighthouse*. Eleanor, the eldest daughter, has a social conscience like Stella Duckworth's, but unlike poor Stella lives on into an adventurous and contented old age. Rose, the youngest daughter, has Virginia's sensitivity and a brush with sexual abuse as a child, but is largely based on Ethel Smyth, the suffragette and composer who Virginia got to know in 1930 (see pp. 154–5). Ethel taught Emmeline Pankhurst how to throw missiles through the windows of prominent politicians, and both women were imprisoned in 1912 for doing so. Rose is sent to prison for the same misdemeanour in the 1914 section of *The Years*. Her love–hate relationship with Martin mirrors Virginia's with her brother Adrian or with Clive Bell. Martin, like Clive, attends smart parties and has a series of love affairs into his sixties.

Sara and Maggie are alternate versions of Virginia and Vanessa. 'Orphaned' as young women, they feel no sentimentality or bitterness about their evident poverty. Sara has other elements of Virginia: her asymmetric body is a physical manifestation of Virginia's mental problems and, like Virginia, she is eccentric and other-worldly, with a quixotic and fantastic turn to her conversation.

North's feelings of strangeness on coming back to a country from which he has long been absent reflect Leonard Woolf's on returning from Ceylon.

Edward's Oxford experiences were inspired by Thoby's at Cambridge, and his ill-matched friends are loosely based on Lytton Strachey and Clive Bell. Milly, fussy and ingratiating, and the conventional Morris represent Woolf's Fisher relatives (the family of Julia Stephen's sister Mary Fisher and her husband Herbert, whose son William had condemned the *Dreadnought* Hoax).

Socialite Kitty Malone is chiefly Kitty Maxse, the model for Mrs Dalloway in the eponymous novel (see p. 87). Kitty's crush on her teacher Lucy Craddock recalls Fanny Wilmot's on Julia Craye in the story 'Moments of Being: "Slater's Pins Have No Points"'. But her straightforwardness and her love of gardening and the countryside recall Vita Sackville-West.

Small touches are also transplanted from real life. Eleanor's memory of a song sung by her old nurse Pippy ('Ron, ron, ron, et plon, plon, plon') is from Virginia's memory of Justine Nonon in 'A Sketch of the Past' (*Moments of Being*). Gossip from the Woolfs' Belgian landlady at 17 The Green, Mrs Le Grys, inspired part of the 1918 chapter, in which Crosby has to clean up after the count. Crosby is a portrait of Sophie Farrell, loyal servant of the Stephens (see p. 155).

## Themes

### Family Saga

The extended Pargiter family has long tentacles, like Virginia's own family, the Stephens, Duckworths and Fishers. At the opening of the novel, the family units seem separate and self-contained, later intermixing progressively (Edward has a youthful passion for Kitty; Abel visits his brother Digby's family) until in the final chapter a family party gathers them all together. More than fifty years have passed, and those whom we first saw as children – Maggie and Sara, North and Peggy – are approaching

### Women's Lives

Virginia's main aim in *The Years* was to tell the story of the lives of women. The prospects for Eleanor, from an upper-middle-class family, look unpromising to begin with, but after her father dies her life opens up into one of adventure and experience. She never marries but travels the world, and evidently has a substantial private income. Her cousin Sara, on the other hand, lives in cheerful poverty in a slum area with no discernible means of support. Sara's sister Maggie, having married, is slightly better off, but not much – she turns poverty into a bohemian lifestyle. Delia and Rose dedicate their lives to causes. Delia, a passionate devotee of Parnell and Irish Home Rule, marries an Irishman but is disappointed to find him a harmless British patriot instead of a dashing rebel. Rose becomes a suffragist and is sent to prison when she throws a brick through a window for the second time. Peggy has had the advantages of education that her aunt Rose and others fought for and has become a doctor, but she is not content. Introverted and depressed, she deprecates the achievements of

middle age. A few relatives merit only a mention. Peggy and North's brother, Charles, dies in the First World War; remembering this prompts Peggy's bitterness at seeing a statue of Edith Cavell, another war casualty. Maggie and Sara have three brothers whose names we never discover. The family network presented to the reader is much broader than it is deep: there are a lot of brothers, sisters and cousins, but the children of Milly, Delia, Maggie and Kitty are only briefly acknowledged and not woven into the fabric of the story.

> 'My dear Nell,' said Peggy, glancing up at her, 'how often have I told you? Doctors know very little about the body; absolutely nothing about the mind.'
>
> (*The Years*, 'Present Day'

science and suffers a kind of existential angst.

### Time and Progress

The relationships between the generations change between 1880 and the present. Abel Pargiter's life was a mystery to his children, who held him a little in awe. In the present day deference is gone; Eleanor is 'Nell' to her niece Peggy, who is impatient with her aunt's short attention span and forgetfulness. The mysteries of private life exist in a different form. After Abel's death Martin feels a little affronted that he was not entrusted with the secret of his father's mistress. Decades later Eleanor's life, with its broad geographical horizons, is a mystery to her relatives, as is that of North, who has been farming in Africa. Some things have not changed. In the 1880 section, Abel Pargiter sits in his club with men who talk of their experiences in the colonies in India and Africa. Subsequent generations – Martin, North – have similar colonial experiences.

Other repetitions are registered in Rose and Martin's eternal quarrelling and in Nicholas and Eleanor's topics of conversation: when North relates their talk to Sara, she is able guess accurately how it ends. Peggy acknowledges that each person has a particular route in their brain by which they think the same thoughts and say the same words. North sees that Patrick is doing just this in his nostalgia for the British Empire. But in a neat reversal of history, the most perceptive of the younger generation are North and Peggy, the children of the conservative Morris, and Celia, whose trite observations in 1911 were silently predicted by Eleanor. This concept of circularity is further explored in Woolf's next and final novel, *Between the Acts* (see pp. 181–6).

Technology, the chief measure of progress in the twentieth century, is highlighted in the final chapter. A basket-mender passes as North parks his new sports car – ancient and modern, juxtaposed. The telephone bell interrupts conversations and Peggy wonders whether in the future it will be possible to see the caller, anticipating the videophone or the webcam. Eleanor has a new shower bath that she shows off proudly to her nephew. She remembers seeing her first aeroplane and muses on what a difference air travel and other innovations – radio broadcasting, domestic hot water, electric lights – have made to the world.

# The Curtain Falls: Virginia Woolf, Mental Illness and Death

. . . . . . . . . . .

From her teenage years, Virginia Woolf suffered from a mental illness that manifested itself in a variety of physical and psychological symptoms: headaches, a rapid pulse rate, sleeplessness, refusal to eat, racing thoughts and an inability to concentrate. There were episodes of depression – despair, guilt and suicidal tendencies; and of mania – visual and auditory hallucinations, euphoria, irrational anger and unpredictable behaviour. Sometimes the episodes were short in duration – perhaps only a day or two of depression – and sometimes they could last for months, or even years. Since Virginia's mental condition affected her life and her work, and eventually prompted her death, it should be explored in detail.

### Diagnoses

A number of theories have been advanced about Virginia's illness. Current psychiatric thinking has it that she suffered from manic depression, or bipolar disorder, a state of chemical imbalance affecting about 1 per cent of the general population, in which the highs and lows of ordinary life are severely exaggerated. Today this can be treated to an extent, but a century ago Virginia's doctors diagnosed 'neurasthenia', a state of fatigue and depression covering a wide range of symptoms (the nearest modern equivalent is chronic fatigue syndrome). The only treatment

for the mind was food and rest. But for the *physical* symptoms, such as headaches and insomnia, there was a cornucopia of drugs available. Recent theories suggest that Virginia's medicines may have done more harm than good, producing a chemical dependency that created further 'symptoms'. And there were a number of different diagnoses: Virginia complained that the heart specialist diagnosed heart problems, the lung specialist diagnosed lung problems; in short, whatever the doctor's specialization, her illness fell within his area of expertise.

## Virginia's Major Breakdowns

### Depression, 1895

The first sign of what was to come was Virginia's prolonged depression after her mother's death in 1895. Virginia was thirteen years old. She could not sleep or eat and became thin and frail. This time there was no manic stage.

### The First Suicide Attempt, 1904

After her father's death in February 1904, Virginia suffered no immediate ill-effects. She travelled to Europe with her brothers and sister, but her behaviour was sometimes odd. Visiting Rodin's studio in Paris she was asked by the sculptor not to touch the unfinished work, and immediately did so, openly and deliberately. She admitted in letters that she was irritable and found it hard to concentrate on writing. On her return

home Virginia's condition grew into full-blown mania, with hallucinations, imaginary voices, violent behaviour and severe headaches. Under medical supervision at the house of her friend Violet Dickinson, she made her first suicide attempt, jumping from a window – fortunately, it was not high up, so her physical injuries were not serious. But her experience of this period of mental illness later fed into Septimus Warren Smith's shell-shock and suicide in *Mrs Dalloway*. While Vanessa, Thoby and Adrian moved into the new house at 46 Gordon Square, Virginia convalesced quietly with her aunt Caroline Emelia in Cambridge. It was the end of the year before she was well enough to go home.

### Two Years of Illness, 1913–15

The next episode was even longer and more severe, and almost ended with

Virginia's death before she had published a single book. Like her 1904 breakdown, the symptoms took some time to develop, but were probably triggered by nervous exhaustion at correcting the proofs of her first novel during May and June 1913. By July, when she had been married to Leonard Woolf for only eleven months, she was suffering from insomnia and stress, and was sent for a rest cure. But her condition worsened into violent mood swings and delusions of a conspiracy between Leonard and the doctors. Virginia's distrust of the medical profession is well known. It may have started with the premature deaths of her mother and half-sister, or with the misdiagnosed illness of her brother Thoby in 1906. It was certainly reinforced when Vanessa suffered a miscarriage in 1911, having been advised by her doctor that it was safe to travel to Turkey while pregnant, and was ineradi-

cably confirmed by her own treatment for mental and physical illness. It was during this period that she began to feel controlled by her doctors.

On 9 September 1913 the crisis came. Leonard, leaving Virginia in Adrian's room in Brunswick Square in the care of Ka Cox, went with Vanessa to consult a specialist about Virginia. In their absence Virginia made a second suicide attempt by taking an overdose of veronal, a sleeping drug. Ka phoned Leonard, who returned immediately. Fortunately Maynard Keynes's brother Geoffrey, a doctor, was lodging temporarily at Brunswick Square. He drove with Leonard at top speed to St Bartholomew's Hospital (where he was a house surgeon) for a stomach pump – his quick actions saved her life.

The following two months Virginia spent convalescing at her half-brother George Duckworth's house. Her

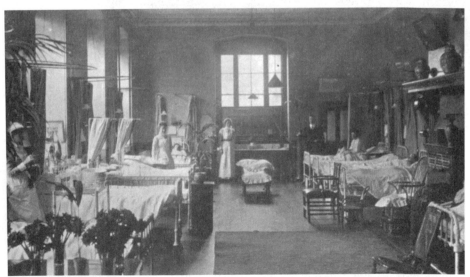

*St Bartholomew's Hospital, London*

breakdown, according to Leonard Woolf, lasted until the following summer. During the second half of 1914 Virginia's behaviour was normal, but then in early 1915 she had a relapse, with headaches and insomnia and hallucinations of her dead mother. Four nurses were engaged, against whom Virginia rebelled violently, and she began to chatter incessantly and incoherently, before falling eventually into unconsciousness. Like Orlando, she underwent a change during her coma – on awakening, she was much more subdued and recovered gradually over the next few months.

## Virginia and Freud

Some Woolf readers think it odd that Virginia never undertook psychotherapy, especially since Freud's influence was so strong in Bloomsbury. Not only did the Hogarth Press publish English translations of Freud's works, but Virginia's brother, sister-in-law and two friends became psychoanalysts in the Freudian mould.

However, there were two good reasons why Virginia was not psychoanalysed. First, she feared being 'cured' of her writing gift along with her mental instability; second, psychoanalysis was considered dangerous for anyone with suicidal tendencies.

## The Final Breakdown and Death

Between the 1913–15 episode and the one that was beginning when she killed herself in 1941, Virginia had no serious breakdowns. She had occasional depressions, some bordering on despair, but dragged herself back from the edge on each occasion. She even found some good in the spells of 'madness', believing that they spurred her creativity, and in her long periods of convalescence, which gave her the time to think and write.

Virginia's final breakdown began during the Second World War, and the air raids, restrictions, rationing and continual threat of invasion must have increased her depression. But there were other stresses and strains, including the aftermath of publishing *Roger Fry*; delving into her memories, not all of them pleasant, to write 'A Sketch of the Past'; and the completion of her novel *Between the Acts*.

During the last few months of 1940 there were ominous signs of instability. Virginia quarrelled with Vanessa and admitted to her diary that she was angrier than she had been for years. In a different mood, she euphorically described to Ethel Smyth how she had fallen into a water-filled hole in a flooded field. A fortnight later she became irrational and hostile, writing resentfully of the acquaintances that were 'leeches' on the Woolfs; John Lehmann, Leonard's partner at the Hogarth Press, was called a 'shark'. In February 1941, women overheard talking on a trip to Brighton were referred to as 'tarts' and 'slugs'. (One of the conversations inspired Virginia's last story, 'The Watering Place', and is transferred almost word-for-word from her diary, retaining the tone of distaste.)

In early March depression descended. One day, Leonard found Virginia wet and shaken after a walk, claiming that she had fallen into a ditch by accident, recalling the incident described to Ethel Smyth a few months earlier. By the 26th, Leonard was certain that she was teetering on the brink. He now faced an unbearable decision – whether to look after her himself or risk catapulting her into breakdown by imposing the strict regime of nurses and constant supervision. Proceeding cautiously, he persuaded Virginia to consult Octavia Wilberforce, a doctor friend. It seemed to him afterwards that Virginia was improving. But he was wrong. On the morning of 28 March, Virginia walked across the fields behind the house, weighted her pockets with stones and drowned herself in the river Ouse, having left letters for Leonard and Vanessa, the two people she loved most in the world, telling them that she feared the approach of a madness from which she would never recover. When Leonard found his letter on the mantelpiece he immediately went down to the river, fearing the worst. He found her walking-stick on the bank and alerted the police.

## Aftermath

Virginia was missing for nearly three weeks. On 18 April her body was spotted floating in the water by a group of children. The identification, inquest and cremation followed within three days, and Virginia's ashes were buried under one of the two elms in the Monk's House garden that had been named, by the Woolfs, after themselves – Leonard and Virginia. In the weeks following Virginia's disappearance and death, Leonard, an intensely private man, mourned alone but could not hide his red eyes and haggard appearance from friends. He was inundated with letters of sympathy and grief. These have been collected and published, and constitute a tribute to Virginia the friend and Virginia Woolf the writer (see *Afterwords* below).

---

### Read On ...

*'All That Summer She Was Mad': Virginia Woolf and Her Doctors*, by Stephen Trombley, London: Junction Books, 1981

*The Flight of the Mind: Virginia Woolf's Art and Manic-depressive Illness*, by Thomas C. Caramagno, Berkeley: University of California Press, 1992

*Virginia Woolf*, by Hermione Lee, London: Chatto and Windus, 1996 (see chs 10 and 40)

*Afterwords: Letters on the Death of Virginia Woolf*, ed. Sybil Oldfield, Edinburgh: Edinburgh University Press; New Brunswick, NJ: Rutgers University Press, 2005

# *Between the Acts* (1941)

· · · · · · · · · · ·

## Origins

Like her heroine, Miss La Trobe, when she completed a work Virginia always had the seed of an idea for a new one in her head. Frequently, she was working on several projects simultaneously. When she began writing her last novel (originally called 'Pointz Hall') on 2 April 1938, she was just beginning *Roger Fry* and was expecting the proofs of *Three Guineas*. The idea for the novel, minus the pageant that was to form the heart of the novel but otherwise surprisingly unchanged, appears in a diary entry:

'I' rejected: 'We' substituted ... we all life, all art, all waifs & strays – a rambling capricious but somehow unified whole – the present state of my mind? And English country; & a scenic old house – & a terrace where nursemaids walk? & people passing – & a perpetual variety & change from intensity to prose.

(*Diary* 5, 26 Apr 1938)

The pageant idea dates from August 1938. By the end of the year Virginia had written 120 pages and envisaged the book as a 'medley' (*Diary* 5, 19

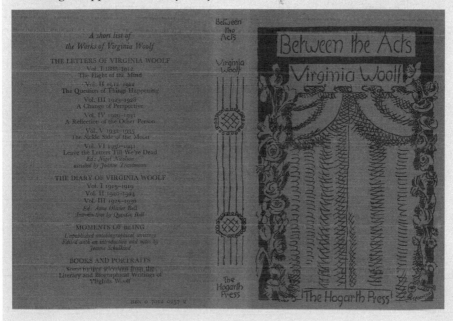

Dec 1938). Later it occurred to her that her diary was a gymnasium for her writing skills:

> Scraps, orts & fragments, as I said in PH. [Pointz Hall] which is now bubbling – I'm playing with words; & think I owe some dexterity to finger exercises here
> (*Diary* 5, 31 May 1940)

Virginia completed the novel on 23 November 1940 and revised it for the next three months. The title change to 'Between the Acts' was made on 26 February, just as Virginia descended into her final illness. On 27 March Virginia, suddenly gripped by an idea that her novel was worthless, wrote to John Lehmann, Leonard's partner in the Hogarth Press, asking him not to publish it. Leonard, believing after Virginia's death that the letter was written in the grip of illness, decided to go ahead with publication and the book appeared that summer.

## Plot Summary

On an evening in June 1939, Bartholomew Oliver, retired from the colonial service, sits talking with Mrs Haines, whose gentleman-farmer husband, Rupert, remains silent. Isa, Bart's daughter-in-law, enters.

The next morning, Lucy Swithin, Bart's widowed sister, reads about prehistoric times. Bart tries to amuse his small grandson but only succeeds in making him cry. Isa daydreams about Rupert Haines. In the library, Bart, Lucy and Isa talk about that afternoon's pageant; Lucy wonders whether it will rain.

The Olivers' lunch is interrupted by the lively Mrs Manresa. Her companion, William Dodge, is younger and more restrained. Isa's

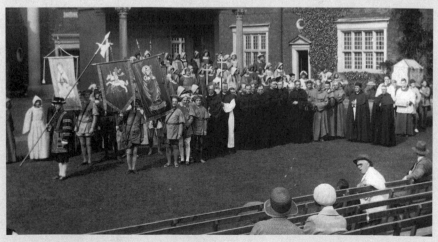

*Pageant, 1930s*

husband Giles, a stockbroker, arrives. They all go to watch Miss La Trobe's pageant.

The play begins, a history of England. Local citizens speak the lines and a faulty gramophone provides background melodies. The age of Chaucer is followed by that of Elizabeth I. A Shakespearean comedy of mistaken identity ensues, then there is an interval for tea. Isa, feeling an affinity with William, shows him round the greenhouse.

The pageant resumes with extended scenes from a Restoration play. During the next interval, Giles shows Mrs Manresa the greenhouse. Lucy, inspired by the play, thanks Miss La Trobe, who sees that her efforts are not being entirely wasted. When the pageant resumes, we are in the nineteenth century, stirring childhood reminiscences among the audience. There is a picnic scene from the 1860s, then a break in the action – unknown to the audience, this represents the present moment.

Mirrors reflect the spectators, who are uneasy, with the exception of Mrs Manresa, who unselfconsciously repairs her make-up. A disembodied voice speaks, then

the play is over. The vicar deduces a meaning, but aeroplanes interrupt him. He thanks Miss La Trobe, who is not present. The national anthem plays, then the audience scatters, talking animatedly about the pageant's meaning. Mrs Manresa and William Dodge drive off.

Miss La Trobe clears up her props and goes to the pub, where she contemplates her next play. At Pointz Hall, the Olivers talk about the play, then settle to reading or napping. Eventually, Isa and Giles are left alone together. They speak, and a new story begins.

## Sources

The pageant, not a well-known form today, was popular in the first half of the twentieth century. In 1934 and 1938 the Woolfs' friend E.M. Forster had written village pageants; the second of these, *England's Pleasant Land*, may have inspired Virginia to include a pageant in the novel she was writing, as the idea dates from around this time. Forster's play was published by the Woolfs in April 1940 under the Hogarth Press imprint, so it is certain that Virginia knew about it. She was also familiar with the

> Holding what? Tin cans? Bedroom candlesticks? Old jars? My dear, that's the cheval glass from the Rectory! And the mirror – that I lent her. My mother's. Cracked. What's the notion? Anything that's bright enough to reflect, presumably, ourselves?
>
> (*Between the Acts*)

village plays that were occasionally staged in Rodmell.

The patriarch of Pointz Hall, Bart Oliver, has in common with Leonard Woolf his ability to control dogs and his grasp of facts – Lucy and Isa may believe it is a hundred miles to the sea, but he knows it is only thirty-five. Lucy Swithin's mind is like Virginia's, moving swiftly from one thing to another, and proficient at conjuring up vivid scenes.

In August 1938, while writing the book, Virginia had a visit from Vita, bringing wine and a basket of peaches, as Mrs Manresa breezily arrives at Pointz Hall with her picnic basket. Mrs Manresa is not a simple portrait of Vita, but a mix of characters. In her desire for attention, there is a hint of Clive Bell; in her liking for lipstick and powder, a faint suggestion of Clive's paramour, Mary Hutchinson. Her name may have been suggested by the former home of Gerard Manley Hopkins, Manresa House, near Richmond Park; or by Manresa Road, off the King's Road, very close to where the MacCarthys and Sibyl Colefax lived. It also implies the quality of a 'man-eater'.

Miss La Trobe, the writer and director of the village pageant, may have been inspired by Vita's friend, the lesbian suffragist Edith Craig (daughter of Ellen Terry), who in 1909 had staged a pageant celebrating women's achievements. In 1929 she built a theatre in a barn at her home,

Smallhythe in Kent, and created the Barn Theatre Society, which Virginia was keen to join. Miss La Trobe, also a lesbian, carries hints of Virginia's friend the composer Ethel Smyth, who knew what it was like not to be taken seriously in her art.

The most mysterious character in the book is Rupert Haines, the gentleman-farmer. His name suggests Rupert Brooke, and Isa, who loves him, bears a physical resemblance to Ka Cox, who loved Brooke. Haines's face is 'ravaged', perhaps in the First World War. But he is a shadowy figure and never speaks. Isa has met him only twice before the pageant, so her fierce yearning for him is based almost entirely on her imaginings. At the pageant, Haines is dressed in grey and seems to fade into the background, like a ghost, or a symbol of the war dead, past and future.

## Themes

### *History*

History and prehistory feature prominently in the novel via two means. Miss La Trobe's pageant is a parade of England's history from when the land mass first formed to the present day. The pageant, the centrepiece of the novel, shows that history is by no means a definitive collection of facts – it dwells at length on certain eras and ignores others completely. Some of the audience reject Miss La Trobe's version of history and construct their own. Lucy is the only person who appreciates Miss La Trobe's intention, even if she does not fully understand it.

Lucy's book, *Outline of History* (H.G. Wells, 1920), is the other framing device. At the beginning and end of the novel, Lucy reads of prehistoric scenes. As she leaves Isa and Giles to come to terms with one another, she has just reached the end of a chapter that introduces the early human. The final scene of the novel suggests that, despite the veneer of civilization, modern humans are much the same as their ancestors. Isa and Giles are compared to foxes, that fight as they mate. Modern humans, however, have one major advantage – speech. We leave Isa and Giles as they begin to talk to one another for the first time in the book, as though they are performing the first scene of Miss La Trobe's unwritten play.

> It was night before roads were made, or houses. It was the night that dwellers in caves had watched from some high place among rocks.
>
> Then the curtain rose. They spoke.
>
> (*Between the Acts*, final words)

### Poetry

The main characters of *Between the Acts* share a fondness for quoting snatches of verse, reinforcing the literary history depicted by the pageant. The romantic Isa, despite her solid and prosaic appearance, even thinks poetic thoughts while she orders the fish for lunch. She is described as 'book-shy' but loves poetry, writing her own in account books so that nobody will find it. Snatches of her poems ('There to lose what binds us here') are interspersed in the text with those of Byron ('She walks in beauty like the night'), Shelley ('the moor is dark beneath the moon'), Shakespeare ('To be, or not to be'; 'I fear I am not in my perfect mind'), Keats ('Fade far away and quite forget') and Swinburne ('Swallow, my sister, O sister swallow'). But 'lower' forms of verse also make their appearance in the book – nursery rhymes and popular songs – and give the pageant an air of the carnival.

The 'scraps, orts and fragments' of the pageant – indeed the whole novel is made up of them – echo T.S. Eliot's *The Waste Land* and Shakespeare's *Troilus and Cressida* ('The fractions of her faith, orts of her love, / The fragments, scraps, the bits and greasy relics / Of her o'er-eaten faith', Act V, sc. 2). There is another echo from *The Waste Land* in Isa's recognition of William Dodge as a 'semblable' (co-conspirator, in this context), an uncommon word that Eliot had himself quoted from Baudelaire. Eliot and his work were much on Virginia's mind in the spring and summer of 1939. A personal friend of the Woolfs, he visited them occasionally, and the Hogarth Press published several of his works. He sent Virginia copies of his new play, *Family Reunion*, and his collection of poems, *Old Possum's Book of Practical Cats*. At least twice during this period, Virginia quoted from 'The Love Song of J. Alfred Prufrock' in her diary.

## Postscript

It was in October 1938, while she was collecting scraps of poetry for *Between the Acts*, and considering all the reading she had done during her life, that Virginia had an idea for a book of criticism. Later she conceived this as a 'grand tour of literature' (*Diary* 5, 17 Feb 1939). She considered it at intervals during the rest of the year and the following year, reading and taking notes. Called provisionally 'Anon', it was never completed. However, posterity must be grateful that another, more important, work was saved. Twenty-four volumes of Virginia's diaries came close to being lost forever when 37 Mecklenburgh Square suffered bomb damage in September 1940. They were found among rubble, broken glass and mushrooms sprouting from the wet carpets and, mercifully, were rescued. Thirty-seven years later they were published.

# Bloomsbury in Popular Culture

· · · · · · · · · · ·

Even in Bloomsbury's time, novels were written with veiled portraits of its members; positive if the author was friendly and sympathetic, negative if the author had seen the satirical possibilities. Some of the books that caricatured Bloomsbury figures contemporaneously have been mentioned on p. 00 in connection with Ottoline Morrell. In these same books appear sketches based on other Bloomsbury figures.

Surprisingly few of the works of Virginia Woolf, given their cinematic qualities, have been adapted for the big screen (only *Mrs Dalloway* and *Orlando*, though *To the Lighthouse*, and *A Room of One's Own* have been televised, and *The Waves* adapted for the stage), but those of E.M. Forster have proved particularly popular.

## Books Contemporary with Bloomsbury

*The Longest Journey* by E.M. Forster (1907). Forster's novel, with its dedication 'Fratribus' ('Brotherhood'), is largely based on his memories of Cambridge and his time in the Cambridge Conversazione Society, the elite group of students known colloquially as the Apostles. Membership of this supposedly secret society was by invitation only, and it was a forerunner of Bloomsbury (see pp. 19–20). Two notable absences from the Apostles were Clive Bell and Thoby Stephen, but most of their friends – Leonard Woolf, Lytton Strachey, Saxon Sydney-Turner, Maynard Keynes and Forster himself – were members. (For other books by Forster, see pp. 108–9.)

*Women in Love* by D.H. Lawrence (1920). Ottoline Morrell, thinly disguised as the pretentious and melodramatic Hermione Roddice, was hurt and angry with the portrayal, but forgave Lawrence in the late 1920s. As is suggested by the similarity in their names, the sculptor Loerke is based on Mark Gertler, and Lawrence casts himself as the hero Rupert Birkin. Philosopher Bertrand Russell appears, arguing with Birkin, as Sir Joshua Malleson. The novel is sometimes seen as an 'exposé' of Bloomsbury sexual mores, but, if so, it is not a very accurate one. The novel was filmed in 1969 by Ken Russell, with Alan Bates, Glenda Jackson, Oliver Reed and Jennie Linden, and is famous chiefly for its nude wrestling scene between the two male leads. (For more on D.H. Lawrence's circle, see p. 112.)

J.M. Barrie's wife. It features portraits of Ottoline Morrell (Lady Rusholme) and Bertrand Russell (Melian Stokes). Cannan also wrote a fictional biography of his friend of Mark Gertler, entitled *Mendel* (1916), which includes an unflattering portrait of Carrington as Greta Morrison.

*Crome Yellow* by Aldous Huxley (1921). Based on the author's visits to Garsington. Priscilla Wimbush, looking like a music-hall transvestite, and the expressionless Henry Wimbush, preoccupied with the history of Crome estate, stand in for Ottoline and Philip Morrell. The lisping and virginal china-doll Mary Bracegirdle is Carrington, and her friend, the deaf but astute Jenny Mullion, is Dorothy Brett. The reptilian and satirical Mr Scogan was inspired by Bertrand Russell, and the handsome and Byronic painter Gombauld is Mark Gertler.

*Pugs and Peacocks* by Gilbert Cannan (1921). The author of this satire became famous for courting Captain Scott's paramour Kathleen Bruce (her second husband was Hilton Young, one of Virginia Stephen's suitors) and stealing

## Later Books Inspired by Bloomsbury

*Lytton Strachey* by Michael Holroyd (1967–8). In the last four decades, there have been many biographies written about Bloomsbury figures. This was the first, written by an up-and-coming biographer with only a book about the little-known writer Hugh Kingsmill to his name. *Lytton Strachey* was to absorb his life for the next five years. Published initially in two volumes in 1967 and 1968, it heralded a renaissance in the fortunes of Bloomsbury, which had been waning throughout the 1950s and 1960s. Some readers were scandalized at the sexual content, especially by Holroyd's revelation that the respected economist John Maynard Keynes had been gay or bisexual (homosexuality was only de-criminalized in the UK in 1967). There was an immediate interest in the story from filmmakers and playwrights – one of these proposed that the hard-drinking macho man Oliver Reed play Strachey, a miscasting of titanic proportions. It would be nearly thirty years before the story was dramatized in the film *Carrington* (see below).

*The Hours* by Michael Cunningham (1998). This Pulitzer prize-winning novel by an American author traces the stories of three women from three eras. Its chief interest to Bloomsbury fans is probably the portrait of Virginia Woolf. It is the early 1920s, she is writing *Mrs Dalloway* (working title, 'The Hours') and is struggling with the severe headaches that herald a bout of depression and a yearning to be in the bustle of London rather than suburban Richmond. Cunningham uses Woolf's words and phrases to great effect to inject her spirit into the 'Mrs. Woolf' sections.

*Mr Dalloway* by Robin Lippincott (1999). As the title suggests, this is a story presented from Richard Dalloway's point of view. It is 1927, four years after the events of Woolf's novel. Richard has a gay lover, with his wife's full knowledge and acceptance. Their marriage is intact; indeed, Richard is arranging a party to celebrate their thirtieth anniversary. Several characters from *Mrs Dalloway* rematerialize, as well as its author. Richard buys *To the Lighthouse* for his wife, and Virginia makes a brief

appearance as one of the spectators of the eclipse that Richard's guests travel to see.

## Films Based on Bloomsbury

*To the Lighthouse* (1983). 115 mins. Television film based on Virginia Woolf's novel. Directed by Colin Gregg, screenplay by Hugh Stoddart. Starring Michael Gough and Rosemary Harris as Mr and Mrs Ramsay, Suzanne Bertish as Lily Briscoe, and an almost unknown Kenneth Branagh as Charles Tansley. This high-quality BBC production is a faithful dramatization of the novel. It was filmed at St Ives, the model for Woolf's story, which she set on the Isle of Skye. Released on DVD, Region 1 format.

*Orlando* (1992). 93 mins. Film based on Virginia Woolf's novel. Directed by Sally Potter and starring Tilda Swinton as Orlando, Billy Zane as Marmaduke Bonthrop Shelmerdine, Quentin Crisp as Elizabeth I and featuring a cameo appearance by Jimmy Somerville in place of the 'wild goose'! A richly coloured and lavish adaptation, made sexy and contemporary without losing Woolf's original intentions. Tilda Swinton's knowing glances into the camera emphasize the humour of the novel. Released on 2-disc DVD set with additional features, Region 1 and 2 formats. (For DVD review, see Stephen Barkway, *Virginia Woolf Bulletin*, May 2004, pp. 64–5.)

*Carrington* (1995). 121 mins. Film based on Michael Holroyd's extensive biography, *Lytton Strachey*. Director and screenwriter Christopher Hampton (who had planned to make the film since 1976), music by Michael Nyman. Starring Emma Thompson as Carrington, Jonathan Pryce as Lytton Strachey, Rufus Sewell as Mark Gertler, Steven Waddington as Ralph Partridge, Alex Kingston as Frances Partridge, Sam West as Gerald Brenan, Penelope Wilton as Ottoline Morrell, Janet McTeer as Vanessa Bell. The touching and unusual love story of Lytton Strachey and Dora Carrington. Pryce almost steals the show, but Thompson plays Carrington with sympathy combined with a refreshing lack of sentimentality. An array of British stars play Bloomsbury luminaries – but unfortunately no Virginia. Released on DVD, Region 1 and 2 formats.

*Mrs Dalloway* (1997). 97 mins. Film based on Virginia Woolf's novel. Directed by Marleen Gorris, screenplay by Eileen Atkins and music by Ilona Sekacz. Starring Vanessa Redgrave as Clarissa Dalloway, Natascha McElhone as young Clarissa, John Standing as Richard Dalloway, Michael Kitchen as Peter Walsh, Rupert Graves as Septimus Warren Smith, Robert Hardy

as Dr Bradshaw, Margaret Tyzack as Lady Bruton. A faithful and atmospheric adaptation of Woolf's novel, well cast and well acted. Released on DVD with additional features, Region 1 and 2 formats. (For reviews of the video and DVD, see Vanessa Channer [Curtis], *Virginia Woolf Bulletin*, Jan 1999, pp. 53–5, and Stephen Barkway, *Virginia Woolf Bulletin*, May 2004, p. 66.)

*The Hours* (2002). 114 mins. Film based on the book of the same title by Michael Cunningham. Directed by Stephen Daldry, screenplay by David Hare, music by Philip Glass. Starring Nicole Kidman, Meryl Streep, Julianne Moore, Stephen Dillane, Miranda Richardson, Ed Harris. Kidman plays Woolf as a humourless depressive with an oversized nose, and Miranda Richardson is an odd choice to play Vanessa Bell, but the three stories intertwine nicely and symbolic touches provide a number of talking points for observant viewers. Woolf fans may not agree with the portrayal of the writer, and the chronological details are unclear, leaving the impression that Woolf drowned herself in 1925. However, the film reignited interest in

Woolf and propelled her novel to the top of the bestseller lists. Released on DVD with additional features, Region 1 and 2 formats. (For a DVD review, see Stephen Barkway, *Virginia Woolf Bulletin*, May 2004, pp. 66–7.)

## Films Based on the Works of E.M. Forster

*A Passage to India* (1984). 117 mins. Directed by David Lean, this epic of racial misunderstanding stars Judy Davis, Victor Banerjee, Peggy Ashcroft, James Fox, Nigel Havers, Richard Wilson, Art Malik and Saeed Jaffrey. Alec Guinness is eccentrically cast as the Indian mystic Professor Godbole. Released on DVD, Region 1 and 2 formats.

*A Room with a View* (1985). 117 mins. Oscar-winning film set partly in Italy. Directed by James Ivory, co-produced by Ismail Merchant and screenplay by Ruth Prawer Jhabvala. Starring Helena Bonham Carter and Julian Sands. A stellar supporting cast includes Maggie Smith, Denholm Elliott, Judi Dench, Rupert Graves, Daniel Day Lewis, Rosemary Leach and Simon Callow. Released on DVD, Region 1 and 2 formats.

*Maurice* (1987). 140 mins. Based on Forster's study of homosexual passion, written in 1914 but not published until after his death in 1971. A Merchant–Ivory production with script by Kit Hesketh-Harvey, known in the UK for light musical comedy. Starring James Wilby, Hugh Grant, Rupert Graves, Denholm

Elliott, Simon Callow, Billie Whitelaw, Phoebe Nicholls, Ben Kingsley and with Helena Bonham Carter as an uncredited extra. Released on DVD, Region 1 and 2 formats.

*Where Angels Fear to Tread* (1991). 112 mins. Also set partly in Italy, this film was directed by Charles Sturridge (of *Brideshead Revisited* fame) and stars Helen Mirren, Helena Bonham Carter and Rupert Graves. As frequently in Forster's writing, the story contrasts the comfortable but strait-laced British with the Mediterraneans and finds the former wanting. Released on DVD with additional features, Region 2 format.

*Howards End* (1992). 140 mins. Another high-quality production from the Merchant–Ivory–Jhabvala team. Starring Vanessa Redgrave, Anthony Hopkins, Helena Bonham Carter, Emma Thompson, Prunella Scales, James Wilby, Jemma Redgrave and Samuel West. A fight over a rich woman's will causes a collision of principles. The usual Forsterian muddles and culture clashes, this time in the home counties. Released on DVD, Region 2 format.

## Plays Based on the Works of Virginia Woolf

A few plays feature Bloomsbury characters, such as Tom Stoppard's *Jumpers* (1972), with an academic philosopher, George Moore, and his ex-cabaret-singer wife, Dorothy (the real names of Bloomsbury's moral mentor G.E. Moore and his wife: see p. 20). One of the play's jokes is that some of George Moore's students think he is G.E. Moore, who had died in 1958. Or Alan Bennett's *Forty Years On* (1968), with a character based on Ottoline Morrell called Lady Sybilline Quarrell. But those below are the main Bloomsbury-inspired plays, based directly on the writings of Virginia Woolf.

*A Room of One's Own* (1989), adapted as a one-woman show by Patrick Garland, starring Eileen Atkins, who won several awards for her performance. It was televised in 1990.

*Vita and Virginia* (1994), dramatized by Woolf fan Eileen Atkins and first performed by herself and Vanessa Redgrave, celebrates the correspondence between Woolf and her intimate friend, perhaps lover, Vita Sackville-West.

*Waves* (2006), devised by Katie Mitchell and performed at the Cottesloe, part of the National Theatre. This clever amalgam of extracts from *The Waves* and others of Virginia Woolf's writings was performed like a radio play, complete with sound effects created on stage, with the addition of live film projected onto a large screen

## Other Bloomsbury-Inspired Shows

Most people know that the Andrew Lloyd Webber musical *Cats*, with its parade of moggies such as Rum Tum Tugger, Old Deuteronomy, Mungojerrie and Macavity the Mystery Cat, was based on T.S. Eliot's eccentric collection of poems, *Old Possum's Book of Practical Cats* (1939). The original 1981 cast included Elaine Paige, Sarah Brightman, Brian Blessed, Wayne Sleep and Bonnie Langford. The musical proved so popular that at any time it is being performed somewhere in the world.

A less well-known fact is that another West-End musical, *Aspects of Love*, has its roots even nearer to Bloomsbury – in David Garnett's 1955 romantic novel of the same name. Incidentally, the novel was dedicated to his wife Angelica, the daughter of Vanessa Bell and Duncan Grant. Andrew Lloyd Webber created the show in 1989, with lyricists Don Black and Charles Hart. It was not the smash hit he had hoped for, but the opening song, 'Love Changes Everything', sung by Michael Ball, became a popular anthem, reaching no. 2 in the British charts.

There is one red herring that we must get out of the way. Edward Albee's play, *Who's Afraid of Virginia Woolf?* (1962), does *not* feature the writer! Her name is used only as a pun – the title of the play is a parody of the song 'Who's Afraid of the Big Bad Wolf?' from the animated film *Three Little Pigs* (Walt Disney, 1933). The plot revolves around a duelling couple and their two unfortunate guests. Laconic George is a history professor at an American college. His ambitious wife Martha thinks he lacks drive and never stops reminding him that he is a failure. The war of words escalates as they begin to play mind games, to which their guests are an unwitting audience. Elizabeth Taylor and Richard Burton played the roles to great acclaim in Mike Nichols' 1966 Oscar-winning film dramatization. The plot twist of the sabotage of a private fantasy by the husband echoes Woolf's 1939 story 'Lappin and Lapinova', in which it marks the end of the couple's marriage; in Albee's play the destruction of the fantasy marks a starting point and the end of the play is more hopeful than was the end of Woolf's story. In a more general sense, Albee uses Virginia Woolf's name to symbolize the mental anguish suffered by the two main characters in his play. By the 1960s she was famous for it.

# Where Now?: Bloomsbury Today

. . . . . . . . . . .

## Visiting Bloomsbury Places

The main houses where Bloomsberries lived and gathered are listed on pp. 147–54. Below are a few places of interest around the UK that Bloomsbury fans might like to visit.

## Freshwater, Isle of Wight

Virginia Woolf's great-aunt, the photographer Julia Margaret Cameron, lived at Dimbola Lodge, Freshwater, on the Isle of Wight from 1860 to 1875. Here she photographed illustrious friends such as the poet Alfred, Lord Tennyson,

*Dimbola Lodge, Freshwater, Isle of Wight*

the painter G.F. Watts and the actress Ellen Terry, as well as local workers and servants, usually in scenes from ancient legends or in melancholy, romantic poses. The house is now run as a museum and education centre, but is closed most Mondays (see www. dimbola.co.uk). Cameron died before any of the younger Stephens were born, but family stories about her abounded, providing Woolf with material for her play *Freshwater*, a comic portrayal of life at Dimbola (see pp. 128–9).

### St Ives, Cornwall

The Stephen family holidayed at Talland House, St Ives, situated on a hill overlooking Porthminster beach, for several months every year from 1882 to 1894. The train to St Ives travels for the last few miles along the coastline, affording spectacular views. Talland House is now six holiday apartments, though the exterior remains intact (see www.tallandhouse.com). The garden is much reduced from the days when the Stephen children played cricket there, but there are good views of the bay and of Godrevy lighthouse from the upper windows. Her St Ives holidays inspired Woolf's novel *To the Lighthouse*, and in her memoir 'A Sketch of the Past' (*Moments of Being*) she says that waking in the nursery at St Ives to hear the waves breaking upon the beach is the basis of all her memories.

### Cambridge

An hour's train journey from London's Kings Cross, Cambridge was where Bloomsbury began. Its core 'members' – Thoby Stephen, Leonard Woolf,

*Talland House, St Ives*

Clive Bell, Lytton Strachey and Saxon Sydney-Turner – met at Trinity College in 1899; Desmond MacCarthy was a slightly earlier graduate. Roger Fry, Maynard Keynes and Morgan Forster went to King's; its imposing chapel is famously the venue for a televised carol service every Christmas. The smaller Trinity Hall is where Leslie Stephen went to college, and there is a room named after him. Opening hours to Cambridge colleges vary, but access is usually permitted during the day. An evocative portrait of Cambridge appears in the third chapter of *Jacob's Room*. The narrator of *A Room of One's Own* complains about the policies of Trinity's Wren Library and compares lunches at a women's college (Newnham, called Fernham in the book) and a men's college (King's). Rupert Brooke lived in nearby Grantchester at the Old Vicarage (now a private house owned by Jeffrey Archer), and Virginia stayed with him for a week in August 1911.

### East Sussex – Lewes, Rodmell, Firle and Berwick

In Lewes itself is the house that Virginia bought but never lived in, the Round House, situated in Pipe Passage, a path off the high street (see pp. 153–4). The current owner has written a book about the house's history; see www.theroundhouseatlewes.co.uk. Four miles south of Lewes is Monk's House in Rodmell, a National Trust property open to the public from April to October (Wednesday and Saturday

only; office: 01323 870001, or see their website www.nationaltrust.org.uk). Several miles to the east is Charleston Farmhouse near Firle (open from April to October, phone 01323 811626, or see www.charleston.org.uk; see also p. 153), where walls and furniture painted by Vanessa and Angelica Bell and Duncan Grant still survive. In Firle is Virginia's first country residence, Little Talland House (see p. 148), and there are simple headstones to Vanessa Bell and Duncan Grant in Firle Churchyard (see p. 80). Also nearby is St Michael and All Angels church at Berwick, with interior decorations by (confirmed atheists!) Vanessa and Duncan. A number of their friends and acquaintances modelled for the figures, including Angelica Bell as Mary

*The Round House, Lewes*

in the Annunciation. (In 1879 her grandmother, Julia Stephen, pregnant with Vanessa, had modelled for Edward Burne-Jones's *Annunciation*.)

## Knole and Sissinghurst Castle, Kent

The childhood and adult homes respectively of Vita Sackville-West (see p. 111). Visiting Knole fed into Virginia's inspiration for *Orlando* (see pp. 128–31), and Sissinghurst houses, among other treasures, the Woolfs' second printing press, given to Vita when they bought a new one (see p. 38). Both Knole and Sissinghurst are now National Trust properties; details can be found at www. nationaltrust.org.uk.

## National Gallery, National Portrait Gallery

Visit the National Gallery, on London's Trafalgar Square (nearest tube and rail station Charing Cross), armed with a copy of Lois Oliver's book *Boris Anrep: The National Gallery Mosaics* (London: National Gallery Company Ltd, 2004). In the foyers and vestibules you will find portraits of Bloomsberries and others representing 'The Awakening of the Muses' (e.g. Virginia Woolf as Clio, Muse of History, Clive Bell as Bacchus, God of Wine, Lydia Lopokova as Terpsichore, Muse of Dancing, Greta Garbo as Melpomene, Muse of Tragedy), and 'The Modern Virtues' (e.g. T.S. Eliot as Leisure, Augustus John as Wonder, Winston Churchill as Defiance).

At the National Portrait Gallery in nearby St Martin's Place, there is a selection of Bloomsbury portraits on permanent display. These include Virginia Woolf by Stephen Tomlin (bust, 1931), Vanessa Bell by Duncan Grant (1918), Lytton Strachey by Carrington (1916), Duncan Grant, self-portrait (c.1909), Clive Bell by Roger Fry (1924), Roger Fry by Vanessa Bell (1912), Roger Fry, self-portrait (1930–4), Maynard and Lydia Keynes by William Roberts (exh. 1932), Desmond MacCarthy by Duncan Grant (c.1942), E.M. Forster by Carrington (1920), the Memoir Club by Vanessa Bell (1943), Gerald Brenan by Carrington (1921), Ottoline Morrell by Augustus John (1919). In addition, scholars may be interested in the extensive photographic collection including Ottoline Morrell's albums, viewable by appointment. (See www. npg.org.uk/live/photcoll.asp for details.)

## British Museum, British Library

The Reading Room of the British Museum that Woolf refers to in *Jacob's Room* is now publicly accessible, with the British Library housed in a new building at St Pancras. Visitors will see that the names of famous male writers that Julia Hedge noticed painted around the foot of the dome are no longer there. The Reading Room has been restored to its original 1857 appearance – the names were added in 1907. In a bookcase near the door there is a small display of Woolf's work, and her name appears in a list of famous library users.

*The British Museum seen from Montague Street*

In the John Ritblat Gallery in the British Library at St Pancras a manuscript handwritten by Woolf is on display (currently 'A Sketch of the Past', but see www.bl.uk/onlinegallery/whatson/exhibitions/ritblat/literary.html for up-to-date details). You can see a photograph of a page from the manuscript of *Mrs Dalloway* on www.bl.uk/online gallery/themes/englishlit/virginiawoolf. html. Occasionally available is the only remaining recording of Woolf's voice, from a BBC broadcast, 'Craftsmanship', of 1937 (the talk is printed in *The Death of the Moth*).

### Mrs Dalloway Walk

Westminster, Regent's Park and Bond Street are, for Woolf fans, synonymous with *Mrs Dalloway*. During the morning in London, Clarissa, Richard and Elizabeth Dalloway, Peter Walsh, and Septimus and Rezia Warren Smith walk or travel past many of London's landmarks, including Queen Anne's Gate, St James's Park, Piccadilly, Bond Street and Harley Street, and many Woolfians want to recreate these journeys, seeing what survives of the places Virginia Woolf wrote about so vividly eighty years ago. Stuart N. Clarke of the Virginia Woolf Society of Great Britain has created a street-by-street walk, following in the footsteps of the characters in the book. Available at: www.virginiawoolfsociety.co.uk/vw_res.walk.htm. Elisa Kay Sparks has colour-coded each journey featured in the novel and has created an attractive slide-show presentation that can be accessed online: http://hubcap.clemson.edu/~sparks/TVSeminar/dallwalkmap.html.

## Societies and Conferences

### Virginia Woolf Society of Great Britain

Founded in 1998, the VWSGB aims 'to present Virginia Woolf in her true light as a great novelist, essayist, publisher and woman of letters'. It is a non-profit organization and holds a number of events including a prestigious annual Birthday Lecture, held on the nearest Saturday to Woolf's birthday, 25 January. Speakers have included Gillian Beer, Julia Briggs, Maggie Humm, David Bradshaw, Lyndall Gordon, Anna Snaith, Sybil Oldfield and Alison Light. There is also a Study Day in July, as well as walks, a Reading Group and specially arranged trips to places of interest to Woolfians. The VWSGB publishes the *Virginia Woolf Bulletin* three times a year (free to members). See the website at: www.virginiawoolfsociety.co.uk.

*VWSGB Birthday Lectures*

### International Virginia Woolf Society

Founded in 1977, the IVWS is affiliated to the Modern Language Association of America, and has a more academic flavour than its British counterpart. It is 'devoted to encouraging and facilitating the scholarly study of, critical attention to, and general interest in, the work and career of Virginia Woolf'. Publications include (annually) two newsletters, a bibliography of Woolf scholarship, and a membership directory. IVWS members receive a free subscription to the biannual *Virginia Woolf Miscellany* (published independently). The IVWS website is at: www.utoronto.ca/IVWS.

### Société d'Etudes Woolfiennes

Based in France, the SEW was founded by academic Christine Reynier in 1996, because, she says: 'at that time, Woolf was not yet considered as a great modernist writer in France; Joyce still tended to appear on every conference programme while Woolf did not'. A biennial conference is held, from which selected papers are published in journal or book form. Links have been established with academics from other countries, particularly the UK and US.

### Virginia Woolf Society of Japan

The VWSJ, founded in 1977, states its aims as 'To foster and encourage the scholarly study of Virginia Woolf, and to provide opportunities for members to share their enjoyment of her writings' (VWSJ President, Noriko Kubota). There are three meetings a year and an annual conference in the autumn. The *Virginia Woolf Review*, containing scholarly articles and reviews in English, is published every October. You can contact the VWSJ by email on: VWoolfSoc-lj@infoseek.jp or see the website: http://wwwsoc.nii.ac.jp/vwsj/index.html.

### Virginia Woolf Society of Korea

The VWSK sprang from an idea in 1994 to publish Korean translations of the works of Virginia Woolf. It was officially founded on 25 January 2003, Virginia Woolf's 101st birthday, and today is run by academics from various Korean universities. It holds regular meetings and conferences and publishes a journal in June and December, carrying scholarly papers and reviews, and a newsletter concerning the VWSK's activities and events. See the website at: http://211.202.2.60/~kykyxz/en_index.htm.

### Virginia Woolf Conference

The annual Virginia Woolf conference has been running since 1990 and is sponsored by a different host institution each year, usually a university based in the US or UK. The conference is international in terms of both speakers and delegates. Recent themes have included 'Woolf in the Real World' (2003), 'Back to Bloomsbury' (2004), 'The Art of Exploration' (2005) and 'Woolfian Boundaries' (2006).

### Charleston Trust

This charitable organization is based at Charleston Farmhouse in East Sussex, the former home of Vanessa Bell and Duncan Grant, and raises funds for the maintenance of Charleston, and the acquisition of items (paintings, etc.) relevant to its history. 'Friends of Charleston' receive a number of benefits including free entry to the house, a subscription to *Canvas*, the Trust's newsletter, priority booking for certain events, and private view invitations. The Charleston Festival, part of the Brighton Festival, is held every May in a marquee in the grounds of Charleston Farmhouse. It has a general literary focus but there are usually one or two Bloomsbury events. See: www.charleston.org.uk.

# Bloomsbury Descendants

Although Virginia and Leonard Woolf, Lytton Strachey, Saxon Sydney-Turner and Maynard Keynes had no children, there were plenty of other Bloomsberries to continue the dynasty. Below are details of a few of the families whose offspring have carried on the Bloomsbury heritage.

## The Bells

Vanessa and Clive's eldest son, Julian, died in the Spanish Civil War in 1937. Their second-born son, Quentin (1910–96), was the author of the first full-length biography of his aunt, Virginia Woolf. In 1972, Quentin's wife, Anne Olivier Bell (the niece of Rupert Brooke's paramour, Noel Olivier), made perhaps an even more significant contribution to Woolf scholarship when she published a highly accomplished, annotated edition of Virginia's diaries in five volumes in the late 1970s and early 1980s. Quentin and Olivier (pron. 'Olivia') had three children, who divide their grandparents' talents between them. Julian Bell, an artist, illustrated an edition of Virginia Woolf's story *The Widow and the Parrot* (1988). Virginia Nicholson has written or co-written a number of books, including *Charleston: A Bloomsbury House and Garden* (with Quentin Bell) and

*Among the Bohemians*. Cressida Bell is a textile designer (see www.cressidabell.com). Her designs can often be found in the shop at Charleston.

Angelica, the daughter of Vanessa and Duncan Grant, became a painter like her mother. She wrote about her unorthodox upbringing in *Deceived with Kindness* (1984). She married David Garnett, her father's former lover, in 1942, and had four daughters, Amaryllis, Henrietta, Frances and Nerissa. Frances Partridge's son Burgo, author of *A History of Orgies* (1958; recently reprinted), married Henrietta in 1962, but died tragically young the following year, just after the birth of their daughter. Henrietta Garnett has written a novel, *Family Skeletons*, and a biography of Anny Thackeray.

A selection of Bloomsbury Heritage booklets

## The Woolfs

Leonard's nephew, Cecil Woolf, is following in his uncle's footsteps. He and his wife, the writer Jean Moorcroft Wilson, run Cecil Woolf Publishers. They publish 'Bloomsbury Heritage', a series of monograph booklets about aspects of Bloomsbury. Jean is the general editor for the series, and is also the author of *Virginia Woolf: Life and London* (1987).

## The Frys

Roger Fry had two children, Pamela and Julian, by his wife Helen Coombe. Julian emigrated to Canada in his early twenties and became a farmer. Both wrote about their childhood memories of their father and life at Durbins, Guildford. Pamela married, and her granddaughter, Rebecca Taber, is herself an artist and held an exhibition of her paintings at Durbins in 2002 (see: www.rebeccataber. com).

## The Nicolsons

Nigel Nicolson (1917–2004), the son of Vita Sackville-West and Harold Nicolson, co-founded publisher Weidenfeld and Nicolson. He was the author of the revealing *Portrait of a Marriage* about his parents (1973), and a book about Virginia Woolf containing some poignant personal memories. He edited Woolf's letters, his parents' correspondence, and his father's diaries. He published his autobiography, *Long Life*, in 1997. Vita's elder son Ben (b.1914) became an art historian and editor of the *Burlington Magazine*. He died in 1978.

Nigel's eldest son Adam Nicolson is a writer, and collaborated with his father on a travel book, *Two Roads to Dodge City*. He is married to the horticulturalist, writer and TV gardener Sarah Raven. Nigel's elder daughter Juliet, formerly a publisher's editor and journalist, is the author of *The Perfect Summer* (2006). She was involved in the making of the documentary *The War Within: A Portrait of Virginia Woolf* (1996), filmed at key Bloomsbury locations, and was the voice of Vita in the film. Her younger sister Rebecca, a former journalist, co-founded publisher Short Books in 2000 (see www.theshortbookco.com).

So the legacy of Bloomsbury is still flourishing, a century after its beginnings, through two world wars, the rumblings of many more, and a wealth of changes in social history, some of which the Bloomsberries would have applauded (equal rights and anti-discrimination laws, the growing understanding of mental illness, the advent of gay marriage), some that they would almost certainly have deplored (reality television, the inescapable mobile phone, the 24/7 society). Things that we now take for granted they had to fight for – from the women's vote to the recognition of homosexuality – yet they still seem like modern, even avant-garde, people to us. It's not difficult to see why they attracted so much interest in their own time, and why they continue to do so in ours.

## The MacCarthys

Character actor Jonathan Cecil is the grandson of Desmond and Molly MacCarthy. His brother Hugh co-wrote with his wife Mirabel *Clever Hearts* (1990), a dual biography of his grandparents.

# Book List

This list contains works of general interest to fans of Virginia Woolf and Bloomsbury that should be fairly easily available. Please note that, since various editions of Virginia Woolf's books have been published, original publication dates are given for those. For work on a more specific topic covered by this book, see the **Read On ...** section in individual chapters.

Bell, Clive, *Old Friends*, London: Weidenfeld and Nicolson, 1988

Bell, Quentin, *Bloomsbury*, London: Weidenfeld and Nicolson, 1997

— *Virginia Woolf: A Biography*, London: Pimlico, 1996

Briggs, Julia, *Virginia Woolf: An Inner Life*, London: Allen Lane (Penguin), 2005

Caine, Barbara, *Bombay to Bloomsbury: A Biography of the Strachey Family*, Oxford: Oxford University Press, 2005

Caws, Mary Ann, and Sarah Bird Wright, *Bloomsbury and France: Art and Friends*, New York: Oxford University Press, 2000

Cecil, Hugh, and Mirabel Cecil, *Clever Hearts. Desmond and Molly MacCarthy: A Biography*, London: Victor Gollancz, 1990

Curtis, Vanessa, *Virginia Woolf's Women*, London: Robert Hale, 2002

Gerzina, Gretchen, *Carrington: A Life of Dora Carrington, 1893–1932*, London: Pimlico, 1995

Glendinning, Victoria, *Leonard Woolf:*

*A Biography*, London: Simon and Schuster/New York: Free Press, 2006

Hall, Sarah M., *Before Leonard: The Early Suitors of Virginia Woolf*, London: Peter Owen, 2006 (contains a chapter on the elusive Saxon Sydney-Turner)

Holroyd, Michael, *Lytton Strachey: The New Biography*, London: Chatto and Windus, 1994

Kirkpatrick, B.J., and Stuart N. Clarke, *A Bibliography of Virginia Woolf*, 4th edn, Oxford: Clarendon Press, 1997.

Lee, Hermione, *Virginia Woolf*, London: Chatto and Windus, 1996

MacGibbon, Jean, *There's the Lighthouse: A Biography of Adrian Stephen*, London: James and James, 1997

Oldfield, Sybil (ed.), *Afterwords: Letters on the Death of Virginia Woolf*, Edinburgh: Edinburgh University Press, 2005

Ondaatje, Christopher, *Woolf in Ceylon: An Imperial Journey in the Shadow of Leonard Woolf, 1904–1911*, London: HarperCollins, 2005

Rosenbaum, S.P., *A Bloomsbury Group Reader*, Cambridge, MA: Blackwell, 1993

— *Edwardian Bloomsbury*, Basingstoke: Palgrave Macmillan, 1994

— *Georgian Bloomsbury*, Basingstoke: Palgrave Macmillan, 2003

— (ed.), *The Bloomsbury Group: A Collection of Memoirs, Commentary and Criticism*, Toronto: University of Toronto Press, 1995

Skidelsky, Robert, *John Maynard Keynes*, vol. 1, *Hopes Betrayed: 1883 –1920*, 1983; vol. 2, *The Economist as Saviour, 1920–1937*, 1992; vol. 3, *Fighting for*

Britain, 1937–1946, 2000; all London: Macmillan

Spalding, Frances, *Duncan Grant: A Biography*, London: Chatto and Windus, 1997

— *Roger Fry: Art and Life*, Norwich: Black Dog Books, 1999

— *Vanessa Bell*, Stroud, Glos: Tempus Publishing, 2006

Woolf, Leonard, *Autobiography*, London: Hogarth Press (5 vols: *Sowing*, 1960; *Growing*, 1961; *Beginning Again*, 1964; *Downhill All the Way*, 1967; *The Journal Not the Arrival Matters*, 1969)

— *The Letters of Leonard Woolf*, ed. Frederic Spotts, San Diego: Harcourt, Brace, Jovanovich, 1989

Woolf, Virginia, *Between the Acts*, London: Hogarth Press, 1941

— *The Captain's Death Bed and Other Essays*, ed. Leonard Woolf, New York: Harcourt, Brace and Co./London: Hogarth Press, 1950

— *Carlyle's House and Other Sketches*, ed. David Bradshaw, London: Hesperus Press, 2003

— *Collected Essays*, ed. Leonard Woolf, 4 vols, London: Hogarth Press, 1966–7

— *The Common Reader* (First Series), London: Hogarth Press, 1925

— *The Common Reader* (Second Series), London: Hogarth Press, 1932

— *The Complete Shorter Fiction of Virginia Woolf*, ed. Susan Dick, London: Hogarth Press, 1985 (revised 1989)

— *The Death of the Moth and Other Essays*, ed. Leonard Woolf, London: Hogarth Press, 1942

— *The Diary of Virginia Woolf*, ed. Anne Olivier Bell, 5 vols, London: Hogarth Press, 1977–84

— *The Essays of Virginia Woolf*, ed. Andrew McNeillie, 4 vols, London: Hogarth Press, 1986–94 (a total of 6 vols is planned)

— *Granite and Rainbow*, ed. Leonard Woolf, London: Hogarth Press, 1958

— *A Haunted House and Other Short Stories*, London: Hogarth Press, 1943

— *Jacob's Room*, London: Hogarth Press, 1922

— *The Letters of Virginia Woolf*, ed. Nigel Nicolson and Joanne Trautmann, 6 vols, London: Hogarth Press 1975–80

— *The Moment and Other Essays*, ed. Leonard Woolf, Hogarth Press, 1947

— *Moments of Being*, ed. Jeanne Schulkind, London: Chatto and Windus, 1976

— *Monday or Tuesday*, London: Hogarth Press, 1921

— *Mrs Dalloway*, London: Hogarth Press, 1925

— *Night and Day*, London: Duckworth, 1919

— *A Passionate Apprentice: The Early Journals*, ed. Mitchell A. Leaska, London: Hogarth Press, 1990

— *Roger Fry: A Biography*, London: Hogarth Press, 1940

— *To the Lighthouse*, London: Hogarth Press, 1927

— *The Voyage Out*, London: Duckworth, 1915

— *The Waves*, London: Hogarth Press, 1931

— *A Writer's Diary*, ed. Leonard Woolf, London: Hogarth Press, 1953

— *The Years*, London: Hogarth Press, 1937

.